Greek Myths for a Post-Truth World

ALSO AVAILABLE FROM BLOOMSBURY

Greek Tragedy in a Global Crisis: Reading through Pandemic Times
by Mario Telò
Queer Euripides: Re-Readings in Greek Tragedy edited by Sarah Olsen
and Mario Telò
Tracking Classical Monsters in Popular Culture by Liz Gloyn

Greek Myths for a Post-Truth World

Yiannis Gabriel

BLOOMSBURY ACADEMIC
LONDON · NEW YORK · OXFORD · NEW DELHI · SYDNEY

BLOOMSBURY ACADEMIC
Bloomsbury Publishing Plc
50 Bedford Square, London, WC1B 3DP, UK
1385 Broadway, New York, NY 10018, USA
29 Earlsfort Terrace, Dublin 2, Ireland

BLOOMSBURY, BLOOMSBURY ACADEMIC and the Diana logo are
trademarks of Bloomsbury Publishing Plc

First published in Great Britain 2024

A catalogue record for this book is available from the British Library.

A catalog record for this book is available from the Library of Congress.

ISBN: HB: 978-1-3503-7657-1
       PB: 978-1-3503-7656-4
       ePDF: 978-1-3503-7658-8
       eBook: 978-1-3503-7659-5

Typeset by RefineCatch Limited, Bungay, Suffolk
Printed and bound in Great Britain

To find out more about our authors and books visit www.bloomsbury.com
and sign up for our newsletters.

Whoever continues to be puzzled by the wonders of the world and recognizes their ignorance in the face of such mysteries is a lover of wisdom. This is why the lover of myth [philomythos] is also a lover of wisdom [philosophos], since myth too is made up of wonders.

ARISTOTLE *METAPHYSICS* 1.982B

To Iason and George whose early and subsequent years kept Greek myths alive in our family life.

Contents

Map

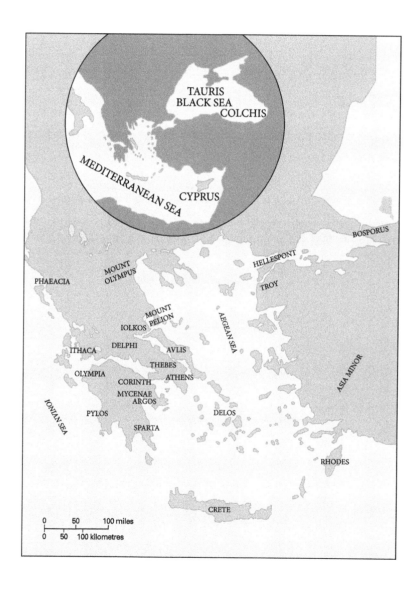

Acknowledgements

Countless friends, relatives and members of my family have joined me as fellow travellers in my mythological explorations. I would like to thank them all, none less than my sister Marianne Gabriel, whose illustrations add a different and profound dimension to the content of this book.

I would also like to thank the three anonymous reviewers of my book at proposal stage for their warm encouragement and insightful observations. Finally, I would like to acknowledge the support and professionalism of my editor and her colleagues at Bloomsbury.

Preface

Ithaca, island of my maternal grandfather. September 2020.

Early afternoon, I am walking with my older son along a rocky path. The Ionian Sea is stretching out to our left, Cephalonia a stone's throw in the near distance. The path is taking us to a cave known locally as the cave of Eumaeus. Eumaeus was Odysseus' loyal swineherd who, in Homer's Odyssey, assisted his master to recover his throne. Returning to Ithaca after a twenty-year absence, Odysseus was helped by Eumaeus and his son Telemachus to kill the suitors who had installed themselves in his royal palace, pestering his wife Penelope, eating and drinking what remained of his fortune.

I am returning to Ithaca twelve years after my previous visit, as the pandemic restrictions have just been relaxed enough to permit travel.

Iason and I walk past a large bank of wild calla lilies, as the trail gets narrower and rockier. We reach a desolate little plateau, from where we will start walking downwards towards the cliff that sinks vertically into the Ionian. The cave is tucked away inside the cliff.

From a distance we hear a rumble. We look up in the sky. There is no evidence of thunder. We walk on as the rumble gets louder.

We reach an ancient and crumbling stone wall to our right – beyond it, the dried up remains of an old vineyard. The rumble has now become a roar, a roar that reaches deep inside our bellies. Beyond the wall, we can now see a darkness, a black shadow moving towards us, or is it *standing still? Is it a shadow or is it the biggest and angriest black creature either of us has ever seen. Or is it the roar that makes it look so enormous? The creature howls in our direction. Is it on a chain or is it unleashed?*

My son and I quickly look at each other in alarm. We make a sharp left turn and walk as fast as our legs will take us away from the creature. The roar grows more distant. We eventually reach the cave, but we are only thinking about our way back and having to meet the creature again.

On our way back, we avoid turning our eyes in the direction of the roar and walk determinedly forward, the roar gradually fading away. 'This is a land of myth,' my son says. 'This was Cerberus himself, the three-headed hound of Hades, we met, was it not?'[1]

This book grew out of my love of Greek myths. These myths have long been part of my life and the lives of those close to me: my parents, my teachers, my children, my friends. I grew up in Greece in the 1950s and 60s, long before television sets, computers, phones or other devices with screens. That was a narrative universe where stories – spoken, written *and sung* – were the main way that people communicated with each other. People told stories to impress others, to pass the time, to educate children, to get their emotions off their chests, to learn from each other's experiences and troubles; or just for the hell of it, simply because telling stories was what people constantly did. Greek myths were an important part of this universe, populated by individuals, children and grown-ups, many of whom had names like Artemis, Athena, Odysseus, Heracles, Persephone and Iphigenia.

I first encountered several of the stories in this book in my childhood. Before I could read or write, my mother told me the story of Phaëthon, the boy who wanted to emulate his father the Sun god and ride his father's blazing chariot across the sky. The scenes of Odysseus sailing past the Sirens' Rock and Troy's old King Priam pleading with his enemy Achilles to return the body of his beloved son Hector featured in two large panels in my family's sitting room. They were painted by my sister Marianne, whose illustrations adorn the pages of this book. I remember my first encounter at the age of eleven with Oedipus, a figure whose name I had heard, sometimes in whispered conversations ('Poor man, struggling with his Oedipus, isn't he?') but one I had somehow avoided. I finally met him in the pages of Stefan Zweig's *Freud and Psychoanalysis* that I found by chance in my father's large library. The book, now part of my own library, was published in Greek in 1938 and has diligent annotations by my father. I spent many sleepless nights imagining myself as Oedipus trapped in a story of my own, unable to escape my fate, doomed to commit unspeakable crimes.

Many years later, when I was a father myself, I remember telling my sons the fable from Aesop that you will find in this book. A colony of frogs, tired of the anarchy in which they lived, asked Zeus to give them a king; it ended badly for the frogs, since the king that Zeus sent them, a stork, gobbled them all up. This story led to different family conversations about whether the frogs deserved their fate, about leadership arrangements in our own household, and the pros and cons of cheerful anarchy versus firm parental rule.

Greek myths surface constantly in my mind, sometimes assuming new forms, merging and fragmenting but always capable of speaking to me, of moving me. At times they turn into mindworms refusing to leave my consciousness, probing deeper into my thoughts and colouring my outlook and my feelings. It is then that I find myself *thinking mythologically*, relating my current experiences to some myth or other and then discovering new dimensions to these experiences – this is what happened when encountering the dark apparition in Ithaca and this is what triggered my discussions of several myths in this book, including those of the tragedy in Tauris and the miasma in Thebes in Chapters 2 and 4.[2]

And then there is the natural landscape of my native country, the physical space and seasons of the year, unchanged since ancient times, that keep these myths alive for me. The snow-covered mountains in winter, the small island coves, the gnarled trunks of the olive trees, the dazzling carpets of flowers in springtime, the ceaseless din of the crickets in the summer heat that deletes the colour green from every landscape, goats and sheep grazing in fields of stone and straw, dilapidated shacks dotted around the countryside that could have been standing there since the days of old Laertes. And, unchanged since times immemorial, there is the immensity of the sea, now diaphanous azure, now viscous wine-coloured, now exploding with fearsome ferocity. These are all things that Greeks since the times of Homer would recognize as their own. Churches apart, once you leave the world of cities, villages and tourist resorts, you can still enter a space that has changed little since the times when Dionysus and his ecstatic followers roamed the countryside, when gods chased nymphs around pine groves and mountain springs, when the sound of Sirens lured mariners to their death.

If Greek myths continue to fascinate and enchant us today, it is because we can well imagine them as actual events in actual places, like Cerberus suddenly emerging to terrify me and my son during our Ithaca walk. These myths play to some of our deeper desires and fears, stirring our emotions and triggering our own imaginations. They are enduring stories, but adaptable and supple, too. Different generations and different people rediscover them, reinterpret them, retell them and reinvent them. My aim in this book is to uncover some of the ways in which they address concerns and anxieties specific to our own times, including environmental degradation, mass migration, escalating inequality, war, exclusion, authoritarianism and bewildering technological developments.

Each chapter starts by recounting a particular myth and then examines what light it can cast on our post-truth times. These are times when the nature of truth itself is contested, when the difference between fact and fiction appears to melt away. These are also times when we agonize over our identities – individual and group – the shape of our bodies, our eating patterns, growing old and infirm. We are worried about what we consume and what we produce. We are fearful of large-scale population movements and having to live with groups and people different from ourselves, the Other. We worry – some more, some less – about climate change and the future of the planet. We witness the rise of populist leaders and mounting questioning over the value and the future of democracy. We are perplexed by the imponderable threats created by scientific discoveries in fields like artificial intelligence, biotechnology and genetic engineering. These are some of the themes that surface as I examine my chosen myths and stories.

My choice of myths is inevitably idiosyncratic – I have chosen myths that speak deeply to me and ones in which I have discovered over the years a great wealth of meanings. The *Iliad* and the *Odyssey* feature in several chapters, magnificent narrative mosaics with many layers and colours. Iphigenia and Oedipus make extended appearances, colossal figures of myth whom we are more likely to encounter in our dreams than in our daily lives. By contrast, Phaëthon and Narcissus, doomed young men whose stories adorn Ovid's *Metamorphoses*, are more likely to match the profiles of people we encounter regularly, even as 'friends' on social media. There are also some simpler stories that maybe stretch the meaning of myth: a contest between two ancient painters casually described by Pliny the Elder, the delightful fable of Zeus and the frogs mentioned above. These, too, will reveal some profound insights on issues that preoccupy us today: the nature of truth and the allure of authoritarianism.

Greek myths cannot, of course, solve the massive problems that confront society today. Nor can they resolve our personal troubles, as we struggle for identity and meaning, as we fight alienation and loneliness. They can, however, give us new ways of addressing our post-truth malaise. They can free our imaginations from some of the stultifying assumptions of our times and allow us to venture into new ways of thinking, new ways of understanding our problems, new ways of seeking answers to the questions that puzzle us. They can educate our emotions into accepting those things that we find hard to accept. They can help us moderate those anxieties that are prompted by our own imaginings, and act on those that call for action, even if our defensive mindsets invite us to ignore them or displace them. They can also warn us against some tempting solutions that would only compound our current problems.

One thing that Greek myths can certainly do is act as fountains of meaning in our post-truth times, when meaning itself becomes precarious and fragmented. The quest for meaning in our personal lives but also as social beings, as ephemeral parts of an enduring entity we call humanity, as inhabitants of a bountiful but fragile planet – this is something which our great recent accomplishments in science and technology have failed to satisfy. If anything, by dislodging that part of our existence that craves for myth, science and technology have contributed to a vacuum of meaning that we regularly experience as alienation, loneliness and existential despair. This book does not seek to diminish or neutralize scientific knowledge but, in its small way, tries to restore myth as a vital part of our day-to-day existence. Myths are not just stories, interesting and moving as they are. They are able to reach further, awakening in us a sense of awe and rapture in the face of the mysteries we face, individually and collectively, and emboldening us to face these mysteries with courage and sagacity.

Recognizing that, in our times, the meanings of myths fragment and diffuse in line with the preoccupations and interests of different audiences, I do not seek to offer definitive interpretations or conclusive answers. I propose instead a kaleidoscope of possibilities and connections, inviting different readers to draw their own conclusions. In doing so, I hope that readers may incorporate these myths or others of their own choosing into their life stories and narratives. They could then discover in myth alternative ways of living and experiencing the world they inhabit.

Like all stories, myths wax and wane, but – at least the best among them – retain their emotional power. Across centuries and millennia, David defeats Goliath, Cassandra makes her unheeded prophecies and Pandora unleashes fresh troubles from her box. Yet, each age discovers new meanings in old stories and different myths come into prominence as they address the aspirations and fears of each. Some myths fade away and die, to be replaced by others. Different ages invent their own myths to supplement, supplant or qualify the myths they inherit from the past. In addition to myths from antiquity, we in the West now also have the myths of Faust striking deals with the devil, Frankenstein unleashing forces he cannot control, Don Quixote heroically fighting enemies invented by his own imagination, and Big Brother watching over our every thought and action. People in other cultural traditions have rediscovered myths from their own pasts or invented new myths drawing on their current predicaments, reflecting their current aspirations.

The world's myths belong to all. But the study of myth has been pursued by many different disciplines, including ethnography, psychology, literature, linguistics, history, archaeology, philology and several more. Greek mythology has long been studied by classical scholars, some of whom have devoted long years of their lives, often to a single work or a single author, making enormous contributions to our understanding. I am not a classicist; although I have some knowledge of this scholarship, I draw predominantly from my own areas of interest and knowledge in social psychology and cultural studies. I therefore approach Greek myths with enthusiasm but also with humility, aware that there is a large area of scholarship that is *terra incognita* for me. I offer my pre-emptive apologies to scholars who may see me as venturing into their patches with scant equipment. But then the world's myths belong to all. Accordingly, I have sought to make a light-touch use of scholarly literature so that the book is accessible to all lovers of myth. Readers interested to expand their knowledge or to learn more about the theoretical foundations of some of my arguments can consult the 'Reading On' section at the end of the book.

It is my sincere wish that this book will inspire readers to embark on their own journeys through the realm of Greek mythology, drawing their own insights and experiences. Inside this realm, they are certain to discover fresh pleasures, intellectual stimulation and, maybe, the kind of practical wisdom and reassurance that we so badly need in our times.

Introduction

Erysichthon, a young prince in Thessaly, enjoyed the good life of pleasure and adventure in equal measure. He decided to build a magnificent new banqueting hall to entertain his guests. He took a party of twenty stout young men, all armed with double axes, to a sacred grove dedicated to Demeter, the goddess of the earth, cultivation and fertility. There, they started chopping down a mighty black poplar tree with their axes. Rising high above all other trees in the grove, this was the tree around which dryad nymphs of the forest would gather under the moonlight to dance in Demeter's honour.

As Erysichthon's axe hit the tree, a deep groan was heard. Feeling the tree's pain, Demeter assumed the form of an old priestess, Nicippe, and gently spoke to Erysichthon. 'My child,' she said, 'pride of your parents, stop hurting this tree and stop your followers from hacking down Demeter's sacred grove.' Erysichthon shook his axe threateningly at the goddess and said, 'Get out of my way, woman. These trees will make a fine banqueting hall to have fun with my friends.'

Demeter, normally a good-natured and benevolent goddess, was incensed and promised revenge. She sent an insatiable hunger to torment Erysichthon. The more he ate, the hungrier he became. Recruiting the support of Dionysus, god of wine-making and religious ecstasy, Demeter also inflicted an insatiable thirst on the young man. He ate and drank all day, yet his hunger and thirst only increased. And curiously, instead of growing obese, he wasted away, growing thinner by the day, until eventually he was reduced to just skin and bone.

Erysichthon sold off all earthly possessions to buy more and more food and drink. It was never enough. The more he ate, the hungrier he got; the more he drank, the thirstier he got. He ended up a beggar eating filth off the streets, scorned by everyone, even by his own parents. In some versions, he sold his own daughter to feed himself but even this was not enough. He ended up eating his own body until there was nothing was left of him.

The story of Erysichthon has reached us from several ancient sources. Best known among them are the accounts of Alexandrian poet, librarian and scholar Callimachus and Roman poet and storyteller Ovid, both in verse. The first was written in Greek in the third century BCE and is titled, Hymn to Demeter. The second is part of Ovid's famous poem, Metamorphoses, written in Latin some two hundred and fifty years later. Although it is highly likely that Ovid was aware of Callimachus' version, there are several differences between the two texts. In one of them, the tree in question is a poplar, in the other it is an oak; Erysichthon is a prince in one and a king in the other; in one account he cuts down a single tree, in the other an entire grove. His punishment is different, too. In Callimachus' account, Demeter recruits the support of Dionysus who inflicts unquenchable thirst on Erysichthon. Ovid's poem makes no mention of this. It concludes with Erysichthon eating his own body in contrast to Callimachus' in which Erysichthon ends up as an emaciated beggar in the streets.

Such discrepancies are as common in ancient Greek mythology, as they are in other mythologies. Long before the story of Erysichthon and most ancient myths were written down, they were parts of an oral tradition, told again and again over many generations. These retellings inevitably resulted in embellishments, omissions and modifications to suit particular occasions and the tastes of different audiences. In this way, myths emerged as products of collective imagination, distillations of shared experiences that were reinforced with every retelling, shedding what was ephemeral and parochial while preserving what was enduring and generalizable. Even the names of some of main characters changed in the course of these retellings.[1] Still, there is something common to all accounts that reached the written stage that help to identify the myth, whether the central character is a prince or a king and whether he is referred to as Erysichthon or Triopas – the sacrilegious cutting down of a holy tree by a powerful and arrogant man against the warnings and pleas of the offended female deity, the punishment of excruciating hunger leading to the demise of the offending character. There is no right and wrong version of the myth. Ancient Greeks were liberal in accepting contradictions and discrepancies in their myths, in contrast to other religious traditions where the alteration of small details could amount to sacrilege in its own right.

The myth of Erysichthon, like other Greek myths, retains some of its meaning and power across different cultures and different historical periods. Even people who do not accept the idea that a tree or a grove can be sacred may relate to the story and maybe discover new meanings in it, consistent with their values and their aspirations. It is a myth that appears particularly in tune with our times. In our consumerist culture, we are struck by the fact that Erysichthon wanted the wood to make a banqueting hall, a place for opulent consumption and feasting. We notice the addictive qualities of consumption as portrayed in the myth and can readily relate to the black hole in the protagonist's stomach. Erysichthon is being consumed by his compulsive consumption. Living in times where eating disorders are commonplace, we can't fail but respond to the nature of the punishment inflicted on Erysichthon, although we may be surprised that over-eating and over-drinking make him waste away rather than grow obese.[2]

Ever more anxious about climate change and the future of the planet, we cannot help seeing the myth of Erysichthon as an allegory for the reckless exploitation of nature by humanity. For centuries now, we humans have treated nature as a limitless resource to exploit, with little concern for the long-term repercussions of our actions. Aware of the vital part played by trees in sustaining our environment, we can readily relate to the pain caused by the tree's wanton destruction; some of us may indeed feel the tree's pain as Erysichthon strikes it with his axe. We may then ponder whether the tree of life has already been brought down and what, if anything, we may do by way of atonement and redress.

Many people will respond to the gendered nature of the myth. Here is a male intruder armed with a brutal weapon, a double axe, accompanied by his hoodlums likewise armed, violating a peaceful female space, wreaking havoc and destruction all around them, all for the sake of 'fun'. Even then, the female deity responds with gentleness only to be pushed away callously by a man who clearly has no respect for what is held holy by someone else.

It is immediately clear that the myth of Erysichthon is a rich one, opening up many lines of interpretation and many ways of reflecting some of our current concerns. Still, immersed as we are in viewing the myth as a parable on consumption and the reckless exploitation of nature, we may fail to observe another possibility. What if the tree that Erysichthon is chopping down is not the tree of life but the tree of truth, a tree that has grown strong and imposing over many centuries? It has resisted storms and droughts, but it is now under constant assault from myriad axes. Losing all faith in truth would leave us gorging ourselves on a diet of junk food – lies, gossip, bullshit, conspiracy theories, fake news and phoney myths. Is there anything then we can still do to protect the tree of truth?

Looking at the tree at the heart of the story as an allegory for nature and looking at it as an allegory for truth may lead to different conclusions. As rich symbolic structures, the meanings contained in a myth can easily change or migrate. The tree of life can become the tree of truth and just as easily it can turn into the tree of freedom or the tree of democracy under threat from the axes of some powerful agent and his cronies. In our post-truth times, we recognize that it is not possible to control or police the meanings of any narrative. We regularly see works of art, dramas, operas, myths and so forth reframed and retold in original and sometimes shocking ways. The characters and the plotlines of the *Odyssey* and the *Iliad*, Homer's two magnificent poems that feature large in this book, have been recast and reimagined in our times by numerous novelists but also by filmmakers, video games creators, conceptual artists and others. This is far from new. The seventeenth-century Italian composer, Claudio Monteverdi, composed an opera, no less magnificent than Homer's work, based entirely on the return of Odysseus to Ithaca. The story of Iphigenia in Tauris, first told in Euripides' play that I discuss in Chapter 2, features in numerous operas of the eighteenth and nineteenth centuries as well as several plays, including a famous adaptation by Goethe. What is maybe new in our times is the degree of freedom that contemporary storytellers and artists claim in adapting old myths to reflect the sensitivities and sensibilities of our times.

Myths and mythology

Etymology is not just incidental in Greeks myths but an important thread of their symbolic tapestry. The very name of Erysichthon, for example, means 'earth-tearer', containing the germ of the man's brutal and sacrilegious character. The word 'myth', for its part, derives from the verb 'myo', originally meaning 'shut tight', especially the mouth or the eyes. It is a particularly productive verb that spawned many words, including 'mystery' and 'myth' as well as the Greek word 'myesis', meaning initiation to a cult or a mystery. This verb also yields the Greek word for mussel ('myax'), a mollusc that shuts tight, as well as the words for bone marrow and brain ('myelos'), substances contained inside tightly shut bone structures.[3]

Myth originally signified authoritative spoken acts, including prophecies, vows and prayers, rich in symbolism, used in initiation rites into mysteries. Such spoken acts served as a collective memory for societies before the invention of the written word and contained a deeper significance like the living organism enclosed in the shell of a mussel.[4] Gradually the word 'myth' assumed the meaning of a traditional narrative dating from before historical times, one that retains authoritative, symbolic and sacral qualities.[5] The story of Erysichthon highlights the sacral quality of the myth, so that even non-religious people will recognize the holiness of Demeter's tree (or grove). Failing to recognize this makes the myth simply unintelligible, which it would arguably become in a world entirely devoid not only of religious belief but also of religious feeling.

In addition to their symbolic and sacral qualities, myths gradually assumed another vital quality that continues to define them today, one which dominated Aristotle's extensive thoughts on the subject – myths have plots. Aristotle, in fact, used the word 'mythos' to denote the plotline of a poetic narrative, such as an epic poem, a tragedy or a comedy. Plots cannot be created willy-nilly by throwing together any random sequence of acts or events. They have a tight logic or grammar of their own, whereby different actions and consequences are woven together, sometimes in unpredictable ways or ways out of line with the intentions of the main characters, but not at random. Events in a myth cannot be rearranged arbitrarily. Plots are unlike lists of bullet points, assortments of paintings in a museum or miscellanies of proverbs where an audience may miss one or more items but grasp the essence of the whole. In a plotted narrative if the audience misses one or two key turns in the storyline or if the storyteller fails to properly relate them, they 'lose the plot' and are reduced to baffled incomprehension.[6]

The plots of myths are woven out of exceptional events that retain their power across time and aim at unravelling something deeper, a mystery.[7] Erysichthon might have cut down an ordinary tree or an ordinary grove and built his fancy banqueting hall. This by itself would certainly not have amounted to a myth. However, he chose to cut down a holy tree in a holy grove and the tree groaned in pain. This is an event unlike any that most of us have ever witnessed – it constitutes a mystery, but a believable one. Far from invalidating the narrative, the mystery defines it as a myth. Erysichthon is then warned by a goddess who assumes the form of a priestess. This is another mystery, but again a believable one. Notice how the etymology of Demeter derives from 'de' which may be linked to the earth or to a definite article and the word 'meter' which very definitely stands for 'mother'.[8] Erysichthon arrogantly dismisses these warnings which result in Mother Earth's anger and his dreadful punishment. The sequence presumptuous act – warning – disregard of the warning – divine retribution/punishment is easily recognizable as a key plotline, featuring as it does in countless myths across many different mythologies.

Mythical plotlines are not, of course, limited to transgressions and punishments. The myths I will discuss in this book deploy a vast range of plotline tropes. Noble achievements, accidents, betrayals, coincidences, conflicts and reconciliations, crises and decisions, encounters, errors and their consequences, escapes, gifts, insults, jokes, journeys, lies and deceptions, losses, love affairs and passions, misunderstandings and mishaps, mysteries and riddles, omens and premonitions, conflicts, cruelties and resistances, prophecies and auguries, promises, rescues, sacrifices and self-sacrifices, secrets, separations, surprise interventions and other surprises, traumas and injuries – this is a very partial list of the prodigious ingredients in the recipes that make up mythical plotlines. The power and reach of each myth depend on how imaginatively these ingredients are woven together in plotlines that continue to resonate across the ages.

Aristotle greatly admired the inventiveness of mythical plotlines, whose logic he did much to uncover. But what made him regard myth as exceptional is its ability to reach for something profound and timeless. In his Metaphysics, he goes as far as to contrast different arts and sciences that develop, grow and eventually decline and perish to myths that retain their power across the ages.[9] Likewise, in a famous pronouncement in the Poetics, he expresses his preference for poetry, which uses myths as its source material, to history. 'Poetry,' he said, 'is finer and more philosophical than history; for poetry expresses the universal, and history only the particular.'[10]

It is certainly remarkable that myths dating from several millennia ago can continue to speak to us today. In spite of the great transformations and upheavals in the structure of our societies, their core values and beliefs, in spite of the rise of scientific knowledge and unprecedented technological advances, urbanization and many other changes affecting people's lives, many ancient myths remain comprehensible and capable of generating meaning. Psychologists Sigmund Freud and Carl Jung attributed this power to their ability to address desires and anxieties embedded deeply in our unconscious mind. Freud turned the stories of Oedipus and Narcissus into foundational myths of psychoanalysis by arguing that they each reflect unconscious mental structures. The story of Oedipus expresses a primal desire for union with the mother and a rivalry towards the father, while that of Narcissus expresses, equally powerfully, the craving for self-love in a generally indifferent world. Jung, for his part, viewed myths as bearers of archetypes which reside in the collective unconscious of humanity, expressing timeless desires and anxieties. Myths, in his view, are conscious expressions of the great stream of unconscious ideas and images that flows through the soul of every human being.

In their different ways, both of these psychologists as well as many others recognized that scientific logic is not enough to comprehend the mysteries of the world; they do not provide the foundation on which to base all of our actions. Mythological thinking is part of our psychological make-up and cannot be replaced or neutralized, even if it can be qualified, tempered and analysed. Freud and Jung also recognized that, by addressing timeless questions about the human predicament, myths have a therapeutic power – they help us endure the many uncertainties, anxieties and troubles that life throws at us.[11] Even in times when science has provided her own answers to some of the mysteries of life and nature, our need for myth persists. We need myths as a means of making sense and enduring the numerous blows we receive from nature, society and fate, as well as to help us manage our own demons, our nightmares and anxieties, our irrational obsessions and aversions. Myths may not undo the injustices and troubles that we experience but can help us put them in context. They can transform our outlooks by placing our own quandaries side by side with the predicaments that have faced humans across vast distances of time and space and can open up new agendas for action. By helping us understand ourselves better, they can release us from some of the surplus suffering that we often inflict on ourselves and on others.

Myths in post-truth times

Myths, of course, are not all good. Myths can inspire empathy and compassion for other human beings but also hatred and contempt. Appropriated by skilful propagandists, myths can unleash destruction and disorder. Even seemingly benign myths may be interpreted in destructive ways. The myth of Erysichthon can conceivably turn into a doctrine of hate for a fanatical group of eco-warriors intent on defending every single tree on the planet, by force if necessary. The chapters that follow will demonstrate the dark side of some myths, their potential to cast other people as inferior, as unworthy of respect or as subhuman, providing the fuel for wars, enslavement and genocide. Acts of religious and political terrorism can seek justifications in old myths hardened into dogma, pseudo-myths cooked up for the occasion, or, alternatively, in the presumed desecration of some ancient sacred myth or tradition.

Myths do not exist in isolation. They are parts of narrative ecosystems of ideas and beliefs that can be thought of as ecologies. Narrative ecologies are spaces where, by analogy to natural ecologies, different narratives and counter-narratives emerge, interact, compete, adapt, develop and die. In addition to myths, these narratives and counter-narratives include images, symbols, stories, 'theories', assumptions, archetypes, plotlines, characters, icons and other narrative devices along with the emotions embedded in them. Within these narrative ecologies, old myths can resurface in different guises and assume new meanings.[12] In a narrative ecology dominated by narcissistic strivings of individuals, the *Odyssey* can re-emerge to signify personal journeys of identity and self-discovery. In a narrative ecology dominated by violence and the Manichean struggle between good and evil, the *Iliad* can be reduced to a series of armed confrontations between the goodies and the baddies in which the goodies eventually prevail.

Different narrative ecologies can also redefine the idea of myth itself – for example, by discarding its sacral qualities or reducing the word 'myth' to a simple, emaciated narrative or just a slogan that feeds different prejudices and political agendas. It is significant that a widespread meaning acquired by the word 'myth' in our times is that of a 'popular untruth'. This is apparent in numerous books with titles featuring the word 'debunked', such as Common Myths About Vaccines Debunked or Ten Myths about Slimming Debunked. Whether these 'myths' are promulgated by conspiracy theorists, cunning operators after a quick profit or people claiming to be scientists, the emphasis here is on their falsity and the damage it causes. Protecting the public against such myths is the purpose of the debunkers.[13]

Debunking has assumed a special prominence in the narrative ecologies of our own times, amid a proliferation of fake news, alternative facts, conspiracy theories and other narratives that blur the boundary between truth and untruth, truth and lies. This accounts for the rising popularity of the word 'post-truth' as an umbrella term to describe our times. 'Post-truth' was declared word of the year in 2016 by Oxford Dictionaries, defining it as 'circumstances in which objective facts are less influential in shaping public opinion than appeals to emotion and personal belief'. In a post-truth society, what counts as a 'fact' depends on one's political, religious and other beliefs, facts turn into stories and stories into facts, and eventually facts cease to matter. Post-truth has spawned numerous books, articles and other publications describing a society in which truth can no longer be authoritatively determined and is no longer a reason for believing or not believing something.[14]

Many reasons have been offered for the emergence of a post-truth society. Chief among them is the rise of social media with their narrative ecologies which allow truths, half-truths and untruths to compete for the oxygen of publicity with 'likes' and the unfathomable quirks of algorithms fine-tuned to promote controversy as the only arbiters of value and importance. Related to this is an information overload which makes it impossible for most of us to check different claims and counter-claims and the ensuing tribalism of individuals isolated in online echo-chambers where their views and prejudices get constantly reinforced by like-minded individuals. Another factor accounting for the rise of a post-truth society is the re-emergence of populist leaders in many countries whose contempt for truth recalls the contempt displayed by Erysichthon towards Demeter. In addition to traditional propaganda, disinformation campaigns are systematically pursued by politicians, lobbyists and all kinds of nefarious organizations, secret and not so secret. These have fomented a deep-seated suspicion, bordering on paranoia, that undermines trust in public institutions in politics, science, education, the established media and culture.

Intellectuals have also shouldered some of the blame for the rise of post-truth. Following the popularity of postmodernist ideas since the 1980s, the view of truth as a universal value was supplanted by the notion of different 'regimes of truth' befitting different discourses and different contexts. 'Absolute truth' came to be seen as a discursive resource in the hands of the privileged few, capable of forcing their definitions, their language and their narratives on others. Far from being a universal value, truth came to be seen as a vital part of the toolkit of a hegemonic elite determined to preserve its power and privileges. By the same token, those excluded from privilege could construct their own stories and counter-narratives resisting the hegemonical ones, making their own claims to truth. In this way, the critical axes of postmodern Erysichthons joined those of lying politicians, conspiracy theorists and various influencers in seeking to bring down the tree of truth and replace it with a plethora of bushes and shrubs of half-truths and lies – pliable, hard to dislodge and easy to replace.

The arrival of post-truth society has coincided with the growth of a wide range of discontents and grievances in the twenty-first century, across different nations, classes and groups. These were prompted by global warming, migration, escalating inequalities, artificial intelligence and other technological innovations, the disappearance of traditional jobs and careers, the effects of rampant globalization, terrorism and so forth. Many niches of comfort and safety have been shaken. Old beliefs about gender and family, about race, age and class, about religion, nations and progress have been dented by challenging new ideas and practices. Several of these will surface in the chapters of this book, as we use the lens of Greek myths to examine our post-truth malaise and, maybe, to reconsider who 'we' are and how 'we' might think ahead and act individually and collectively towards a better and more equitable future.

Instead of conclusion: A last look at Erysichthon

What do we feel when we look at Erysichthon and reflect on his predicament? Do we feel loathing for his violation of a holy space? Do we feel anger and dismay for his arrogance? Or, do we feel pity for the insatiable hunger that consumed him and for his miserable end? Do we feel morally superior, confident that we would never have been as foolish as he was? Or, do we recognize in him a fellow human being, fallible and blinded by his own desires and ambitions?

And what do we feel about Demeter or Mother Earth? Is she a generous and bountiful provider for our material needs or is she a vengeful deity concerned with protecting her own domain from presumptuous intruders? Do we need such a deity to protect our planet, or could we manage it ourselves with the help of reason and science? Does Mother Earth have to be a 'goddess' at all or could she, as the Gaia theory claims, be a single, self-regulating but fragile living system that sustains life? Does it make a difference whether Gaia's revenge is the revenge of an angry goddess or the response of a living planet unable to cope with the strains that we humans have inflicted on it?

My reflections on each of my chosen myths in the chapters that follow took my own feelings as their point of departure. I scrutinized my feelings about the main characters, the plot, the objects and settings that define it. Feelings are a good starting point for the exploration of myths, especially if we continue to probe them with questions like 'Why am I feeling this way?' 'Why am I feeling so strongly about this?' 'What if X, instead of being Y, was Z?' and so forth. We then discover that the feelings stirred or aroused by Greek myths are often ambivalent or contradictory, as are their characters and plots. A character like Erysichthon can be both responsible and not responsible for his predicament. A goddess, like Demeter, can be both kind and vindictive. As Beethoven wrote in an enigmatic little note on the manuscript of one of his songs, 'Sometimes the opposite is also true.' This applies to feelings aroused by myth as well as to those aroused by music.

If a myth can arouse complex and ambiguous feelings, it is because it is still alive. It is because it has not been reduced to dogma with an unequivocal plot, crude characters (good and bad) and a sanctimonious moral message. It is my sincerest hope that readers of my book will be encouraged not only to explore these myths further, but also to explore further the feelings these myths arouse in them along with the fantasies they stir in their imagination. In doing so, I am confident that they will discover many more ways in which these myths can shed light on the world we are sharing than my own discussion could ever be capable of.

1

The Narrative Veil: Truths and Untruths, Facts and Fantasies

It is said that an old Greek painter, Parrhasios, was challenged to a painting contest by a younger rival, Zeuxis. He readily accepted.

The younger man painted a tableau of grapes so realistic that it attracted the attention of a flock of birds that started pecking at it. Confident of victory, Zeuxis invited Parrhasios to reveal his own painting covered by a magnificent veil.

The older man asked Zeuxis to lift the veil himself, whereupon the young man realized that the veil was itself the painting. He at once acknowledged the superiority of his rival. 'I deceived the birds,' he said, 'but you managed to deceive me, an artist!'

I first came across this story in my childhood. It had been stored in some recess of my mind, from where it was suddenly awakened one day as I was jogging. I had been thinking about the Greeks' artistic ideal of perfect representation, according to which the perfect painting is one that is so realistic that we don't realize it is a painting. The perfect representation is also perfect deception, as it conceals its own standing as representation. The closer it gets to the truth, the more it deceives. This is the paradox of verisimilitude, the veil of deception, a veil that in our post-truth times we encounter constantly in the form of scams, hoaxes and fakes.

I found the story of Parrhasios and Zeuxis enjoyable but also profound. It is not a sacral myth in the manner of Erysichthon, but it acted as a brainworm that kept raising questions in my mind. One set of questions is factual or forensic – note how the story started with 'It is said'. Who said it? Was the incident based on an actual contest between two historical figures?

The story also raises psychological questions about the motives of the characters. Zeuxis painted some grapes trying to make them look real. He felt that he had succeeded brilliantly by deceiving the birds. He had not intended to deceive the birds but the fact that he did was a measure of his success. Parrhasios, on the other hand, painted a veil. What makes someone choose to paint a veil? Of course, we can never enter the mind of Parrhasios, but we can be sure that the painter of veils, unlike the painter of grapes, never has deception far from his mind. Did he paint the veil mischievously or otherwise, intending to deceive the viewer? If so, why?

Consider now how an authenticator of art might approach the story. Could the veil itself be a cover for another painting or an image hiding beneath it? Imagine for a moment that beneath the veil there is another image – maybe an image so powerful, like the head of Medusa or Edvard Munch's *The Cry*, that all who cast eyes on it are forever haunted by it? Or perhaps there could be another veil. This would amount to a double deception, since not only did the veil pass itself for real, but it masked something else behind it, something that is thereafter consigned to oblivion, unless some future generation equipped with x-rays could discern it on the canvas. What then if we, the viewers, are so fascinated by the veil that we fail to probe what lies behind it, even after we realize that we have been victims of deception? What if the narrative veil stops us seeing what lies concealed in the story itself?

Let us keep interrogating the story. What if our fascination with the veil has already made us forget the grapes? The grapes in the story, so realistically painted, deceived the birds, but have they deceived us, too? Has anyone ever seen birds go for a set of painted grapes or even a perfect photograph of them? Do birds ever attack the numerous mouth-watering images of fruit on advertisers' roadside posters or on the sides of supermarket lorries?[1] Is it plausible then that they went for the grapes of Zeuxis' painting? Did the author of the story deceive us with a story whose plausibility is paper-thin? Or did we suspend our disbelief as a condition for understanding and appreciating the story? And then, what about the contest's outcome? Why should the image of grapes, brimming with the young artist's life juices, be regarded as inferior to the old man's depiction of the deadness of a veil?

And what about me? Am I, too, in the process of deceiving you, the reader? Did I recall the story from memory as I was jogging, or did I find it by putting a few well-chosen words in Google? Try 'painter, grapes, birds' and you will quickly find the story as told by Roman polymath, natural historian and general Pliny the Elder (23/4–79 CE) in his celebrated *Natural History*. You will also discover an image of *Still Life with Grapes and a Bird* by Italian painter Antonio Leonelli (also known as Antonio da Crevalcore) (1443–1525), an early pioneer of *trompe-l'oeil* techniques. Such questions begin to undermine our confidence in the story itself as being a representation of some truth.

What if the point of the story itself is to deceive us? Are we perhaps even dumber than those birds which mistook the painted grapes for real? And then, if the story deceived us so easily, in what ways have we colluded with the deception – just like audiences of a 'magic show' colluding with the wiles of the magician? What makes us so susceptible to such deceptions? Surely the birds had no reason to wish to be deceived by the grapes – but could it be that when listening to stories, watch a play or observe a work of art, we actively *desire to be deceived*?

Stories, fictions and facts

The old story of the two painters quickly alerts us to the twin possibilities of deception and seduction, our willing treatment of appearances as realities and our joyful surrender to the veil of the surface. Far from art imitating life, it is life that imitates art, argued Oscar Wilde, a meticulous observer of veils. In a little-known but delightful essay called 'The Decay of Lying', written as the nineteenth century was coming to its close, he wrote:

> Art finds her own perfection within, and not outside of, herself. She is not to be judged by any external standard of resemblance. She is a *veil*, rather than a mirror. She has flowers that no forests know of, birds that no woodland possesses. She makes and unmakes many worlds, and can draw the moon from heaven with a scarlet thread. Hers are the 'forms more real than living man' and hers the great archetypes of which things that have existence are but unfinished *copies*.[2]

For Wilde, 'lying, the telling of beautiful untrue things, is the proper aim of Art.'[3] It is by lying that the painter, the dramatist, the poet, the storyteller makes us see the world with new eyes. We learn to observe things that had not existed earlier, so that life and nature imitate art rather than the other way round. Ever since the impressionists started to paint dreamy images of the Thames, people started to notice the brown fogs over London with different eyes. Even more audaciously, ever since Sophocles created Oedipus, relations between young boys and their mothers lost something of their innocence. For Oscar Wilde, the veil deceives not because, like the one painted by Parrhasios, it is very lifelike, but quite the opposite, because it is pure artifice, pure invention. If the veil entrances us, if it paralyses our critical faculties, it is because of its ability to speak to our hidden desires.

Oscar Wilde was alarmed at the thought that art was losing its ability to lie as people lost their desire to be deceived by the artist. Why? Because of the arrival of modernity, its rationality, its scientific theories and its bludgeoning champion, *the fact*, the enemy of art, artifice and deception, the killer of romance, desire and magic. Under the 'monstrous worship of facts',[4] he argued, artists were losing their ability to lie and to create art. Wilde was not alone in lamenting what he saw as a future of technology, science, information, facts, cold and clinical precision. This is what Max Weber, one of the founders of modern sociology, referred to as the 'disenchantment of the world', the stripping away of layers of magic, imagination and artifice under the rising hegemony of rationality.

Yet, as we now know, this is not what happened. Far from facts swamping art, a truce was declared. What we, our media, our politicians and even our scientists now routinely call 'the story' is a product of this truce. This is a type of story that is explicitly not 'just fiction' or 'just invention' – it is not like a Grimm Brothers' folk tale or a Disney fairytale. Instead, 'the story' preserves the memory of an actual occurrence, something that happened or at least is believed to have happened. Such stories have become a mainstay of our culture, popping out of most web pages and platforms, exploding out of television screens, and screaming out of the pages of newspapers, magazines and books. They come in bewildering varieties ranging from the foibles of the rich and famous to scare stories and conspiracy theories, from heroic achievements to sordid tales of crime, injustice, scandal and fake scandal. Stories are also vital ingredients through which we create our sense of selfhood and our identities, both individual and collective. We swap them in our daily lives and use them to reinforce our sense of self-worth and value.

Whether in the public domain or in our private lives, stories are privileged by a unique combination of two qualities that make them different from simple information or data. They have plots and at the same time they claim to represent reality. Stories create meaning by placing facts in storylines with characters, heroes and heroines, cowards, victims, tricksters, imposters, fools and so forth. In this way, as Walter Benjamin succinctly put it, stories communicate *facts as experience*, not facts as information.[5] This accords every storyteller a unique narrative privilege, the privilege of *poetic licence* that enables them to twist the material for effect, to exaggerate, to omit, to draw connections where none are apparent, to silence events that interfere with the storyline, to embellish, to elaborate, to display emotion, to comment and to interpret even as they claim to represent something that happened – in this sense, something 'real'.

Poetic licence is something that both the teller of the story and the audience of the story recognize. It is part of a psychological contract or a narrative contract between storytellers and their audiences that enables storytellers to buy the audience's suspension of critical judgement in exchange for pulling off a story which is at once meaningful and plausible or verisimilar. This calls for skill and ingenuity on the part of the narrators who must walk a tricky tightrope across two potentially undermining questions – the 'So what?' question and the 'Did it really?' question. The 'So what?' question indicates that a story is failing to carry meaning, while the 'Did it really?' indicates that it fails to sound plausible. Treading effectively this tightrope with the support of poetic licence gives storytellers considerable latitude in constructing plots and creating meaningful narratives. Does this amount to falsification? Undoubtedly, if the criterion of truth is accuracy of reporting. If, however, the criterion of truth is something different, then it may be that distortions, omissions and exaggerations serve a vital purpose, that of reaching for a deeper truth.

What could such a deeper truth be? The usual answer to this question is that *the truth of the story lies not in its accuracy but in its meaning.* Poetic licence and all the falsifications that it justifies aim at generating a deeper truth, something that reaches beyond the superficial and the temporal. As one of the characters in Pirandello's *Six characters in search of an author* says, 'Let us create a fiction that is truer than truth,' echoing Aristotle's foundational argument. Reality as represented by the work of the artist, the poet, the painter, the storyteller, in this view, is more true because it reaches deeper than the work of the historian and the chronicler – instead of imitating mere appearance, it unveils the essence. A literal untruth may be closer to the true nature of things than a literal truth which remains at the superficial and the mundane. Where literal representation accurately imitates the veil, art and poetry and storytelling use imagination to reach out for what is hidden from sight and timeless.

Behind the narrative veil:
Hoaxes and scams

The story of the two painters, however, raises another possibility. Could instead of seeking a deeper truth, a plausible and attractive story seduce us by paralysing our critical faculties? What if a story deceives us precisely because it rings true? Could it be that the more authentic a story sounds the more we should mistrust it? Isn't this the kind of story what we call a hoax, a genre that in our times has become part of our daily diet of disinformation and fake news?[6]

Consider the case of the award-winning memoir, *Fragments: Memories of a wartime childhood*, by Binjamin Wilkomirski, published in 1996, which described his experience of surviving the terror of the Holocaust as a child. The book gave voice to the author's sufferings that had scarred his entire life. His fragmented narrative through a landscape of horrors invited the reader to identify with the child whose innocent eyes are witnessing unspeakable inhumanity. The power of the memoir was overwhelming. Only someone who had lived through it, the reader felt without needing to have it stated, could tell such a story. On publication, the book was widely acclaimed and showered with awards. A few voices expressed reservations about its accuracy,[7] but these were brushed aside as insignificant when compared to the book's moral as well as literary power. And yet, the book turned out to be a fake. Largely through the efforts of Swiss journalist Daniel Ganzfried and historian Stefan Maechler,[8] it emerged that Wilkomirski (real name Bruno Doesseker, born Grosjean) was not a Holocaust survivor nor even a Jew. His story was entirely the product of his imagination.

As the product of imagination rather than lived experience, it could be argued that the memoir was an even more brilliant piece of literature. Some defended Wilkomirski. Israel Gutman, for example, the director of Yad Vashem and himself a Holocaust survivor, argued: 'Wilkomirski has written a story which he has experienced deeply; that's for sure ... He is not a fake. He is someone who lives this story very deeply in his soul. The pain is authentic.'[9] Others argued that Wilkomirski spoke not just for himself but in a collective voice on behalf of a whole class of silenced victims. 'I was there, not you,' exclaimed Wilkomirski to his detractors, without specifying where 'there' was, but implying that no historical research could deny his experience which was authentic through and through. Yet, the narrative contract between the author and his audiences was irreparably damaged. Wilkomirski had abused his readers' trust. His book was discredited *even as a literary document* and withdrawn from the market, as were many of the awards that it had received. As Maechler argued, 'Once the professed interrelationship between the first-person narrator, the death-camp story he narrates, and historical reality are proved palpably false, what was a masterpiece becomes kitsch.'[10]

The Wilkomirski case demonstrates what happens when, under the narrative veil of poetic licence, products of the storyteller's imagination are presented as facts. Verisimilitude gives way to dissimulation. If we hesitate to see Wilkomirski as a hoaxer, it is because his deception was, by all accounts, a self-deception as much as a deception of his readers. This in turn generates two types of literary narrative. The first is the literary exposé, which has emerged as the antithesis of the memoir, establishing its own psychological contract between authors and their audiences. The second is the psychological analysis of the motives and intentions of authors who overstep the boundaries of poetic licence and enter the realm of hoax.

What makes such breaches of the narrative contract possible? One important factor is the ability of certain narratives to inoculate themselves against criticism, precisely by emerging as the voice of *authentic experience*, an experience that cannot be denied, without violating the personhood of the narrator. This is especially true when the experience is one of suffering and victimization, in which case questioning the narrative amounts to compounding the injury through its denial. Wilkomirski's 'I was there, not you' rings with an authority that is very hard to contest. This inoculation of a claim from legitimate scrutiny, its elevation to incontestable truth, is the product of an unquestioned respect for the personal experience of a victim, who 'discovers their voice' by articulating an experience that enables them to cease being a victim and become a survivor. The story is therapeutic even if it is not true.

What is true of literary memoirs is true of stories in general. We can no longer uncritically believe that the 'truth of stories lies in their meaning, not in their accuracy', since the meaning of stories is radically different, depending on whether the facts reported were experienced at first hand or not. The trauma experienced by individuals like Wilkomirski may be real in some way, but the meaning of the trauma is different, depending on whether they actually experienced the ordeal at first hand or whether they imagined it. What we learn from the Wilkomirski affair is that to the two questions feared by every storyteller, 'So what?' and 'Did it *really* happen?', we must now add a corollary, 'On what *authority* do you claim to speak the truth?'

Truth, post-truth and postmodernism

Over the long centuries of human history, there have been numerous sources of authority – the authority of the prophet and the priest with their direct line to the divine, the authority of tradition emerging from customs and practices whose origin is lost in the mist of time, the authority of the military leader, the statesman, the artist or the intellectual resting on their own qualities and skills. Modernity, the period that saw the rise of capitalism and the nation-state, industrialization and rapid urbanization, elevated the authority of the scientist, the expert and the specialist above all others. Its fruits, whether technological, political or cultural, were celebrated (and lamented) as the products of reason, scientific reason. One of modernity's sharpest observers and critics, Max Weber, saw it all as part of a gigantic process of rationalization that swept everything, good and bad, along its path.

In the latter part of the twentieth century, modernity and her champion, reason, faced a sudden challenge with the rise of postmodernism. Fuelled by a belief in the power of words to create reality, postmodernism argued that words like reason, truth and reality are themselves human creations rather than absolute concepts. They assume different meanings in different situations and different narratives. Suddenly from the 1980s on the words 'postmodern' and 'postmodernism' could be found everywhere, in literary discussions, political arguments, marketing campaigns and every type of cultural commentary and artefact. The mere application of the word 'postmodern' magically turned everything postmodern. Accordingly, it was argued that there is no such thing as a single uncontested truth; everything is relative and depends on how we approach it, including postmodernism itself. All meanings are relative and unstable and so, too, are values and value systems. Facts don't exist outside narrative; they are themselves stories and images. Whoever controls the narrative controls the facts. Jean Baudrillard, one of several French philosophers associated with the rise of postmodernism, mischievously argued that the 1991 Gulf War did not take place; it was, instead, a virtual war conducted on television monitors for the benefit of television viewers.[11] His claim was something of a high-water mark for postmodernism. Maybe it was also postmodernism's moment of hubris when facts decided to reassert themselves.

Following the horrors of 9/11, there was a reawakening to the recalcitrance of facts. Thousands of people dying – whether in New

York, Afghanistan, Iraq or Africa – were no virtual deaths, irrespective of whether those dying were cast as victims, martyrs, heroes, villains or collateral damage. Facts cannot be modified at will, although they may be interpreted, contextualized or challenged. Saddam Hussein did not possess weapons of mass destruction, no matter how these are defined. And Wilkomirski had not been a Holocaust survivor, even if he insisted that his experiences were authentic. Facts may be concealed or choked in a morass or disinformation and subterfuge. They may be challenged by patent falsehoods masquerading as 'alternative facts', but they cannot be wished away.

Many of those who had previously joined the postmodernist bandwagon quickly jumped off it and the words 'postmodernism' and 'postmodern' have been in decline ever since. One legacy of postmodernism, however, has endured and thrived, the belief that the way we use words is deeply political and shapes the realities that we experience. Words like 'identity', 'civilization', 'gender' and even the once straightforward word 'woman' lost their innocence and became terrains of contest and argument, feeding the controversies of the culture wars. Many of us in Western countries nowadays take greater offence over an insulting word or phrase than over blatant extremes of inequality, injustice and oppression. In contrast to the decline of postmodernism, the term 'post-truth' is still on the ascendant. Post-truth does not deny the existence of facts as such but emphasizes the ability of emotions, fantasies and wishful thinking of every kind to cancel them and cast patent falsehoods in their place. In a post-truth world, global warming, the outcomes of democratic elections, the origin of epidemics and much else are shrouded in suspicion and uncertainty fuelling different stories, hoaxes, conspiracy theories and so forth.[12]

The voice of experience and the voice of the expert: Can they speak to each other?

Science and scientists are now routinely subject to suspicion. Scientists make mistakes, and they often disagree among themselves. They make false pronouncements and issue exaggerated warnings. They are political players with vested interests of their own. Their authority and their arguments are now regularly questioned, sometimes rightly and sometimes wrongly. Some of this questioning comes from other scientists who take opposing views. Some comes from lobbyists and spokespeople of political and economic interests threatened by a particular scientific opinion. Conspiracy theorists routinely challenge virtually every scientific argument for reasons of their own. One of the biggest challenges to scientific authority in our times comes from the authority of personal experience, the authority of the person who has lived and witnessed events at first hand. The authority of personal experience, as demonstrated by the Wilkomirski affair, has in our times acquired a sanctity of its own and is difficult to gainsay. 'Thou shalt not deny my experience; thou shalt not silence my voice!' becomes an incontestable proclamation in our culture where the therapeutic discourse of earnest confessions and pained disclosures reign supreme.[13]

Personal or lived experience, especially experience of injustice and discrimination, when shared with those of other people facing the same situation, has become the bedrock of 'identity politics', itself a term of much controversy. Someone whose identity has been forged by living through a particular experience or from belonging to a particular group can speak authoritatively about it. 'Speaking as a(n) X' where X can be gender, race, class, age, (dis)ability or any other identifier provides a bedrock of a shared experience and creates a platform of authority. Speaking from that platform a person can expect, if not to be respected, at the very least to be believed.

The Wilkomirski affair and many other hoaxes and scams like it, some of which become notorious while many remain unnoticed, suggest that if science can no longer be fully trusted, neither should the voice of experience be elevated to unquestionable authority. There is indeed a great deal we can learn from direct experience, ours and other people's. Science can no longer disregard lived experience in many fields including environmental science, medicine and all the social sciences. Equally, however, knowledge from experience cannot be accepted without questioning and criticism. Descartes's rationalism has lost much of its appeal in our times, but we would do well to remember his warning about some 'deceiver or other, very powerful and very cunning, whoever employs his ingenuity in deceiving me'[14] and approach all experience, including our own, with a healthy dose of scepticism. Experience, including our own, very often deceives us and cannot be regarded as the final arbiter of truth. No matter how accurately we register our observations and our feelings, no matter how authentically our experiences gush out in words and sentences written and spoken, they are coloured by all kinds of desires, fantasies and resistances that remain hidden from view. Experience is itself a veil. It is a veil that conceals things from others but also from ourselves. Probing what lies under the veil or maybe the different layers of veil that make up experience requires courage, wisdom and an affinity for brutal self-examination that few of us possess.

Instead of conclusion

Maybe Parrhasios did not seek to deceive us after all. The veil he painted was an invitation to reflect. It is a veil of many layers and many meanings. It is a veil that alerts us to the various narrative seductions and deceptions that give us solace and pleasure. It is a veil that warns us against trusting unconditionally what our eyes or our hearts dictate. Maybe, after all, Parrhasios' intention was to invite viewers of his canvas to imagine what lies behind the veil he had so brilliantly painted, the dreams and nightmares that loom deep in their fantasy lives. Maybe, too, it was Zeuxis who, dazzled by his rival's ability to create a lifelike effect, saw the veil as a successful attempt at dissimulation. Or maybe, it was the shrewd Pliny who turned the entire incident into a story of deception.

We, by contrast, have the privilege of reflecting on the story and probing the meanings lying behind the veil. We can project our own desires and fantasies onto it. We can even liberate the narrative from its original framing as a contest and view it, with Oscar Wilde, as a beautiful lie that invites us to ponder the meaning and value of truth.

2

Iphigenia: Escaping from the Shadows

Iphigenia, daughter of King Agamemnon of Argos, finds herself in a distant, foreign land on the Crimean Peninsula. Assisted by a chorus of female Greek captives, she is the chief priestess in the temple of Artemis. There, as per the local custom, she presides over the sacrifice of captured foreigners to the goddess. This is part of the Artemis cult practised by the Taurians, the land's barbarian inhabitants. Her temple is covered in blood and the rotting remains of many victims who have died there. Iphigenia hates her duties but performs them diligently, earning the respect of the locals and their barbarian king, Thoas.

How did Iphigenia end up in this distant and dark land? Iphigenia was herself a sacrificial victim, sacrificed to Artemis by her father Agamemnon to ensure favourable winds for the armed expedition to Troy. But at the moment of the sacrifice, Iphigenia was seized by Artemis and magically transported to the land of the Taurians to become her virgin priestess and chief executor of her cult. Those left behind in Aulis had no idea that Iphigenia has survived the sacrifice or what happened to her subsequently. In her place on the altar, they discovered the dead body of a magnificent stag.

Many years later, Orestes, son of Agamemnon and Iphigenia's brother, arrives in Tauris in a fifty-oared ship after a dangerous journey from Greece. He is accompanied by his faithful friend Pylades. Orestes is nearly mad, pursued by the implacable Furies for the murder of his mother Clytemnestra and her lover who had themselves murdered Agamemnon following his return from Troy. As the only way of expiating his guilt, Orestes was ordered by Apollo, the god of prophecy and brother of Artemis, to seize the sacred statue of his sister from Tauris and bring it to Athens. Only then will he finally find peace and solace.

Orestes and Pylades are captured by the Taurians and sentenced to be sacrificed to Artemis. The priestess presiding over their sacrifice is, unbeknown to Orestes, none other than his sister. After various complications, Orestes and Iphigenia recognize each other as brother and sister who last saw each other when Orestes was only a baby. They fall into each other's arms and, in tears of recognition, tell each other the stories of their tragic lives during the long years of their separation.

They then make a plan to escape from Tauris together with the goddess's statue. Outsmarting the Taurian king Thoas, they reach the deserted bay where Orestes' ship is moored. Their escape, however, is noted by local herdsmen and is further delayed by a freak storm at sea which throws the Greek ship back on the beach. A messenger reports the news to Thoas who is about to send his army and navy after the Greeks.

At this point, the goddess Athena appears in full majesty in front of the king, ordering him to stop his pursuit of the strangers. She demands that the women prisoners held by the Taurians be escorted back to their Greek homelands. She also instructs Orestes to return to Athens and build a temple near Brauron where the statue of Artemis is to be placed and worshipped. Iphigenia will serve the rest of her life as temple warden and will be buried there when she dies. In her honour, the finest garments of women who die in childbirth will be placed on her tomb.

King Thoas duly agrees and is praised by Athena for his wisdom, as she urges favourable winds to take Iphigenia, Orestes and Pylades back to Greece. The chorus of captive women laud Athena and rejoice at their imminent return to their own homeland.

Tauris: Land of exile, danger and savagery

Tauris. A land beyond the dreaded Clashing Rocks of the Bosporus, lying at the edge of the Greeks' known world. Sitting at the very top of the Black Sea, the dangerous, unfriendly sea,[1] it was known up to Byzantine times as the Tauric Peninsula, gradually assuming the name by which it is known today, Crimea.[2] Colonized by a scattering of Greek settlements from about the fifth century BCE, its local inhabitants were never assimilated to the Greek or, later, the Roman world.[3] In our days, less than two hundred years after the horrors of the Crimean War with its more than half a million dead, the land has become the terrain of new horrors and new atrocities. At the time when Euripides wrote his tragedy, in *c.* 414–412 BCE, Tauris could be seen as a land shrouded in near perpetual darkness, whose population could easily be cast as savage cowherds, engaged in human sacrifices, worshipping the cult of a brutal virgin goddess.[4]

This is the land where Iphigenia and her female companions find themselves captive and exiled at the start of the tragedy. The word 'exile', used repeatedly throughout the drama, suffuses it with the deep nostalgia of the exiled. In introducing herself, Iphigenia laments:

Exiled from Greece. Forgotten by Greece.
I sing no songs for Hera at Argos.
I weave no more.

My shuttle does not sing upon the loom!
It does not weave in many colours
the pictures of Pallas Athena and the Titans.[5]

Iphigenia's companions, assisting her in her macabre duties at the temple, are captive women from different parts of Greece. Enslaved in a dark, inhospitable country, they are dreaming against hope of returning home one day. Their chorus of brooding nostalgia evokes the spirit of enslaved and uprooted people and exiles across the ages:[6]

How I wish I could fly!
Follow the paths of the Heavens above where the sun spreads his sweet light . . .
Where he urges the fleetfooted steeds of his chariot.
Then, by beating the wings on my back, I could go and stop above our own home.
If I could only stop high above the place where the chorus dances . . .
. . . there where, as a young girl, worthy of a handsome groom, I would dance with my girlfriends,
all of the same age, my mother swelling with pride nearby.[7]

Tauris is also the land where Orestes is washed out, tasked with the bizarre mission of stealing the goddess's statue and bringing it to Athens. Like Iphigenia, he uses the word 'exile' with great anguish and repeatedly to describe his fate. Having killed his mother, he is hunted down by the Furies wherever he goes. Addressing Apollo, shortly after landing in Tauris, his words suggest a deeper exile, an exile from all humanity, an exile from himself, an inability to escape the moral chaos which engulfs him:

I had become a wandering exile until I went to your temple and asked you for a way to escape their [the Furies'] frenzied anger and that's when you told me to come here. [8]

And later, to his sister, whom he has not yet recognized as such, he says:

I am an exile, yes. Of my own will . . . and yet not.[9]

Iphigenia in Tauris is first and foremost an exile drama, driven forward by a painful longing for the homeland, for home. For this reason alone, it cannot fail to move us from the very start.

Iphigenia: Tragic but resourceful, rational and practical heroine

Who are the protagonists, who find themselves in this dark and inhospitable land?

Iphigenia. Doomed princess, daughter of doom-laden king of kings, Agamemnon. Enticed to Aulis on the pretence of marrying super-hero Achilles, slaughtered by her own father to expedite the brutal expedition against Troy, transported to a savage land to preside over cult human sacrifices. In the earlier tragedy, we met her as a young girl, a sacrificial victim in the pitiless world of men, deceived and manipulated, eventually rising to nobility by resolving to die willingly for the honour of Hellas. It is a very different Iphigenia we encounter in *Iphigenia in Tauris*. A mature woman, she is uprooted, homesick and vulnerable but she is no damsel in distress. The locals, including their savage king, respect her, if only because of her special relation with Artemis, herself a cruel and wayward deity.

Iphigenia is confused and overwhelmed at times, in the grip of powerful and conflicting emotions, including anguish, terror, despair, revulsion and loathing. But she is also resourceful, rational and practical. Once, she recognizes in Orestes and Pylades her kinsmen in dire straits, she takes over the initiative in planning their escape and becomes the main driver of the drama. In assuming responsibility for the dangerous mission ahead, she displays both inventiveness and courage to match any male hero, living fully up to the etymology of her name which means 'born strong'.[10] She also shows prudence, resisting her brother's reckless impulse to kill Thoas, just as Odysseus resists the temptation to kill the Cyclops. Instead, she outwits the king by using her own unique craft, her religious authority with Artemis. She asks to purify the strangers as well as the goddess's effigy which they have supposedly defiled by taking them to the beach where the Greeks' ship is waiting. Thoas obediently complies, an easy victim to Iphigenia's ploy.

One element that gives Iphigenia's plan for escape its unique pathos and power is the support she demands and gets from her assistants, the other enslaved Greek women. She appeals to them in solidarity as fellow women, promising to use her own powers to ensure their future freedom. Her plea to the chorus of deracinated and defenceless women like her has an unmatched eloquence and beauty:

> My dear friends, I turn my eyes towards you.
> My hopes and my Fate rest with you. Whether I succeed in this effort or I die by it; whether or not I lose my country, my beloved brother and my beloved sister, it all rests with you.
> Let the first words of my plea be these:
> We, women, are wise, we support and trust each other and we defend our common interests with all our might. Keep these events a secret and help us with our escape.
> A disciplined tongue is a noble thing.
> You see before you three close friends united with one Fate:
> Either to return home or to die. If I succeed, then I will make sure you get your share of my luck. You, too, will return home, back to Greece.
> So, my dear friends, I beg you. I swear by your right hand –

And yours, and yours, too! And by your sweet cheeks!

By your knees!

By whatever you hold dear, back home: a mother, a father, children, those of you who have them.

What do you all say, then? Speak! Who among you says, yes, who says, no?

If you do not agree with us then I am lost. As well as my poor brother. [11]

These words alone raise Iphigenia to a cosmic level of heroism, a heroism whose combination of daring and plea for solidarity takes her beyond that of any male hero in Greek mythology. But there is one additional feature that sets Iphigenia, as she features in *Iphigenia in Tauris*, apart from other heroines of Greek mythology. Unique among such heroines, she is the only protagonist of a drama whose plot, as Hall points out, 'does not involve sex, marriage, a male partner or becoming a mother'.[12] Instead, the plot is driven by love of different kinds – the love between Iphigenia and her attendants, the love between childhood friends Orestes and Pylades (which inspired many subsequent dramatists and illustrators), but above all the sibling love between Iphigenia and Orestes. It is no accident that when their escape is about to be foiled by an enormous wave that throws the Greek ship back to the beach and to the hands of the waiting Taurians, Iphigenia prays to Artemis by invoking the goddess's love for her own brother, Apollo:

Goddess! I am your priestess. Forgive my theft and please take me away from this barbarian land and bring me safely back to Hellas! You, too, have a brother whom you love, so you must know that I also love mine![13]

The love between Iphigenia and Orestes has nothing of the wild and primal qualities of the love for Orestes shown by his other sister,

Electra, who saw in him a messiah, an avenger of their father's murderer and the redeemer of Argos. Instead, Iphigenia's level-headedness and fundamental sanity stand in opposition to her brother's propensity to madness induced by the Furies. Her love for Orestes whom she remembers as a mere infant finds its ultimate expression in the words with which she greets him in the famous recognition scene, a scene that greatly impressed Aristotle as well as countless painters of frescoes and ceramic vases:

Iphigenia

My dear brother! The dearest man in my life!

You have sailed here, so far from your land, Argos!

Let me hold you!

Orestes

And let me hold you, too, my dear sister. You, who people say are dead!

Tears stream down my face! I grieve and I rejoice, just like you!

Iphigenia

Oh! You were a tiny baby, a tiny, tiny baby when I left you in the arms of your nurse.

The tiniest little being in the palace!

Oh! My heart! You are more joyful than words can express!

What can my lips say?

All this was beyond hope. Beyond miracles, beyond words![14]

When Orestes arrives in Tauris, accompanied by the faithful Pylades, he is in what we would recognize today as a state of post-traumatic stress disorder (PTSD). He has done the second worst thing that any man[15] can do, apart from killing his father and marrying his mother. He has killed his own mother, avenging his father's murder by her and her lover. Orestes is now haunted by the implacable Furies, periodically plunging into abject depression or exploding in delirious mania. To redeem himself, he has been ordered by the god Apollo, or so he believes, to steal the hallowed artefact of Artemis, presumed to have fallen from heaven, from its legitimate if unpleasant owners, the Taurians. In the state he is in, his friend Pylades is more of a carer than a partner. And Iphigenia is the driving force of the escape rather than the captive princess being saved by the two gallant men.

Once the identities of the Greeks have been revealed to each other, the drama unfolds as a pure escape story. Having outfoxed Thoas and his followers, the Greek trio of Iphigenia, Orestes and Pylades escape from the barbarian land with the effigy of Artemis, but not without an intervention at the critical moment of another goddess, Athena. It is her sudden appearance that brings the story to its happy conclusion.

Both the drama's happy end and the *ex machina* intervention by the goddess jar with modern audiences. Is *Iphigenia in Tauris* a tragedy at all? Different scholars have described it in different ways as a tragicomedy, a tragedy manqué, a romance, or an escape play.[16] Aristotle, however, had no hesitation in singling it out as a tragedy and an exemplary one at that. For Aristotle, as for ancient Greeks in general, a tragedy was not a story necessarily ending up in disaster. He would have been surprised at the way the word 'tragedy' is used today to describe any and every event that results in extreme suffering. Instead, a tragedy, for the Greeks, was a narrative that involved a rapid transition or reversal from good to bad or from bad to good (and often to bad again) brought about by accident (what the Greeks called 'Tyche') or by the unexpected consequences of the protagonists' actions. Aristotle contrasted *Iphigenia in Tauris* to the other exemplary tragedy which he held in great esteem, *Oedipus Rex*. Both these works, he argued, make optimal use of surprises, in which a set of vital recognitions brings about the protagonists' sudden reversal of fortune – but while in *Oedipus Rex* the plot moves from light to darkness, Iphigenia's plot moves from darkness to light.[17] All the same, the Aristotelean emotions of pity and fear that engulf the audience at the end of a performance of *Iphigenia in Tauris* are tempered by the drama's happy ending, as the chorus praise Athena, rejoice in the deliverance of Iphigenia, Orestes and Pylades, and their own imminent salvation.

And what of the *deus ex machina* device, where a god descends literally with the help of a mechanical hoist to bring about the resolution of the drama? Interventions by a superior agent to bring about closure have been used in different kinds of fiction for centuries. It is Athena's intervention (again) that restores peace at the end of the *Odyssey*, a peace that seems too precarious to last. Several of Euripides' tragedies concluded in this way, most notably *Medea*. This is something for which he was criticized already in ancient times, not least by Aristotle, who argued that a play's resolution is best accomplished 'as a result of the plot itself, and not from a contrivance'.[18] In more recent times, the role of *deus ex machina* can be performed by the accidental discovery of a magical tool, the arrival of the all-conquering US cavalry, or an inheritance from a rich uncle in America. In all of these cases, an external and unexpected factor enters the plot in the nick of time to provide a resolution and a final dramatic twist. Does the plot of *Iphigenia in Tauris* call for such an intervention? Goethe did not think so and brought his own play of *Iphigenia in Tauris* to its happy conclusion with a reconciliation between Greeks and barbarians. This clears an old misunderstanding and allows for reason and universal brotherhood and sisterhood to triumph.[19]

Euripides, too, could have brought the story to its happy conclusion without the help of a metaphysical intervention by Athena. It is only the unexpected sea storm just as the Greeks have boarded their ship and are escaping that throws the plot wide open again and calls for Athena's *ex machina* appearance to bring about the final resolution. In spite of its 'contrived' nature, this resolution accomplishes several important results which would not have been achieved without that final plot twist. First, it ties the events in Tauris with the subsequent cult worship of both Artemis and Iphigenia in Brauron and other sites in eastern Attica which would have been familiar to the audiences of Euripides. In this way, the tragedy becomes an origin or a 'just so' story,[20] accounting for subsequent practices and institutions. Second, the divine intervention ensures the liberation of the remaining captives, the Greek women of the chorus who have supported Iphigenia risking their own lives. Iphigenia's pledge will be fulfilled, and the women will return home from their exiles. Third, Athena's intervention legitimizes the theft of Artemis' effigy from its rightful owners. By establishing a new setting for the cult of Artemis near Athens, it provides some rationale for Apollo's earlier command to Orestes. Finally, and most importantly, it allows Thoas to have a change of heart sending his captives off in good grace, earning the praise of Athena, a Greek goddess, and showing himself to be a man capable of transforming himself. He, a barbarian, confronted by the majesty of Greek divinity, can act in a noble way.

Barbarians and exiles

Barbarians. The word, used repeatedly in Euripides' tragedy, whether in performance or in written text, creates an unpleasant jolt. Already found in Homer,[21] the term 'barbarian' may have been used originally to describe someone who didn't speak Greek or who spoke Greek badly. *Bar-bar* may well have been what foreign languages sounded to Greek ears at the time. By the time Euripides was writing, the word's negative associations had already hardened.[22] Barbarians were typecast as primitive and cruel, as impulsive and unable to control their urges, alternately as cowardly and effeminate or brutal and pitiless, as indolent and luxurious or primitive and uncultured. A key feature of barbarians as typecast by the Greeks was their inability to develop political institutions and act as citizens of a 'polis' (city-state). This finds its pinnacle in Iphigenia's utterance in Euripides' earlier tragedy, approvingly cited by Aristotle, 'It is right ... that Hellenes should rule barbarians, but not barbarians Hellenes, those being slaves, while these are free.'[23]

The portrayal of the Taurians in *Iphigenia in Tauris* weaves together nearly all the stereotypes of barbarism.[24] A population of cattle farmers, practising human sacrifices, without institutions or social relations to speak of, they feature in the drama as 'little more than ventriloquized, animated puppets designed to make the Greeks' intelligence and emotional range appear to the best advantage'.[25] Their king, Thoas, until Athena's final intervention, is the stereotype of a brutal despot, thirsting for the foreigners' blood, his only redeeming feature being the respect in which he holds Iphigenia in as much as she acts as an effective conduit to Artemis. He is easily outsmarted by Iphigenia's ploy of having the strangers and the effigy of the goddess purified, displaying a primitive gullibility and piety.[26]

In all of these ways, the description of the Taurians by Euripides are direct projections of Greek ethnocentrism, a postcolonial mindset, and a classic example of 'othering'. This is the process of casting a group, an individual or an object into the role of the Other and establishing one's own identity in opposition to and, frequently, vilification of this Other. The ease with which the adjective 'other' has generated the verb 'to other' in the last twenty years or so is indicative of the power of a term that now occupies an important position in feminist, postcolonial, civil rights and sexual minority discourses. Othering is a process that goes beyond denigration – it denies the Other those defining characteristics of the Same: reason, dignity, love, pride, heroism, nobility and ultimately any entitlement to human rights.

Whether the Other is a racial or a religious group, a gender group, a sexual minority or a nation, it is made rife for ridicule, exploitation, oppression and indeed genocide by denying its essential humanity. As the philosopher Richard Rorty argued, 'Everything turns on who counts as a fellow human being, as a rational agent in the only relevant sense – the sense in which rational agency is synonymous with membership of our moral community.'[27] Maybe the most pernicious aspect of othering is trapping the Other into a distorted mode of existence from which it is impossible to escape.[28] Virtually anything the Other says or does simply reinforces this othering. The process of othering has been a defining feature of colonization and colonial and postcolonial mindsets where a primitive, uncivilized, indolent, deceitful (the list can be extended almost indefinitely) 'native' provides the reference point against which a European identity of the civilized, disciplined, rational and moral man is constructed, an identity that is not discomfited when inflicting any kind of humiliation on the Other.[29]

The fact that the barbarians themselves in Euripides' tragedy accept the designation of barbarian is indicative of its power and reach. The Taurians have accepted the Greek projection and see themselves as 'barbarian'. But this, too, is a Greek projection, hence part of the othering process – the Other is denied a voice and can only speak with the voice of the Same. Even so, Euripides' well-known propensity for mockery at times subverts the othering logic of his plotline. It would not have escaped Greek audiences of the fifth century BCE that human sacrifice, a cornerstone of the othering logic which the Greeks of the time attributed to barbarians, was precisely what was done to Iphigenia by her own father. Or again, consider the drama's most amusing incident, when Iphigenia tricks King Thoas by claiming that she must purify the two strangers before sacrificing them because they are tainted. 'Why?' asks Thoas. 'Have they killed one of our

barbarians in the beach?' delightfully using the barbarian moniker for
his own people. Upon hearing that one of the strangers has killed his
own mother, Thoas exclaims, 'O, dear Apollo! This is something that
even we, barbarians would never do!'[30] This line still generates laughter
in performance – whether his statement is an instinctive expression
of revulsion or an ironic aspersion against the noblest of Greece's
civilized deities.

The theft of the statue of Artemis by the Greeks is another classic
example of Greek ethnocentrism. The two heroes are instructed to
recover the effigy from the barbarian land where it has 'fallen from the
sky'. The barbarians are clearly unable to recognize its real value and
Apollo himself commands Orestes to seize it and bring it to Athens.
Lord Elgin could not have invented a better justification for seizing
the Parthenon marbles and relocating them in the safe and cultured
spaces of the British Museum. Even so, Euripides' barbarians, as they
fight the Greeks on the beach, reproach them delightfully: 'What gives
you the right to come here and steal our statues and our priestesses?'[31]
The use of the hyperbolic plural for 'statues' and 'priestesses' may
suggest the barbarians' outrage at the Greeks' sacrilegious theft as
much as their unsophisticated emotional repertoire.[32]

The Shadow

In spite of Euripides' attempts to scatter the seeds of doubt and
subversion in his text, in spite of his subtle ambiguities and ironic
detachment, *Iphigenia in Tauris* presents an unbridgeable gulf between
Greek and barbarian, between the cultured and the primitive. In
projecting all the undesirable qualities of the Greek onto the barbarian,
the barbarian becomes the Shadow of the civilized person, just as it
does in Hans Christian Andersen's 1847 short story, *The Shadow*.[33] In

this story, a cultured man, a 'young and clever scholar from the colder north', travels to a sunny foreign land and is exposed to fascinating new sights and new experiences. He takes ever greater notice of his shadow than he did in his sunless homeland. Gradually he realizes that the shadow assumes an independent existence. At some point, the shadow becomes entirely separate from the man and it eventually disappears altogether. The anonymous man returns home without his shadow but, years later, the shadow comes back and is reunited with him. Only now, the man realizes that, instead of being the master of the shadow, he has become its slave. In the story's grim end, the shadow marries a hard-nosed princess, while the man, who is no longer young, is summarily executed.

Andersen's story has been interpreted in different ways,[34] but it must have exercised a fascination on Carl Jung who theorized the Shadow as one of the core archetypes of humanity.[35] It is a primordial image, part of our symbolic and spiritual legacy and a foundational element of our collective unconscious. The archetype of the Shadow stands for the dark side of every human being, a part of ourselves that is not just unknown to us but actively repressed from our conscious mind.[36] Onto the Shadow, we project all those qualities that we disavow in ourselves, including brutality, envy, hate and so forth. Thereafter we live most of our lives as if these qualities exist in others but not in ourselves. The Shadow, as theorized by Jung, cannot be experienced directly. It is deeply unconscious. But it surfaces regularly in dreams, fantasies, powerful experiences and feelings as well as neurotic symptoms. At times, the Shadow can appear suddenly in our lives, as it does in Andersen's story, overwhelming us through spasms of irrationality, self-harm, depression, horror and violence.

In addition to its individual manifestations, the Shadow has collective manifestations. Groups, families, communities and nations all possess Shadows that are cast over the entirety of their members.

Collective Shadows are expressed in myths, rituals, group fantasies, religious and political beliefs and so forth. They are composed of shared but disavowed psychic contents, including collective traumas and failures, shameful events in a group's past, unrealized ideals and ambitions, shared fears, obsessions and suspicions. In common parlance, we often refer to these as the 'dark side' of the group, the community or the nation.

Groups collectively seek to manage their Shadow by keeping it firmly subordinated to idealized collective achievements and triumphs, expressed in myths and stories, commemorations, historical relics, national museums and celebrations and so forth. These bind groups together, acting as anchors for group identities and also as standards to uphold. In addition, however, groups seek legitimate expressions for their Shadow. This is where othering becomes very effective, since in addition to anchoring group identities in shared achievements and triumphs, othering enables groups to base their identities in opposition to the Other, the conscious expression of the group's unconscious Shadow. In Joseph Conrad's famous novel of 1899, for example, the 'heart of darkness' of the title, located in Africa, represents in an archetypal way the Jungian Shadow of the 'civilized' European collective identity. In our times, the collective Shadow can be directed by populist leaders at the corrupt and malevolent elites in opposition to the purity and goodness of 'the people'.[37] Alternatively, the Shadow can be cast onto the needy and undeserving outsiders and shirkers, the 'parasites' who suck the life out of the nation. While the elites become the targets for projections of greed, arrogance and contempt for the people, the parasites are targeted for their ingratitude, their envy and their neediness. All of these are projections of disavowed elements that enable an idealized image of the people as authentic, pure and wholesome.

Could the Greeks have found a more hospitable sanctuary for their collective Shadow than the Scythian shore, Tauris, the land of shadows and human sacrifices, shrouded in near-perpetual darkness? Remember that Euripides was reinventing the myth of Iphigenia during or shortly after the disastrous expedition of the Athenian forces to Sicily (415–413 BCE) during the Peloponnesian War which signalled the collapse of Athens and its Golden Age. Writing at a time of desperate danger, in Athens, a city whose citizens were dying in their thousands in the quarries of Syracuse, when Greeks were massacring and enslaving each other in an orgy of fratricidal carnage, it is the Taurian that Euripides cast as the barbarian, the Shadow, the Other.

A short digression: Tauris in a hospital emergency ward

At this point I have a confession to make to the reader. In spite of the recognition scene between Iphigenia and Orestes that I always found deeply moving, the story of *Iphigenia in Tauris* was never one of my favourite Greeks myths. Its implausible start (Iphigenia magically transported by Artemis at the moment of her sacrifice in Aulis), the heroics of the Greek duo of Orestes and Pylades, and especially the equally implausible happy end through an *ex machina* intervention, all conspired to diminish the story in my eyes. I also found myself little affected by the live performances of Euripides' tragedy and Gluck's opera I had attended, which left me cold and dissatisfied. I am now approaching both of these works with a fresh mind. The reason for this was a story I heard as part of a research project in a London hospital, one that evoked the story of the Taurian Iphigenia, prompting me to look at it more carefully and in greater depth.

The story was told by a male junior hospital doctor during a group interview, in which my colleagues and I were trying to elicit examples of good quality patient care. The story was enthusiastically endorsed by other participants, all junior doctors, as an excellent example of good patient care and also as typical of the sort of situation they faced on a daily basis during their night shifts. Here is the junior doctor's story, verbatim:

> A pregnant woman came in through A&E [Accident and Emergency]. She was having problems with her pregnancy. I asked the registrar [senior clinician] what to do. They decided that the best thing to do was get the woman scanned to find the problem. However, being a night shift there were no porters to be seen and the scanning units were closed. I felt that the anxious woman could not stay in A&E surrounded by drunks and druggies as it was inappropriate. Instead of calling for porters, which would have taken time, I and the registrar moved the pregnant lady to the maternity ward ourselves where we opened up a scanning unit to find out what was wrong with the lady's pregnancy. I was proud of the leadership that I had received from my registrar; not every registrar would have done this, but he solved the problem and delivered good patient care in the process. The problems were resolved within an hour with only skeletal night staff.

On first reading this story with its simple plot, its rudimentary characters and its limited emotional range, one finds little to connect it to the complexities of Greek myths with their superhuman heroes and dark passions. Yet, the story immediately triggered mythological thinking, linking it to the myth of *Iphigenia in Tauris*, partly because of its rescue theme and the presence of two male protagonists and a woman in trouble. Of course, unlike Iphigenia, the woman in the story is entirely passive, saved by the two gallant doctors. The story is not an escape story but a highly gendered rescue story. In it, two male characters save the damsel in distress by *going beyond the call of duty*.

This is what accords the two doctors a heroic quality. The woman, for her part, turns, in the course of the narrative, into a 'lady', whose plight calls for individualized care from the doctors. This contrasts to the plight of the anonymous 'drunks and druggies', whose treatment was negatively affected by the preferential treatment offered to the pregnant woman.

The story immediately reveals a division – at least in the mind of the narrator and his audience – between the deserving and the undeserving patient. The former has a human face as an individual with unique needs who evokes empathy and care. The Other is the impersonal patient, who, the story suggests, is undeserving and even parasitical. Their plight evokes indifference or even resentment on the part of the doctors; they can be *sacrificed* in the interest of rescuing the pregnant woman. This sacrifice causes no discomfort for the narrator or his audience, all junior doctors who responded to the story enthusiastically, exclaiming at its conclusion, 'Yes, yes, this is exactly the sort of incident that demonstrates good patient care in our hospital!'

It is telling that the narrative is quiet about the nature of the problems that afflicted the woman's pregnancy, as if these were irrelevant to the story. They may have been serious medical issues or exaggerated fears on her part. What is relevant is her distress over the possibility of losing her baby, a distress that affects the narrator directly. His use of the slightly odd expression 'proud of the leadership I . . . received from my registrar' suggests a level of gratitude towards his senior colleague who stepped in to support him in his own moment of acute need and vulnerability. In this way, the clinical senior is also seen as someone going beyond the call of duty to support his junior just as they both go beyond the call of duty to help the pregnant woman. Caring is offered to the woman in need, but it is also extended to the junior by his senior. In this way, the three of them become a single entity bound by ties of solidarity in the face of a common predicament.

Another reason why the A&E story may have awakened the myth of the Taurian Iphigenia is its dark and at times macabre quality, alluded to in the expression 'skeletal night staff'. The story is set during a night shift, when anxieties and fears are exacerbated, when porters are simply nowhere 'to be seen' and managers and administrators are absent. It is also a time when conventional hospital routines and procedures on triage and priority of care are loosened, allowing for personal heroism to surface. The doctors' heroics of going beyond the call of duty in assisting the pregnant woman relegates the 'drunks and druggies' to the part of lost souls whose fate is indifferent to the narrator. Unlike the chorus of *Iphigenia in Tauris* who will be saved from captivity and exile by Athena's divine intervention, they are a silent chorus, left to suffer in solitude and neglect.

Without reaching the tragedy's emotional range and plot complexities, the story mirrors, if imperfectly, several of the features of the ancient myth – the gendered nature of the rescue mission, the split between Same and Other, the emotional bonds that unify the Same in opposition to the Other, and the sacrifice of the Other in the interest of the Same. In this way, Euripides arguably helps us make sense of the story's key elements that might have gone unnoticed had we limited ourselves to applying conventional techniques like narrative or discourse analysis. Maybe the biggest assistance that Euripides provides us is in helping us understand why in the darkness of the night, in a high anxiety environment like that of a hospital A&E department, things do not follow the rules and procedures of a bureaucratic organization. These rules and procedures, meant to ensure the fair and equal treatment of all patients by a state organization, are suspended. Instead, the well-being of some is sacrificed in the interest of another at the discretion of the doctors, whose action is hailed as heroic.

Conclusion

Confronted with the complexities of the Taurian Iphigenia in performance or simply by reading Euripides' text in translation, contemporary audiences will respond in different ways. Much of it will depend on the quality of the performance or the translation as well as the audience's own circumstances, the troubles and anxieties that afflict them.

Young people may recognize in Iphigenia, Orestes and Pylades young people suffering for the crimes of earlier generations, wondering whether their own troubles may not be rooted in the actions of their parents and grandparents. The theme of exile and unbearable homesickness will move many people, especially those living in foreign countries away from their homeland to escape war, persecution or poverty. The setting of the drama in the Crimea, the epicentre of one of today's darkest tragedies, a war between people sharing a common faith and many cultural traditions, will inevitably shake Europeans who thought that such horrors no longer had a place on their continent. There are parts of the story that may leave us perplexed or indifferent. The caprices of the gods (like Apollo's command to Orestes or his sister Artemis' overbearing silence throughout the drama) and their *ex machina* appearances and disappearances may strike us as implausible. The self-sacrificing friendship between Orestes and Pylades which entranced earlier generations may leave most of us cold, unless it is presented in sexual terms, an irresistible temptation for today's directors and translators. Even the deep and passionate sibling love between Iphigenia and Orestes may not speak to most of us with the force it once held. By contrast, the powerful sisterhood that binds Iphigenia with her companions will move many of us deeply.

Maybe above all else, and along with Edith Hall,[38] most of us will recognize and celebrate Iphigenia's uniqueness in Greek mythology, as a woman who combines passion and courage with outstanding resourcefulness and intelligence, pursuing goals other than those of romance, marriage and motherhood. In this way, as Hall has noted, she stands as an archetype for today's quest heroine. In all these ways, Euripides dark tragedy offers a rich narrative tapestry of images and events that still resonate today, capable of arousing passions, including the classical Aristotelian mixture of pity and awe.

The story's most unsettling aspect to modern sensibilities is Euripides' brutal caricature of the barbarians and the gulf that separates them from civilized people, a gulf that we have rightly learnt to mistrust after discovering that civilized people are capable of atrocities and cruelties every bit as hideous as those of the worst barbarians. More than two thousand years after Euripides, another Greek, the Alexandrian poet Constantine Cavafy, returned to the divide between civilization and barbarism in a poem whose pre-apocalyptic imagery accords perfectly with the gloomy mood of our times. In his 'Waiting for the Barbarians', Cavafy imagines himself as one of a huge crowd that has gathered in a city's large central square. Is it Rome? Is it Athens? It doesn't matter. The crowd anxiously awaits the arrival of the barbarians. Who are the barbarians? What are their intentions? Such is the state of decadence, meaninglessness and loss among the population that they seem not to care; they need something, anything, even the barbarians to come and bring change and renewal.

The kingdom's emperor has woken up early and has placed his throne next to the city gates where the barbarians will arrive. He has prepared a special scroll to offer them. A surrender? An abdication? It is not clear. The legislators and other dignitaries and notables, too, are waiting expectantly for the barbarians, in all their regalia. They hope to impress the barbarians with their emerald and amethyst jewellery, their scarlet-embroidered togas, the golden staves and maces. Only the orators have stayed away. It seems that the barbarians do not care for public speeches.

Then the crowd is seized by uncertainty and confusion. As darkness comes, they begin to drift away from the square, returning to their homes. Why? The answer comes in the poem's unexpected conclusion:

Night has fallen and the barbarians haven't come.
Some people have arrived from the frontier towns,
And said that there are no barbarians to be seen any longer.
Now what will happen to us without barbarians?
Those people were a solution of sorts.[39]

As in Beckett's *Waiting for Godot*, Cavafy's narrative is built around the escalation of an expectation and then the sudden but weary disappointment resulting from its non-realization. As with Godot who doesn't turn up, the failure of the barbarians to show up casts the whole preceding narrative in a new light. Who are the barbarians? Were they expected as conquerors or as liberators? Did they simply vanish or were they always a figment of the city's imagination? And what kind of a solution would they be?

At first sight, the barbarians are the conquerors who have finally reached the gates of a decaying and helpless empire, its armies and defences overrun, its population ready to submit to them. They have lost their appetite to fight as well as their faith in their own institutions. The crowd is fatalistically waiting for the city's final capitulation. Yet, the failure of the barbarians to show up and the crowd's disappointment suggests that the barbarians were throughout a creation of their own imagination. But what kind of creation? Commenting on his own poem, Cavafy offered a surprising interpretation. He suggested that the barbarians may represent a popular desire for radical change and for a simpler life. 'Society,' he wrote, 'reaches a level of luxury, culture and irritation (=torpor), where, despairing of a state in which no solution compatible with everyday life is possible, it decides to opt for a radical change – to sacrifice, to transform itself, to go backwards, to simplify.' He proposes that, at the end of the poem, people realize that this longing for the life 'of a simple and uncultured person for whom things have the pleasure and charm of the unexplored' is 'utopian'.[40] This realization that the desire for simplicity is utopian results not in despair, but in disappointment. The dream of a simpler life represented by the barbarian will remain a dream.

Whether the barbarians represent something brutal and primitive or something simpler and closer to nature, the poem leaves no doubt that people who consider themselves cultured *need* the barbarian. By casting the barbarian in this light, Cavafy meets Euripides and reaches beyond him. The barbarians are always part of us, as every age and every society reimagines them according to their own dreams and nightmares. Our own times, with their Manichean splits between good and bad, their all-pervading fears and anxieties, their conspiracy theories, their inability to communicate and understand the Other, and their nostalgia for times that were simpler and kinder, create their own barbarians.

In the realm of myth, barbarians of different ages meet, cohabit and mutate. In our collective unconscious, the barbarian as threat whom we want to annihilate, the barbarian as an inner demon from whom, like Orestes, we desperately seek to flee, but also the barbarian as a life-sustaining dream of a simpler and happier life, these and other images of the barbarian exist together, always as the Other, the Shadow. Euripides and Cavafy have started a conversation about the barbarians. Whether we encounter them out there in flesh and blood, whether they are projections of our minds, or inhabitants of the deeper recesses of our heart, we should continue this conversation.

3

Phaëthon: Flying High before Crashing

Phaëthon, young son of the Sun god Helios, was unsure about his father's true identity. With good reason. He was growing up in the court of King Merops of Ethiopia who treated him like his very own son. Yet, his mother Clymene regaled Phaëthon with stories of his real *father, the god who rides his blazing chariot across the sky every day, surveying everything that happens in heaven and on earth. To make matters worse, one of Phaëthon's young playmates, Epaphus, son of Zeus and one of his countless 'conquests', taunted him mercilessly. One day, his insults were more than Phaëthon could bear: 'You are a fool,' Epaphus said, 'to believe all that your mother says; that divine father you boast about is all nonsense – he is not your* real *father!' Flushed with shame, Phaëthon asked his mother to prove that his father truly was the Sun god. Moved by her son's distress, Clymene, with tears in her eyes, turned at the sun's beaming blaze and swore a solemn oath that he who 'governs the whole globe' is his true father and the father of his sisters, the Heliades, too. If, however, he wanted confirmation, why did he not visit Helios in his shining palace in the east and put the question to him.*

Whether Phaëthon's journey to the east was a long or a short one is debated. He did eventually reach his father's dazzling palace of gold, silver and bronze and met Helios dressed in magnificent purple robes, surrounded by his entourage of the Seasons, the Hours, the Months, the Years and the Centuries. Helios received him kindly and immediately confirmed what Clymene had said. 'Truly, you are my son, just as your mother said. But to remove any doubt from your mind I will give you proof. Ask anything you want of me, and you will have it.' Helios affirmed his promise by making the greatest oath a god or a mortal could make – swearing on the water of the river Styx. At once Phaëthon responded that he wanted to drive his father's golden chariot across the sky for a single day. At once Helios realized the folly of his promise. In vain he pleaded with the boy to relinquish this dream. No god, not even Zeus himself, let alone any mortal, could control the four fiery steeds that pulled the chariot. The more desperate Helios became seeking to dissuade Phaëthon from his foolish desire, the more doggedly Phaëthon stuck to his request. Taking his father's place, even for a single day, surveying the skies and the earth from high above, was all that mattered to him and filled him with delirious excitement.

Helios concedes. He has no other option. Even he, a god, is bound by an oath he has given. More as a token than as serious advice, he counsels Phaëthon how to follow the charted path, not too high, nor too low. Above all, he urges the boy to spare the whip and keep a firm rein on the horses. Phaëthon hardly listens, exhilarated as he is at the prospect of the journey ahead. Soon he climbs on the chariot, the four horses already yoked and raring to go. The gates of the palace stable open and the horses burst out into the open air, gaining height rapidly. Barely for a moment does Phaëthon feel the joy of the ride, the inebriation of height, the glory of speed. Barely a moment does it take for the horses to realize that something is wrong, that there is no proper ballast in the chariot, no firm hands on the reins. In panic, they run wild, quitting their usual path, pulling hither and thither, now climbing up to great heights and nearly missing the Crab and the Scorpion constellations, now diving low and *scorching huge areas of land. Pale and shaking in terror, Phaëthon now wishes he had never had this crazy dream, he had never doubted his mother and had never left the comfortable palace of Merops.*

There are many different accounts of the damage that Phaëthon caused during his calamitous ride. Some say that the inhabitants of Ethiopia turned black under the blazing heat as the chariot scorched their land and that the Sahara turned into a permanent desert. Lakes and rivers dried up, all vegetation was destroyed, every single mountain from the Alps to the Caucasus and mighty Olympus were set ablaze. The sea was boiling, dolphins dared not leap and Poseidon himself had to flee to its deepest recesses to escape the conflagration.

Life on earth is in danger of imminent and total destruction. In despair, Mother Earth pleads with Zeus: 'If land and sea, if heaven's high palaces perish, prime chaos will all confound. Save from the flames whatever's still alive, and prove you mean Creation to survive.' [1] *Zeus, greatly alarmed, and after a hasty consultation with the other gods, has to act. He quickly picks up one of his thunderbolts and strikes Phaëthon and the chariot. The last thing the young man sees as he hurtles to the ground, his auburn hair on fire, is the whole earth on fire. He falls headlong, like a streaming trail of light into the water of the river Eridanus. Still smouldering, his remains are found and buried by some kindly Hesperian nymphs. The horses, relieved of their unreliable master, gradually settle down, resume their routine and make their way peacefully to the west.*

Phaëthon was mourned. His sisters, the Heliades, grieved for months on the shores of the river, shedding bitter tears. Finally, the gods took pity on them and turned them into poplar trees, their tears becoming amber pearls dropping into the water. Phaëthon's dear friend, Cygnus (not the cruel Epaphus), sat by the river's edge and mourned him for years, until his hair was white and the gods took pity on him turning him into a swan. Phaëthon's father, the great Helios, sick with grief, took days off work, leaving the earth in total darkness. His poor mother Clymene, overwhelmed with sorrow, roamed the earth until she found Phaëthon's tomb on the river's bank where the Hesperian nymphs had buried him. Prostrate and drenched in tears, Clymene hugged the marble tombstone. On it, the words were carved:

> *'Here Phaëthon lies, who drove his father's the Sun god's chariot, Great was his fall, yet greatly did he dare.'*

Phaëthon: Identity troubles and dreams of flying

Confusions over identity are central to the story of Phaëthon. Who is Phaëthon and who is Helios? Phaëthon's name, meaning 'radiant' or 'shining', derives from the Greek word *phaos* meaning 'light'. Confusingly, his father, too, is occasionally referred to with the epithet Phaëthon, 'the shining one'. Besides Phaëthon in our story, there is another mythological Phaëthon, son of Eos, the goddess of Dawn, whose story occasionally merges or is confused with that of the son of Helios. And what of Helios himself? In Ovid's telling of the story, Helios is the same god as Phoebus Apollo, the god of light, the arts, archery and prophecy, medicine and healing. The Greeks, by contrast, could not envisage Apollo with his enormous portfolio of responsibilities being also in charge of daily dragging the celestial chariot across the sky. This vital but rather routine responsibility was assigned to a different deity, the Titan Helios, his name meaning 'sun' in Greek, son of the titans Hyperion and Theia. Still, there is extensive conflation of Apollo and Helios in Greek as well as in Roman mythology, something that is not uncommon in the realm of myth where different characters and archetypes regularly merge and separate.

The story's driving force is Phaëthon's quest for his true identity. Accused of being a mere mortal, he seeks to establish the immortal quality of his lineage. Doubts over the real identity of his father sow the seed for his own troubled psychological identity. Illegitimate he may be, but this is preferable to being just another ordinary princeling; and it is infinitely preferable to not being sure who his true father is. Epaphus' insults, reminiscent of the insults that took Oedipus to Delphi and to his own demise, set the whole story in motion.

Anxieties over fatherhood have plagued human beings since the beginning of time; it is only recently with the advent of DNA parenthood tests that it has become possible for individuals to reliably identify their father. Not surprisingly, a large number of people have discovered that their biological father is not the person they regarded as their father. One of those was Justin Welby, 105th Archbishop of Canterbury. In 2016, at the age of sixty, Welby discovered that his biological father was not Gavin Welby, the man he had regarded as his father, but Sir Anthony Montague Browne, the private secretary to Churchill, with whom his mother had had an affair. At the time, he accepted what for most people would have been a shocking discovery with considerable grace but also a degree of ambivalence, commenting: 'Although there are elements of sadness and even tragedy in my father's [Gavin Welby's] case, this is a story of redemption and hope from a place of tumultuous difficulty and near-despair in several lives. It is a testimony to the grace and power of Christ to liberate and redeem us, grace and power which is offered to every human being.' He added: 'My own experience is typical of many people. To find that one's father is other than imagined is not unusual. To be the child of families with great difficulties in relationships, with substance abuse or other matters, is far too normal ... This revelation has, of course, been a surprise, but in my life and in our marriage Caroline and I have had far worse. I know that I find who I am in Jesus Christ, not in genetics, and my identity in him never changes.'[2]

It is hard to overemphasize the importance of the anxiety over fatherhood and its effects on our emotional lives.[3] Is our father an impostor? Are we illegitimate? Are we different from who we think we are? Have we been the victims of deception throughout our lives? These anxieties feed a set of fantasies known to psychoanalysis as the 'family romance'.[4] In the classic version of this fantasy a child imagines that their real parents are a king and a queen, their actual parents mere impostors who seized them at a young age.[5] The case of Phaëthon, while expressing the same anxiety, is the exact opposite of this – he believes that he is the son of a god but is afraid that his real father may be a mere mortal. The meeting with Helios clears this uncertainty – almost too easily. After all, Helios has offered no cast-iron proof that he is indeed Phaëthon's father, but this does not trouble the young man. He wants to believe that Helios is his father and he believes him. Henceforth his doubt over his father's true identity turns into doubt whether he can live up to such a father. His quest for identity is no longer a forensic one; it becomes a psychological one. Having a famous father is not enough. If anything, now that he knows who his father is, his quest to prove himself worthy of such a father becomes even more pressing.

The curse of having a famous parent is one that frequently plagues their offspring who struggle to fashion an identity of their own, away from the shadow of their parent. This theme was explored with great insight by Diana Winstanley,[6] herself the daughter of a celebrity father. She argued that for many such children creating an identity of their own is a journey fraught with dangers.[7] Some children take ever greater risks in a desperate attempt to impress their parents, themselves too preoccupied with their own celebrity. Alternatively, they may seek to attract their parents' attention and draw love upon themselves by adopting a victim position, harming themselves and hurtling from one disaster to another. Phaëthon undoubtedly opted for the heroic path to identity. He sought to emulate his father even for a single day. His request, as Ovid describes it, has all the qualities of a kneejerk reaction to his father's promise to grant him anything he wanted:

[Helios] scarce had ended [talking] when the boy declared
His wish – his father's chariot for one day
With licence to control the soaring steeds.[8]

Dreams of flying

Phaëthon's wish is undoubtedly impulsive and audacious. But in addition to emulating his father, in that split second it took him to make his request, another burning desire had surfaced – the desire to fly. This desire, found in countless stories and myths, suggests something deep-seated and primordial.[9] It has fuelled attempts to create flying machines, to rise above the clouds, to reach out into space and view the earth from afar. The adventures of aviators and astronauts have long excited the public imagination and endowed their protagonists with heroic capacities;[10] today, ordinary mortals have dreams of going into space, the ultimate in adventure tourism.

There is something about Phaëthon that casts him apart from other flying heroes and makes him the ultimate archetype for those who love to fly. Alone among Greek heroes, he flies *because he wants to fly* – not to escape from prison like Daedalus and Icarus, to flee from trouble like Phrixus and Helle, or to kill monsters like Perseus and Bellerophon. He just wants to fly.[11] He does not seek emulate his father yoked to the chariot. He wants to breathe the fresh air high above the earth, to feel freedom like the birds, the flying gods Hermes and Iris, the stars themselves. He wants to escape gravity and earthly burdens. He wants to see from high up what the eye cannot observe from the hurly-burly of life on the ground. His demise is inescapable. Without adequate preparation or forethought, his father's last-minute desperate advice is no substitute for training. He is doomed to failure from the moment he utters his wish. Maybe he knows it, too, but it is too late to change his mind. If we hesitate to refer to Phaëthon's tragedy as the result of hubris, it is because he is too young and too innocent to make a preposterous boast. No god wishes to see him punished and Zeus himself is reluctant to use the might of his thunderbolt until the survival of life on earth is in jeopardy.

Poor Phaëthon. His is the tragedy of a youth who went on a quest to resolve his identity crisis and failed to do so. He died too young. He tried heroism and ended up a tragic victim, like so many adolescents who die in the flower of youth joyriding a motorcycle or their father's car, since identity crisis is not the exclusive preserve of the offspring of famous parents. Ironically, it was after his death that Phaëthon acquired an unassailable identity of his own, as the subject of other people's bitter tears and grief. It is that epitaph written on his tombstone that turned a foolish youth into a cosmic symbol, one after whom an asteroid was named, 3200 Phaëthon – one that apparently will always pose a remote but real hazard to life on earth.

Identity and choice

Anxieties about identity plague us today more than ever before, not only during adolescence but throughout our lives. We agonize about our personal and collective identities, our sexual and gender identities, our professional and work identities, our family and political identities, our national and race identities, and many others besides. Presented with choices that were inconceivable to earlier generations, our identities are no longer bestowed on us at birth. Instead, they become projects that many of us pursue throughout our lives with greater or lesser success.

Choice is the bedrock of our identity projects. Today we are presented with a constant array of choices, many of which would have baffled earlier generations. We constantly face the choice of objects and services to buy, but also the choice of occupation, of partner or partners, of sexual, political and every other kind of orientation. These choices open up new possibilities of identity construction but also create pressing new anxieties. The consumer culture we inhabit, with its glut of goods and services, promises to assist us in making us unique and special but it also fuels constant insecurity and anxiety. Do our choices represent our 'real, authentic self' or are they mere slap-ons, futile and desperate attempts to turn us into something we are not, to cover the deeper void that engulfs us?

Many of us try to counteract our insecurities over our identity by creating identity anchors, fixed reference points on which we try to build our sense of selfhood. Identity anchors can take various forms, such as religious and political beliefs, national and other allegiances, groups with which we identify, family and other relations, hobbies and interests. One of the commonest identity anchors is the occupation or profession with which we identify. For one particular group of professionals – airline pilots – the dream of flying itself provides a unique identity anchor from a very young age. In my research with Amy Fraher, an airline pilot, we interviewed many pilots who were laid off following the 9/11 terrorist attacks, when world aviation ground to a halt.[12] We discovered that nearly all of them had dreamt of flying since their earliest childhood. Becoming a pilot was not so much a career choice as the fulfilment of a childhood dream, the Phaëthon dream. This dream continued to be the rock on which their identity was built, and they were willing to endure many hardships to defend it.

Many of these pilots resisted moving to better-paid and less taxing jobs 'on the ground' and resigned to long periods of being furloughed. During these periods, some of them lapsed into considerable hardship, making ends meet by doing the most mundane manual jobs or drawing unemployment benefit and surviving on their savings. This was a far cry from the $300,000 per year job, villas with swimming pools and every conceivable amenity, unlimited respect, power and comfort, all of which they had tasted previously in their careers. Throughout these hardships and adversities, the dream of flying again was what sustained them. There is no greater insult for a pilot than to be likened to a glorified bus driver. This simply denies the elemental quality of the dream that inspires them. Even when, Phaëthon-like, their careers and livelihoods crashed due to redundancy, illness or old age, many pilots found it hard to let go of the dream. Having been at the controls of a mighty flying machine, with hundreds of passengers on board, and seeing the sun rise against the skyline of San Francisco is an image that would continue to define them long after their careers had sunk to a permanent twilight zone.

Helios and the sins of the father

Phaëthon flying his father's chariot ended in disaster. Was he a fool? A spoilt youth, oblivious of the real dangers of life? An impulsive teenager unable to resist his primitive desires? Or was he a dreamer who, in his folly, managed to express something eternal and universal – the fantasy of flying and, maybe by extension, the wish to be free from the earthly constraints of gravity, toil and neediness, to see and explore what has never been seen before? Whichever way we choose to view Phaëthon, the bitter tears shed by his grieving sisters and his adoring mother reveal the devastation left behind by the premature death of an innocent, the broken hopes and unlived futures. And what of Helios, Phaëthon's father? In Ovid's telling of the story, he, too, is devastated by the death of his son. His grief is tainted by overpowering guilt, too:

> Subdued as in the gloom of an eclipse,
> Loathing himself, loathing the light, the day,
> Gives way to grief, and grief rising to rage,
> Denies this duty to the world. 'Enough',
> He cries, 'Since time began my lot has brought
> No rest, no respite. I resent this toil,
> Unending toil, unhonoured drudgery.
> Let someone else take out my chariot . . .'[13]

Has there ever been a more powerful, a more astute psychological description of a father's despair in recognizing his own responsibility for the demise of his child? Helios, furious at the world and at himself, retreats into the darkness of his grief. It takes the combined pleading of all the deities of Mount Olympus to persuade him to return the light to earth and her inhabitants. He then resumes what now has become a thankless task, but not without first venting his fury on the horses, cursing them, and whipping them savagely.

Phaëthon is undoubtedly the protagonist of the story, but Ovid's psychological portrait of the father is every bit as insightful. There can be few finer accounts in mythology of the tenderness of paternal love than the description of how Helios received Phaëthon in his palace.[14] His impulsive offer to grant Phaëthon any wish he has and to affirm it with the most solemn of oaths was every bit as reckless and as foolish as the young man's subsequent demand. It is also typical of a father who has failed to stay in touch with his son, an absent father like so many fathers in our times who seek to compensate with inordinate gifts and favours their failure to offer what their children crave – presence, constancy and love. Helios may be a touchingly loving father but, for all his splendour, he is an inadequate and immature father, one who has failed to help his son through the difficult transition from childhood to adulthood.

The failure of a father to act as a father when his son most needs him is a central feature of the analysis of the Phaëthon story by that great student of mythology, Joseph Campbell. In his classic work, *The Hero with a Thousand Faces*, he describes the myth of Phaëthon as a

> tale of indulgent parenthood [that] illustrates the antique idea that when the roles of life are assumed by the improperly initiated, chaos ensues. When the child outgrows the popular idyll of the mother's breast and turns to face the world of specialized adult action, it passes, spiritually, into the sphere of the father – who becomes, for his son, the sign of the future task.[15]

Far from foolish, Campbell views Phaëthon's wish to emulate his father as entirely natural and commendable. He is a child living in a child's world of fantasy, where a wish has only to be spoken to turn into reality. The role of the father, of other adult males and of society at large is to provide the child with the help they need in order to make the transition to adulthood. This calls for what Campbell calls the purging of the child's infantile impulses, including all illusions of 'good' and 'evil', through rites of passage necessary before the father can properly transfer the power of his office to his son. Helios was too absorbed with his daily job, his own career and all its trappings – the golden throne, the palatial abode and the adoration of his retinue – to reflect on what it means to be a father and what his son's real needs were. There is a tragic anguish when Helios belatedly recognizes his failure and desperately pleads with Phaëthon to give up his doomed desire:

'Sure proof you seek of fatherhood;
indeed my dread sure proof affords:
a father's fear proves me your father.
Look into my eyes!
Would you could look into my heart and see
And understand your father's agony!'[16]

There is tenderness, too, when Helios coats his son's face with magic balm to stop it being seared by the flashing sunbeams and when, too late, he offers the paternal advice that should have come much earlier. Few fathers in our time will fail to be moved by the anguish of Helios – how many of them will also learn the difficult lesson of the hard work it takes to help a boy enter an adult world?[17]

The environmental Leviathan

The story of Phaëthon is a tragedy that engulfs an entire family. But it is also one in which a boy's capricious actions threaten to destroy life on the planet. Living in the midst of unprecedented anxieties about global warming, species extinctions and the rising levels of the sea, this is a theme that is unlikely to leave us unmoved. It certainly a theme that preoccupied Plato who was a keen observer of the natural environment and its effects on the welfare of a state and its citizens.[18]

Plato refers to the story of Phaëthon in the dialogue *Timaeus*, one of two in which he discusses the fate of the lost island of Atlantis. One of the characters in *Timaeus*, Critias,[19] reports a conversation between the Athenian sage and lawmaker Solon and a priest in the temple of Sais whom he met during a visit to Egypt, more than two centuries before Plato's time. During the conversation, the Egyptian tells Solon:

There is a story, told in Greece as well as here in Egypt, that once upon a time Phaëthon, the son of Helios, yoked the steeds in his father's chariot, but was unable to drive them properly along the course normally taken by his father. He ended up burning almost everything on earth and was himself destroyed by a thunderbolt. Now this is a myth, but the truth of it lies in the fact that, over long periods of times, there are great conflagrations on earth, caused by the shifting movements of the sun and other celestial bodies that destroy much of life on earth. In such times, people who live on mountains or in dry countries suffer greater destruction than those living near the great rivers or the sea. This is a calamity from which the Nile, our great saviour, protects us by rising high.[20]

The Egyptian sage attributed the destruction of life on earth to the movement of celestial bodies. The myth of Phaëthon, by contrast, attributes it to human actions against warnings of imminent danger. This may be more appropriate for our times when global warming caused by humans has emerged as an unprecedented threat for the survival of human life on earth. Extreme weather events, forest and bush fires, floods, tornadoes, and freak storms that were meant to happen every hundred years have now become regular events, causing frequent devastation, threatening large parts of humanity.

Global warming and its effects are no longer *future* threats. They are part of the lived reality for millions of people on the planet. Drought, floods, crop failures, coastal erosion, desertification, deforestation, industrial and other pollution are causing extinction and migration of many species as well as human misery, poverty, wars, homelessness, population dislocation and mass migration on an unprecedented scale. The Sixth Assessment Report (AR6) of the United Nations Intergovernmental Panel on Climate Change (IPCC),[21] published in 2021–2 and described by the Secretary General of the United Nations, António Guterres, as 'an atlas of human suffering and a damning indictment of failed climate leadership', documents the extensive damage already suffered by humans as well as other animal and plant lives on the planet. Unlike earlier reports by the same body, the latest one established that environmental destruction is not lying waiting in the future. It is happening now. Nearly half of humanity are currently living in conditions of extreme environmental vulnerability. Most of them live in poor countries that are disproportionately affected by the greenhouse gas emissions of rich countries.[22] Whether described as a crisis or as climate chaos, this is something that we can no longer ignore and the vast majority of us do not.

In his widely read book, *Collapse: How Societies Choose to Fail or Succeed*, Jared Diamond analysed numerous cases of societies that perished due to environmental collapse.[23] They include the Greenland Norse, the Easter Island society and the Mayan empire. He also discussed various societies in our times that are witnessing extensive environmental degradation, including Haiti, Rwanda and the US state of Montana. Various factors are responsible for environmental collapses, but it is generally recognized that once a tipping point is reached, the end comes quickly. What seems like a disaster in slow motion can turn into a sudden and catastrophic collapse. Are we now past the tipping point when, Phaëthon-like, the steeds of the Sun god have burst uncontrolled out of their celestial stable? What is certain is that there is no Zeus wielding a thunderbolt capable of stopping them. Arresting the climate change and mitigating its effects calls for concerted political action, scientific and technological research, and visions of a future in which we let go many of the assumptions and beliefs that have brought us to this state.

The myth of Phaëthon moves us with its evocation of planetary devastation and alerts us to the dangers facing humanity now. The plight of Mother Earth in her desperate appeal to Zeus is one that we cannot afford to ignore. But the myth of Phaëthon does not point the way forward to a solution. Environmental destruction cannot be arrested by a god or a superhero, Greek or otherwise. The challenges facing us now are complex and there is no single solution to them. Science and technology have an important role to play and have already made major steps. A large part of scientific research across the globe is dedicated to discovering realistic solutions, often partial and piecemeal, to mitigate the effects of environmental degradation. But in addition to science, what is required is concerted political action, the building of alliances and the continuing pressure to reduce the extent and effects of global warming, to mitigate its human costs and to find new ways of adapting to the environmental realities of the future.

Apocalyptic visions of the future are a popular theme in many old mythologies. In our times, these visions are helpful in raising consciousness but they can be counterproductive. They all too often spread fatalism and despondency which, in turn, sustain an unsustainable status quo. Narratives of an imminent apocalypse are part of a catastrophology that has become a regular feature of our daily lives. In addition to science and political action, it is vital to develop new stories and myths, genuine counter-narratives that challenge the defeatist and doom-laden narratives that choke action at the collective and the individual levels. These counter-narratives need to celebrate successes of collective action, no matter how limited, challenge the falsehoods disseminated by established interests and create solidarity across people and across differences and disagreements. Maybe above all, these counter-narratives must neutralize the belief that there is no alternative and excite the imagination of the masses in a different future across social classes, nations and interest groups. We need new stories of how to coexist in greater harmony with nature and with each other. We need a new idea of 'we'.[24]

Conclusion

The myth of Phaëthon speaks to humanity's immemorial fascination with flight, literal and metaphorical, and the dangers of this fascination. It can be invoked to enrich discussions of great aviation and space disasters like the 1986 Space Shuttle Challenger disaster. At a deeper level, this myth offers a graphic illustration of the risks facing young people struggling to establish an identity of their own, especially when neither parents nor society at large offer them adequate support. The Phaëthon dream can illuminate some of our contemporary anxieties about identities and careers, especially those of 'high-flyers' who crash-land when they find themselves redundant or downgraded as a result of social and technical developments and the highly uncertain circumstance of today's job market. Finally, the story of Phaëthon indirectly addresses some of the environmental challenges life on earth is facing as a result of global warming, itself the result of profligate exploitation of the earth's resources. In all these ways, Phaëthon's tale can inform, alert and educate us. While it cannot directly point us to the future, it can act as a strong simulant for concerted action and rouse us out of our daily complacency of living our lives under the banner of business as usual.

4

Oedipus and Thebes: Miasma, Contagion and Cleansing

A plague has brought devastation and death to the proud city of Thebes, birthplace of the god Dionysus as well as of Greece's greatest hero, Heracles, and a city whose citadel with seven gates was second only to Troy's mighty fortress. Animals are dying, nothing grows in the fields, children are still-born and the bodies of dead citizens lie unburied in the streets. Lamentations and crying resound throughout the city.

Years earlier, Thebes was ruled by Laius who was married to beautiful Jocasta. Laius was haunted by a curse cast on him in his youth for defying the sacred laws of hospitality. A son born to him would grow up to kill his father and marry his mother. Laius was terrified when Jocasta gave birth to a son. He hurriedly had the child's feet pierced with a metal pin, strapped and bound. He then ordered one of his herdsmen to take

the child to Mount Cithaeron and abandon him to die. *The baby's life,
however, was spared by the herdsman who was not as comfortable with
infanticide as his master. He delivered the baby to another shepherd in
the service of the king and queen of Corinth, Polybus and Merope. Being
childless, they brought up the boy lovingly as their own son, naming him
Oedipus after his badly swollen feet.*

*Oedipus grew up in Corinth. Neither he nor any of his friends knew
his true origins. One day, he was taunted for being illegitimate, just as
Phaëthon had been. Oedipus went to Delphi where he consulted the
oracle of Apollo. He then heard a chilling prophecy, the same one that
had terrified his Laius – that he was destined to kill his father and marry
his mother. Terrified and believing that this referred to Polybus and
Merope, he vowed never to return to Corinth. During his wanderings
not far from Delphi, he was assaulted by a rich lord on a chariot, who
set his servants upon him. In the fight that followed Oedipus killed the
lord and all but one of his attendants, little realizing that the first half of
the prophecy had already been fulfilled.*

*Oedipus then visits the city of Thebes, tyrannized by the Sphinx, a
monster with the head of a woman, the body of a lion and the wings of
a bird. Oedipus saves the city by successfully answering the riddle of the
Sphinx. In recognition, the citizens of Thebes make him king of their city
in place of Laius, their recently deceased king. They offer him in marriage
the hand of Jocasta, their recently widowed queen. Without knowing it,
Oedipus fulfils the second part of the prophecy, by marrying his own
mother. He remains ignorant of this fact for many years during which he
rules Thebes as* tyrannus *(the word originally meant an absolute ruler
who had not inherited his kingdom from his father). He proves to be a
wise and kind ruler and his city thrives. With Jocasta, Oedipus has two
sons, Eteocles and Polyneices, and two daughters, Antigone and Ismene.*

*Oedipus is now presented with another challenge, the plague that
afflicts his city. As a caring ruler, he determines to do everything he can*

to discover the cause of the calamity and restore his city's prosperity. Little does he realize that it is he who is the cause of the plague, the bringer of the miasma to Thebes. Eventually, the truth comes out. Oedipus is the last to realize what he has done. Jocasta hangs herself. In despair, Oedipus snatches the golden brooches from Jocasta's dress and thrusts them into his eyes. His face, a gory mess, he has the courage to face the citizens of his great city one last time before he goes to exile. The chorus of old men lament:

> People of Thebes, my countrymen, look on Oedipus.
> He solved the famous riddle with his brilliance,
> He rose to power, a man beyond all power.
> Who could behold his greatness without envy?
> Now what a black sea of terror has overwhelmed him.
> Now as we keep our watch and wait the final day,
> Count no man happy till he dies, free of pain at last.[1]

Oedipus is gone but the miasma over Thebes persists. Oedipus' two sons, Eteocles and Polyneices, quarrel over the succession to the throne. Eteocles refuses to honour an agreement of ceding the throne to his brother whom he sends to exile. Polyneices then raises an army with seven chieftains who attack the seven gates of Thebes. During the battle that ensues the two brothers kill each other. The new ruler, Creon, forbids the burial of Polyneices, deeming him to be a traitor who had attacked his own country. Defying Creon's decree, Antigone secretly buries the body of her brother in obeisance of timeless sacred rites. She, in turn, is punished by Creon who has her buried alive for defying his orders. In despair, Haemon, Creon's son and Antigone's lover, kills himself. Euridice, Creon's wife, hears the news and kills herself. Creon, a broken man, continues to rule a devastated city.

Oedipus. Has there been a man more wretched than him? Foredoomed at birth by a curse for crimes he had no part in, mutilated as an infant and abandoned to die, the unwitting bringer of miasma and death to his city, the father of doomed children, the ruler of a state in noxious agony.

Is Oedipus a hero at all? Unlike other Greek heroes his story is left out of children's Greek mythologies on heroes and monsters. Unlike Theseus, Heracles, Iason and other illustrious heroes, Oedipus was not on a mission – unless his mission, one in which he failed dismally, was to avoid his destiny. However, in line with Joseph Campbell's *The Hero with a Thousand Faces*, his life was undoubtedly a journey during which he won a decisive victory when he answered the riddle of the Sphinx and delivered Thebes from her monstrous rule. Again, unlike Theseus, Heracles, Iason and other illustrious heroes, with the possible exception of Odysseus, his victory did not require physical strength and physical courage. Nor did he receive assistance from any god or human. No Athena, Medea or Ariadne came to his aid. As he proudly claims in Sophocles' *Oedipus Rex*,[2] he vanquished the Sphinx with no help from auguries and soothsayers but with the power of his intellect alone.

Come to think about it, the Sphinx's riddle is not impossibly difficult. This is, in fact, the one part of the story that features in some children's compilations of myths and is likely to delight them. 'What is the animal that walks on four legs in the morning, on two at mid-day and on three in the evening?' The answer is, of course, 'man', who walks on all fours in infancy, on two legs in much of his adult life and needs the help of a walking stick in later life. On the surface of it, the Sphinx's riddle does not compare with some of the thorny situations from which Odysseus successfully extricated himself. And yet, as Roberto Calasso explained in *The Marriage of Cadmus and Harmony*, by answering the riddle, Oedipus creates a new riddle, 'And what animal is man?', one whose answer Oedipus will discover years later when he seeks to deliver his city from the miasma that plagues her.[3]

Still, what defines Oedipus as a hero is neither his mental acuity nor the wisdom with which he ruled his city which prospered under him. What defines him as a hero is the tragedy of his life. As Aristotle very clearly saw, his is not an epic story that can be spun out in many chapters, involving many incidents and adventures. Instead, the tragic hero's story is best presented in a drama 'concisely told' when the reversal of his fortune and the sudden recognition of the truth have the most devastating impact on the audience.[4] What makes Oedipus a tragic hero is the belated and shattering realization that he, whose fame rested on solving the Sphinx's riddle, has been ignorant of the biggest riddle, that of his own destiny. His fall is both cataclysmic and terrifying.

The story of Oedipus is not an ordinary story of a mighty ruler's fall, although this is certainly a theme that underpins many tragedies. It is the story of a man in the grip of forces greater than himself, who is entirely ignorant of these forces. His actions, as when he leaves Corinth to avoid sinning against the people he believes to be his parents, end up with precisely the opposite consequences of what he intends. More than any other hero, Oedipus acts out his deeds *unknowingly*; as he himself claims in Sophocles' *Oedipus at Colonus*, 'As for my deeds, I hardly acted them at all, rather they happened to me.'[5]

Still, we cannot say that Oedipus is an entirely innocent victim of circumstances. Many commentators have noted his irascible character, his proneness to losing his temper – something that surfaces repeatedly in the course of Sophocles' drama and would have been at play when he killed the lord who turned out to be his father. If you have a prophecy, as he does, hanging over your head, do you go and kill a 'lord'? And do you marry a woman who, for all her beauty, is old enough 'to be your mother'? And what about Jocasta herself? She knew the prophecy. What business does she have sharing her bed with a man half her age and, on top of this, with still visible scars on his feet? Did neither of them suspect anything during their amorous embraces in Thebes's balmy summer evenings? And what about his scarred feet – did neither of them give them a thought? Throughout Oedipus' long and unwavering search for the truth, the truth about his own parentage and the truth about the bringer of miasma to Thebes which amount to the same thing, his eyes were firmly focused outwards. As if to demonstrate how hard it is to live up to the Delphic maxim 'Know thyself', little did he realize that the critical evidence for the truth was carried all along on his own body.

Oedipus fathers the Oedipus Complex

What casts Oedipus apart from other mythological heroes and most other humans, too, is that the deeds for which he became famous, slaying his father and sharing his mother's bed, are no ordinary deeds. Even in our times, they make us flinch in horror. But why indeed do we flinch in horror at these deeds? This was the starting point for Oedipus' great Freudian adventure, long after his fate in Sophocles' tragedy had been sealed.

Freud was fascinated by Oedipus even before he turned it into the centrepiece of his psychology. Jones, his friend and biographer, tells of an incident at his fiftieth birthday in 1906, when he was presented with a medallion, which bore the inscription from Sophocles' *Oedipus Rex*: 'He who divined the meaning of famous riddles and was a man most mighty.' On seeing the inscription, Freud became pale and agitated. He explained to those present that as a young student at Vienna University, he would stroll around the Great Hall, examining the busts of famous professors. 'He then had a phantasy, not merely seeing his own bust there in the future, which would not have been anything remarkable in an ambitious young student, but of it actually being inscribed with the *identical words* he now saw on the medallion.'[6]

Undoubtedly, Oedipus was a mythical character with whom Freud had established a deep identification. In a letter to his friend Wilhelm Fliess, written in October 1897, a few days before the first anniversary of his own father's death, Freud described what he would later view as his greatest discovery. The reason why the story of Oedipus has held such a powerful emotional grip over people across the ages, he ventured, is that it awakens memories of wishes which once dominated our emotional lives but were subsequently repressed and obliterated from memory:

> Being entirely honest with oneself is a good exercise. Only one idea of general value has occurred to me. I have found love of the mother and jealousy of the father in my own case too, and now believe it to be a general phenomenon of childhood . . . The gripping power of *Oedipus Rex*, in spite of all the rational objections to the inexorable fate that the story presupposes, becomes intelligible, and one can understand why later fate dramas were such failures. Our feelings rise against the arbitrary, individual fate . . . but the Greek myth seizes on a compulsion which everyone recognizes because he has felt traces of it himself. Every member of the audience was once a budding Oedipus in phantasy, and this dream-fulfilment played out in reality causes everyone to recoil in horror, with the full measure of repression which separates his infantile from his present state.[7]

Like Oedipus, we are blind to our past. What sets us apart is the fact that he acted out what for the rest of us is a powerful, if unconscious, phantasy.[8] There was a time in our past when our mother was the object of our total and complete infatuation. The technicalities of sex were certainly beyond our comprehension but wanting to be with our mother, to share her every moment including her time in bed, to be one with her, these were not beyond our desires or our imagination. It is then that our father (or some other adult) came to be seen as a rival, a barrier between ourselves and the mother, a blockage between ourselves and the realization of our desires.

This is the period of our psychological development, around the age of four or five that, in Freud's view, is dominated by a complex of phantasies, desires and feelings which he termed 'the Oedipus Complex'. Each individual lives through their distinct version of this Complex, depending on the family into which they are born, their gender, the actions of the parent(s), the presence of siblings and other significant figures in their home environment and, of course, the social and economic conditions in which they grow up. What is common is the intense sensuous and incestuous love for the mother and the extreme hostility towards the obstacle to this love. What is also common is that we subsequently forget or, to use the proper psychoanalytic term, 'repress' in our unconscious mind nearly everything that pertains to this period. 'Me, wanting to sleep with my mother? NEVER! And kill my father? What nonsense, I love my father and never wished him any harm!' is our common response in later life when we first come in contact with Freud's theory. Freud would view this as the sign of how effectively we repress what was a painful and terrifying period in our life. Yet, for some of us, our first encounter with Freud's ideas may also prompt the response, 'Could it possibly be true?' We each emerge from the Oedipus Complex different from the way we entered it. We emerge having learnt that there are powers in this world greater than ourselves; we have learnt that it is often better to suspend our desires than give free vent to them; we have learnt that it is often better to control ourselves than to have others control us.

The Oedipus Complex and its resolution may be repressed, argued Freud, but they leave various residues or traces in our subsequent development. They will influence our attitudes to authority, our gender identities, our propensity to different types of mental disorder and the mechanisms of psychological defence we adopt when confronted with danger and anxiety. They will affect the amounts of guilt and anxiety we feel, often for reasons we don't understand. They will affect our dreams and nightmares. They will affect the extent to which we succumb to different mental disorders, small and large, and the extent to which we are incapacitated by these disorders.

Freud's theory of the Oedipus Complex has been one of the most fiercely debated and fought-over in psychology. To an early generation of psychologists and psychoanalysts, the Oedipus Complex appeared to hold the key to virtually every psychological phenomenon, normal and pathological. Historians and biographers started to pay special importance to their subjects' childhoods and their relations with their parents. Artists, writers, filmmakers and dramatists discovered striking new possibilities for their creative imaginations. Max Ernst's surrealist symbolism in his painting 'Oedipus Rex' (1922), Woody Allen's film *Oedipus Wrecks* (1989), George Lucas's portrayal of Luke Skywalker in his epic franchise *Star Wars*, Steven Berkoff's no-holds-barred drama *Greek* (1980) and its operatic adaptation by Mark-Anthony Turnage (1988) as well as innumerable other works of art all bear the heavy stamp of the Oedipus Complex.

Still, from its early days, the Oedipus Complex has been subjected to intense criticism, both from within and from outside psychoanalysis. Carl Jung, Alfred Adler, Otto Rank and several other of Freud's early disciples disagreed with Freud's conception of the Oedipus Complex and with the prominence accorded to it. From outside psychoanalysis, ethnographers since Malinowski questioned its universality and proposed that many cultures, notably those with more permissive and relaxed child-rearing approaches, do not inflict the heavy Oedipal dramas on every child. Critics of psychoanalysis have argued that there is an absence of concrete empirical evidence for the Complex, or even more gravely, that the theory is non-falsifiable – any refutation of the Oedipus Complex can be explained away as evidence of Oedipal denial and repression. Feminist critics have denounced Freud's account of the Oedipus Complex, especially the idea of penis envy, forcing his defenders to develop alternative and ever more elaborate explanations and justifications.

The heyday of the Oedipus Complex as an explanatory theory in psychology and in psychotherapy is long gone but many of the controversies it conjured up have continued. If anything, these controversies are a testament to the power of the original myth of Oedipus and its ability to open up different retellings and interpretations. Psychoanalyst Bruno Bettelheim, for example, pointed out that the entire story of Oedipus is built on the cruelty of parents who want to get rid of their unwanted child. It is the father (with the mother's consent) who orders his son killed. No child, argued Bettelheim, however gifted and noble, can ever escape from the injuries caused by parents who withhold their love and care. In this way, he turns the myth on its head, the real crimes being those perpetrated by parents on their children, which in the real world are often actual ones rather than imaginary ones.

A very different line of interpretation was offered by Marxist critic Herbert Marcuse who highlighted the political dimensions of the story at the expense of the familial triangle. The Oedipus myth, he argued, stands for the rebellion against an oppressive patriarchal rule,[9] and demonstrates the folly of believing that 'reason alone' can be the driving force in human affairs and politics, in particular. Oedipus pays the price for presuming that humans can be ruled through the force of reason, disregarding the political realities of the city he rules. What

Marcuse does is to remind us that the story of Oedipus is not just the most tragic of Greek tragedies but also one of the most political ones. This political dimension of the story is what differentiates the Greek myth, especially as told by Sophocles in his *Theban Plays (Oedipus Rex, Oedipus at Colonus, Antigone)*, from other, merely 'folkloric' renderings of the story in which a man unknowingly kills his father and, at least in some of them, goes on to marry his mother.[10] The plays of Sophocles[11] were addressed at a sophisticated, urban, democratic audience who could immediately see how private dramas can be intertwined with politics. The killing of Laius is not only parricide but it is also regicide, the violation of Creon's decree by Antigone is not only an act of personal defiance but contains the kernel of all political rebellion. All three plays of Sophocles are replete with references to the implications of the central characters' personal tragedies for the political and moral welfare of Thebes.

There are very few references to Thebes in the *Iliad* and the *Odyssey*. This is remarkable considering that Thebes was one of the country's oldest, biggest and most famous cities. In the *Iliad*, both the Boeotian Thebes in Greece and her famous Egyptian namesake are briefly mentioned, along with the allusion that Tydeus, the father of the Iliadic hero Diomedes, had been one of the seven chieftains who had sought to restore Polyneices to the throne of Thebes.[12] This leaves no doubt that the Trojan War and its aftermath happened a generation or more *after* the Oedipus tragedy. And yet, in the *Odyssey*, when Odysseus meets Oedipus' mother in the underworld, Homer suggests that Oedipus may still be ruling Thebes, 'despite his misery' in the midst of troubles and misfortunes.

Poor Thebes! As the war at Troy rages on for ten years and as Odysseus wanders the high seas for the next ten, Thebes in smouldering in miasma. Did she ever recover from the misfortunes brought to her by Oedipus?[13] Thebes enjoyed a brief moment of glory in the fourth century BCE when, under the leadership of Epaminondas and Pelopidas, it emerged dominant among Greek city-states, with Athens, Sparta and Corinth all ruined by the fratricidal Peloponnesian War that had preceded it. But Theban hegemony didn't last long. Destroyed by Alexander the Great in 335 BCE, the city sunk more or less permanently into the provincial anonymity that characterizes it to this day. Unlike her African namesake, and in spite of hosting a splendid museum, she is rarely visited by tourists today, not even the multitudes that pass through it on their way to Delphi. Today, it is regularly voted as one of the five ugliest Greek cities, even by its own inhabitants.

Miasma and tragedy

The devastation wrought by the Covid-19 pandemic makes us more sensitive to the predicament of a society, like the one ruled by Oedipus, in the grip of a deadly plague or what is referred to in the play as a 'miasma'.[14] The study of miasma as it features in Sophocles' drama can shed much light on the consequences of the acute state of social anxiety caused by an affliction for which there are no precedents or blueprints. It can also help us understand some of the effects of the pandemic, such as the collapse of trust in social institutions and leadership, the proliferation of conspiracy theories, the quest for guilty parties, the exacerbation of social inequalities, the divisions between the vaccinated and the unvaccinated, the mask-wearing and the mask-dodging, the science-trusting and the science-mistrusting.

The word 'miasma' features regularly in Greek tragedy to indicate a state corruption resulting from an abominable crime or violation.

Once it has taken grip, miasma is highly contagious. It is for this reason that medical science embraced the term to explain a particular type of infection carried by putrid, poisonous vapours identifiable by their foul smell. This miasmatic theory of infection was at its peak in the nineteenth century when it was used to explain the spread of cholera in large metropolitan centres, prompting a series of public health measures.[15] Like many theories, it had numerous beneficial applications before it fell out of favour by the discovery that germs have a wide variety of transmission mechanisms. All the same, the awareness of miasmatic infection has persisted – for example, in our concerns about different pollutants in the air we breathe. In the aftermath of the Chernobyl disaster and different chemical accidents, local inhabitants suffered from debilitating symptoms even after the ostensible pathogens had disappeared, attributing them to silent killers like radioactivity and toxic chemicals released in the air. In the wake of the Covid-19 pandemic, miasma tentatively regained entry into mainstream medical science as airborne transmission was acknowledged to be the major route for infection. After an early scepticism, the World Health Organization recognized aerosol transmission as the main form of infection by the virus. The ventilation of closed spaces, social distancing and especially the generalized wearing of masks, something so alien to Western cultures, became core elements of public policies to contain the disease and shaped the daily habits of individuals and organizations.[16]

Miasma is a dominant theme in tragedy and not only Greek tragedy. 'Something is rotten in the state of Denmark,' says the Guard in Shakespeare's *Hamlet*, alluding to a corruption that is not just political, but spiritual, ethical and even physical. In Aeschylus' trilogy, the *Oresteia*, it takes hold of the house of Atreus in Argos through a series of killings culminating in the murder of Clytemnestra and her lover Aegisthus by Orestes, in revenge for the slaying of his father

Agamemnon. Still, there are few descriptions of miasma afflicting an entire state as powerful as that offered by Sophocles at the start of *Oedipus Rex*:

> Our city –
> Look around you, see with your own eyes –
> our ship pitches wildly, cannot lift her head
> from the depths, the red waves of death . . .
> Thebes is dying. A blight on the fresh crops
> and the rich pastures, cattle sicken and die,
> and the women die in labor, children stillborn
> and the plague, the fiery god of fever hurls down
> on the city, his lighting slashing through us –
> raging plague in all its vengeance, devastating
> the house of Cadmus. And black death luxuriates
> in the raw, wailing miseries of Thebes.[17]

This then is what faces King Oedipus. When he asks Apollo what he should do, the god commands unequivocally:

> Drive the corruption [miasma] from the land
> Don't harbour it any longer, past all cure,
> Don't nurse it in your soil – root it out.[18]

Miasma is both the state of corruption and the bringer of this state, an individual whose actions have offended a deity by defiling a sacral command or broken a vow. As historian Mario Vegetti has argued, miasma results from

> a sin that goes beyond the ordinary legal and moral limits and brings divine vengeance on the head of the guilty person, spreading out to affect the whole community . . . and passing inexorably from one generation to the next. The idea of miasma probably has a

concrete origin, representing the filthy, soiled state of someone who lives outside the standards of his or her community. In its most powerful sense, it refers to the bloodstained hands of the murderer or the sores of someone who might be seen as the victim of divine punishment.[19]

Several features of miasma, as a social condition, set it apart from mere distress or crisis. One is the absence of serious organized resistance. Like a virus that afflicts people from within, miasma paralyses people's fighting spirit. Like a virus, miasma does not discriminate between the deserving and the undeserving. Once unleashed, the miasma is capable of afflicting everyone but also of sparing some people in an arbitrary manner – as Dodds wrote, it operates 'with the same ruthless indifference to motive as a typhoid germ'.[20] Its suddenness, its infectiousness, its arbitrariness and its deadliness make it similar to the sudden onslaught of an epidemic, like the one that struck Athens in 430 BCE, the second year of the Peloponnesian War and the year before the first performance of *Oedipus Rex*. The similarities between Sophocles' description of the Theban plague and Thucydides' description of the actual plague that killed thousands of Athenian citizens are extensive – Sophocles does with poetry what Thucydides does with factual description. Performed a year or so after the start of that epidemic, it is very likely that *Oedipus Rex* failed to win first prize at the city's *Dionysia* festival because its depiction of the plague was far too close to the bone.

A city in the grip of miasma is like a city in the grip of a deadly and contagious disease. Indeed, disease is one, but only *one* feature of miasma. Like an epidemic that strikes people arbitrarily, miasma demolishes people's faith in their gods, their institutions, their identity. Like an epidemic, miasma cannot be fought or resisted with heroic gestures. Initially, individuals may think that they can protect themselves and their families by raising barriers and constructing safe refuges. Some people may believe that they can continue to live their lives but isolation is rarely effective. As vividly depicted in Edgar Allan Poe's macabre 1842 tale, *The Masque of the Red Death*, attempts at creating impermeable boundaries and safe areas are vain as the disease learns to cross all boundaries – physical, emotional and moral.

Miasma is a toxic state that corrupts the institutional and moral fabric of a social unit, but it goes well beyond toxicity. Toxicity can be metabolized and neutralized; it lacks the contagious properties of miasma. Miasma brings about a state of moral and spiritual decay, a corruption of all values and relations of trust, love and community. People suspect their neighbours of being the cause of the misfortune; scapegoating and witch hunts are rife, as paranoia mixes with depression and cynicism with fatalism. These and other aspects of the effects of an epidemic on a society are brilliantly depicted in Camus's *The Plague* (1947).

In seeking to understand the deeper causes of miasma and the attempts to deal with it, classicist Robert Parker[21] started with the observation that it is likely to take root in periods of transition, notably birth, death and marriage. The purpose of rituals in different cultures is to prevent contamination during these dangerous transitions. Funerary rites, for example, are meant to help remove a dead person from the world of the living and consign them to the world of the dead. Mourning, argued Parker, is a period when the living enter the same 'between' land as the dead before burial or cremation. During mourning, familiar activities like eating and clothing are heavily regulated and 'a two-way transition occurs; the dead [person] moves from the land of the living to that of the spirits, while the survivors return from death to life. The last rites finally incorporate the dead and the living in their respective communities.'[22] Unless surrounded by such rituals, persons in transitional positions, such as corpses before burial and newly born babies before they have been named, as well as all those who come into contact with them, become potential causes of miasma for all others. In extreme cases, miasma is exacerbated by the presence of a murderer or murderers whose hands are dirty with blood, irrespective of their motives or rationalizations. As Parker notes, the 'two typical sources [of miasma] are contact with a corpse, or a murderer'.[23]

Miasma: The dynamics of mourning, depression, scapegoating and purification

Miasma results from a failure to honour a death or a loss through a suitable period of mourning and appropriate separation rituals.[24] This failure ties it to three other features that underline its emotional dynamics: depression, scapegoating and the quest for purification. The relation between mourning and depression was studied by Freud in a well-known essay, 'Mourning and Melancholia'.[25] He observed many similarities between mourning and melancholia, an early term for what we now call depression: both of these are responses to loss; they both involve feelings of sadness and meaninglessness, physical and emotional fatigue, inactivity, and a withdrawal of interest from the world.

There is, however, a key difference. In mourning, and with the help of different funerary rituals, all emotional attachments are gradually withdrawn from a lost object that no longer exists. This requires a great deal of psychological work that leaves the mourner exhausted and drained. Melancholia, like mourning, is a response to a loss or a separation, but one where the subject does not know what it is that has been lost. Even when the sufferer is aware of the loss, Freud suggests, he knows whom he has lost but not what he has lost in him … In mourning it is the world which has become poor and empty; in melancholia it is the ego itself. The patient represents his ego to us as worthless, incapable of any achievement and morally despicable; he reproaches himself, vilifies himself and expects to be cast out and punished.[26]

Freud did not exactly see mourning and depression as alternatives, but this is now widely recognized.[27] The fundamental emotional mood of miasma is depression, a depression that results from an inability or unwillingness to mourn. The appropriate separation rites have not been observed, the loss has not been honoured, the pain has not been recognized. Instead, there is a hurried attempt to find the guilty parties and punish them. Apollo's command to Oedipus, 'Drive the miasma from the land', prompts Oedipus to start his own quest for the guilty party. In a similar way, the Covid-19 crisis sparked a quest for the source of the virus and those who kept it hidden or, worse, knowingly or not unleashed it on the planet.

If there is one thing that tragedy teaches us it is that miasma inevitably leads to scapegoating and that scapegoating leads to more scapegoating, exacerbating the miasma. Following Apollo's command, Oedipus announces his intention to discover and banish those responsible for introducing the pestilence that afflicts Thebes. The tragic irony, of course, lies in the fact that it is he who, through his deeds of incest and parricide, has unwittingly incurred the wrath of the gods. It is he who is the miasma. All his threats and curses are therefore aimed at himself, something he realizes at the end of the drama, whereupon, in abject despair, he blinds himself.

But Oedipus' contrition, self-punishment and banishment are not enough to relieve the city of the miasma. He is succeeded in the scapegoating stakes by his son Polyneices, deemed to be a traitor, whose dead body lies unburied and prey to the vultures outside the city's gates. Creon, the new ruler, decrees: 'There shall be no public act of grieving!' Antigone disobeys Creon and buries her dead brother. She now becomes the new scapegoat, blamed for rekindling the miasma. She is buried alive, once again as an attempt to isolate the perceived cause of the pestilence. Far from redeeming or purging the city, this brings about the apocalyptic conclusion of Sophocles' Theban plays. At every turn of the drama, attempts to protect the city from miasma through banishment or isolation lead to the miasma taking a firmer grip, eventually bringing about devastation and death.

Judith Butler[28] provides the crucial link between melancholia (she reverts to Freud's original term) and scapegoating, by noting that 'prohibitions on avowing grief in public [like those imposed by Creon] are an effective mandate in favour of a generalized melancholia'. A scapegoat is someone whose life has no meaning other than to expunge the miasma, yet whose unmourned elimination has precisely the opposite effect. Scapegoating is an effort to create such an agent and hold him or her responsible for the loss. As a social condition, melancholia becomes a political force that drives witch hunts, pogroms and persecutions whose irrationality is matched by their brutality. 'It is not that mourning is the goal of politics,' she notes, 'but without the capacity to mourn, we lose that keener sense of life we need in order to oppose violence.'[29]

The search for someone to blame for misfortune and then to sacrifice or banish them in the belief that this will bring about the lifting of the misfortune can assume different institutional and ritual forms. In ancient Greece, it assumed two complementary forms. The primitive ritual of *pharmakos* involved the sacrifice or banishment of a marginalized member of a community as the price for purification for the rest. In classical times, the political process of ostracism, widely practised in Athens and elsewhere, involved the banishment of someone, generally an eminent politician or a general, for a period of ten years from the city-state, following a majority vote by the citizens. Historian Jean-Pierre Vernant[30] observed that while ostracism was aimed at those perceived as threatening the state from above, *pharmakos* targeted those seen as menacing it from below, the lowlife so to speak. Those bringing miasma from above do so through hubris, words and acts resulting from an excessive pride, often at a moment of manic elation, that end up offending some god who seeks retribution. Those bringing miasma from below do so by infecting the others and surreptitiously contaminating the body of a state or a community, in short by acting as parasites.

The parasite, the person or group who takes and does not give back, the person who sucks the blood out of a community, is the pathogen who, it is claimed, poisons its entire social fabric. This is what makes the parasite so repellent and its elimination so pressing. At its most extreme, this leads to ethnic cleansing and genocide, which are not just murderous spasms but also attempts at purification. As psychiatrist Robert Jay Lifton, who conducted a thorough study of the Nazi genocide of Jews, Roma and others wrote, 'genocide is a response to collective fear of pollution and defilement. It depends upon an impulse toward purification resembling that given collective expression in primitive cultures. But it brings to that impulse a modern, much more deadly stress on health and hygiene – for the Nazis, racial hygiene.'[31]

In our times, the parasite that has assumed great prominence is the economic parasite, the individual or group who feeds on the hard work of others, fails to create value and is a burden to society. In Western consumerist cultures that lionize economic independence and self-sufficiency (the 'hard-working families' so beloved of British politicians of every political hue), the needy, the weak and the poor are readily cast into this role as scroungers, loafers and even as prolific breeders. Parasites are viewed as unwelcome guests at our party, people who arrive uninvited, consume our largesse, offer nothing but trouble in return, show no gratitude and, at the end, impudently voice dissatisfaction with our hospitality.

At the height of the Greek financial crisis in the second decade of this century, the populist media in Germany and other northern European countries cast Greek people as living beyond their means, sucking resources from the omnibenevolent European family and giving nothing back.[32] The Greek debt crisis in these narratives turned into a morality tale of the grasshopper and the ant, a story of the evils of hedonistic living and reckless borrowing set against virtuous prudence and hard work. 'Greece must honour its obligations' and 'Greece must fulfil its undertakings' became constant refrains and Greece's perceived unwillingness to honour these obligations placed it squarely in the role of Europe's parasite. In this view, paying one's debts and the ensuing politics of austerity have a purifying effect; suffering has a redemptive quality. The rules of the game are not mere inventions of Brussels bureaucrats defending the sanctity of markets; they are a civilizing force behind the European project, a force whose violation threatens this project. The suffering of the Greek people was the price Greece had to pay in order to stay inside the European family, the alternative being still unacceptable – throwing the parasite out in the wilderness and letting it find its own way to survive outside the citadel of European institutions.[33]

Even this type of scapegoating, however, is as nothing compared to what is endured by various groups of immigrants, refugees and displaced persons. Vilified for taking without giving, bringing crime, drugs, disease and corruption to the hosting societies, they are regularly cast as the parasites who threaten the state from within. The narrative of parasitism now dominates the rhetoric of many right-wing political parties throughout Europe and the policies of several governments. It is a narrative that sees citizens of European countries fearful of being swamped by various aliens who threaten their well-being, their traditions, their financial comfort and their purity. It would be premature to claim that Europe is currently gripped by miasma as it once was in the living memory of many of the continent's older citizens. Yet, the picture I have painted suggests that the resurgence of miasma in Europe is a distinct possibility. Instead of solidarity and compassion, the poor, the weak and the dispossessed are increasingly met with fear and disdain, cast as parasites that arouse primitive impulses of purification and cleansing. It is ironic that the European project that sought to put an end to centuries of hate and violence is currently discovering new ways of targeting groups and populations. Unless European citizens can find ways of opposing scapegoating with solidarity and enmity with compassion, they risk sinking once again into the condition which the European project sought to extinguish.

Conclusions: Tragedy, catharsis and healing

Confronted with the certainty of death and the many troubles that life heaps upon us, different cultures have sought to offer consolations, notably through the certainties embedded in religious faith. The Greeks gave up the search for such consolations and ended up with two things, philosophy and tragedy – the gifts of Apollo and Dionysus, respectively. Philosophy stemmed from the view that certainty and truth should be sought in rational argument rather than in divine revelation. Tragedy was the fruit of the discovery that truth is unstable and unable to offer the certainty they craved for. What seems true turns out to be an error and what seems to be good turns out to be bad. Worse, the distribution of happiness and misfortune is not governed by any just calculus. This is what makes the fate of humanity tragic, as Freud never tired of repeating. When people act in confident knowledge of furthering their interests, their desires and their aims, they end up with outcomes they had never imagined. There is a vast and tragic discontinuity between the proclaimed intentions of our actions and the outcomes of these actions. Suffering in tragedy is not merely incidental – it is brought about by the actions of the protagonists themselves. Tragedy is never far from human affairs, even if we fail to observe it when it is staring us in the face. This is central to all tragedy – the participants' incapacity to recognize the true significance of what engulfs them. Immersed in illusions, they seek to escape through actions that lead to their escalating entrapment.

Tragedy helped ancient audiences make sense of the prolonged and disproportionate sufferings of the protagonists. It helped them cope with the cruelties, injustices and sorrows that they watched. It helped them reach catharsis, an emotional purgation brought about by witnessing terrible things befalling others with no harm to themselves. The marble seats on which they sat offered a sterile environment protecting them from the horrors that saturated the heart of the theatre, the orchestra. By contrast, for the protagonists of the drama there was no catharsis, only suffering and belated recognition. Catharsis is the privilege of audiences that witnessed their suffering, their folly and their downfall. In the social theatres that become sites of miasma, there are no spectators (unless maybe visitors from outside) and therefore there is no catharsis. If this chapter has established something, it is that the search for catharsis merely reinforces the miasma.

How, then, can miasma be forestalled or sidestepped? The story of Oedipus is not encouraging in this respect. As we saw earlier, miasma persists across time and space, and actions aimed at lifting it have the opposite effect. Individuals may escape from its grip but attempts to eliminate it through decisive heroic action are doomed. If we return to the vital part played in the dynamics of miasma by the inability to mourn and consequent lapse into depression and scapegoating, it would seem that any attempt to transcend these dynamics must start with a recognition of what has taken place, a recognition of the loss, the pain, the tragedy. Recognition of what has been lost is a precondition for turning depression into mourning, and failed cleansing into partial healing. As psychoanalyst Vamik Volkan argued,

> Mourning allows us to accept that a loss or a change has occurred. Without mourning we are trapped in the struggle to accept the tragedy and to adjust to life after it. If that struggle is not won, we cannot move on with our lives. We metaphorically remain hiding in the basement after the tornado has passed over and fair weather has returned. An individual, or a society, traumatized deliberately by others has a tendency to remain in the basement. The sense of shame, humiliation, and helplessness may become internalized, which consequently complicates the survivors' guilt.[34]

Mourning can help us come out of the basement and resume our lives, not without scars, but maybe without open wounds. Learning from societies that have managed to recover from profound trauma, injustice and pain, we can maybe move away from the heart of darkness by acknowledging past injustices without vindictiveness, past mistakes without shame and past losses without despair.

5

Zeus and the Frogs: Craving for Strongman in Times of Uncertainty

In ancient times, a colony of frogs, 'annoyed with the anarchy in which they lived', asked Zeus to give them a king. 'Give us a king, give us a ruler,' they all croaked.

Seeing that they were simple creatures, Zeus dropped a large log in the pond where they lived. The frogs were initially impressed by the splash made by log. They recoiled in fear.

Gradually, however, they grew bolder and started moving closer to it. They soon realized that the log kept floating inertly on the pond's surface. They started climbing on the log and pushing it around. After a while, they were disappointed that the log did nothing – it did not speak, it did not move, it did not rule.

They then pleaded to Zeus again to send them a new king, a 'real king' this time.

Zeus got impatient with the frogs' nagging and sent them a stork; in no time at all, the new leader had eaten up all the frogs.

Does this simple morality tale count as a myth at all? The characters, the frogs, the stork or, in other versions, a water serpent sent by Zeus, and even Zeus himself are simple and direct, almost as simple and direct as the inert log. So, too, are their motives, their emotions and their actions. Yet, this simple narrative has endured through the ages, resurfacing especially in times of political uncertainty and strife.

This fable was composed by Aesop, who did not write down any of his famous stories. It came to us in a written version by the first-century CE fabulist Phaedrus and was then retold and reinvented by several others including the seventeenth-century French poet Jean de la Fontaine. The story is alluded to in Martin Luther's chilling line: 'The world is too wicked and does not deserve to have many wise and pious princes. Frogs need storks.'[1]

In our times, King Log became the protagonist in a short story by Margaret Atwood while the frogs' chorus was central to Paul McCartney's little paean for human solidarity, 'We All Stand Together'. A much earlier frogs' chorus featured in Aristophanes' fifth-century BCE comedy of the same name. In it, the frogs taunt the god Dionysus, driving him to distraction with their cacophony and prompting a mock debating contest.[2] Whether pleading to Zeus, singing in solidarity or mocking the follies of gods and humans, the frogs' chorus suggests a deeper symbolism, one that touches something primal and enduring.

A simple morality tale, a simple political tale

The story of the frogs who desired a king is from its inception a political tale. Its message would not have escaped the Athenians of the sixth century BCE freshly liberated from the tyranny of the Peisistratids, the dynasty that ruled Athens in the second half of that century. Peisistratus the tyrant is, in fact, directly mentioned in Phaedrus' version of the story when Zeus sums up the moral of the story to the Athenians:

'You scorn'd the good king that you had,
And therefore you shall bear the bad.'
Ye likewise, O Athenian friends,
Convinced to what impatience tends,
Though slavery be no common curse,
Be still, for fear of worse and worse.'[3]

The same political message would not have escaped French people from the seventeenth century who would have known the story from de la Fontaine's sharp rendering and the numerous pictorial illustrations it inspired. People are better off sticking with the rulers they have rather than crave a messiah who could just as easily turn into a tyrant. Better the devil you know is its deeply conservative message. It is not surprising that this was one of Aesop's fables that pleased Louis XIV of France enough to include it in his famed labyrinth in the gardens of Versailles.

In our times, the simple morality tale of the frogs' foolish desire and its disproportionate punishment seems neither attractive nor convincing. Simple morality tales, especially of the scaring and sanctimonious sort, hardly resonate with us. We certainly don't need preachers to teach us right from wrong. Our sympathies in the tale veer towards the frogs, simple creatures, maybe vain and stupid, too, but hardly meriting the carnage they suffer.

What makes the story quite interesting to us is the *allure of the powerful leader*, an allure that underpins the rise of populism and populist leaders like Putin, Trump, Orban, Erdogan and their ilk.

These leaders have emerged in numerous countries by aggressively flaunting their masculinity and making promises of restoring former glories and standing up to metropolitan elites and established interests. They either directly repudiate democratic procedures, or they castigate them as being fatally flawed and corrupt. These leaders, now referred to as 'strongmen', are authoritarians, but are also able to make their authoritarianism attractive and present it as the answer to their followers' anxieties and discontentment.[4]

The Stork: Strongman leaders

Strongman leaders are a twenty-first-century phenomenon but their models can be firmly established in the period following the First World War and the rise of Mussolini, Hitler and several other fascist dictators. In fact, following the emergence of strongman leaders in our times, Hitler and Mussolini can no longer be seen as aberrations or exceptions in leadership studies but must be viewed as prototypes liable to surface from time to time in democratic and other societies. Strongman leaders are most visible in the political arena, but they are also found in business, educational and other organizations, in NGOs and the not-for-profit sector. What distinguishes strongman leaders is a combination of three things: first, their routine allusion to violence, their relentless threat of using violence and their actual, regular and visible use of violence; second, their ability to rouse powerful passions and direct these passions to political ends; and third, the personality cult they create with the help of propaganda.

Violence is the sine qua non of the strongman's character. Without violence, his claims are pure bombast. Violence takes a huge variety of forms, individual and collective, physical, political, economic and psychological. The strongman's repertoire of violence includes verbal abuse and public humiliation, blackmail, slander, intimidation, bribery and extortion, sackings, disappearances, as well as incitements to beatings, murders, insurrection, rioting and war. Strongman violence can also take numerous institutional forms including the dissolution, discrediting or emasculation of democratic institutions and procedures, the packing of public bodies with supporters, or their systematic abuse and side-lining.

Violence leaves the strongman's followers and opponents alike spellbound. But while opponents generally recoil from violence, followers are energized and inspired. Violence appals the liberal mind – think of the frogs' brutal ending. Yet, for the strongman and his followers, violence is mother's milk. It bonds them and sustains them. It makes the impossible possible; it makes the fantastic realizable. Violence certainly creates 'developments' in a matter of days or weeks that democratic processes take years or are altogether unable to deliver.

Violence presents any democratic opposition to strongman with a dilemma – should they fight the strongman directly, deploying all means fair and foul, or should they try to sidestep him by offering a forward-looking agenda of progress, unity, healing and truthfulness? Many progressive and democratic opponents of strongman politicians will avoid direct fight following the adage, 'Never wrestle with a pig. You both get dirty and the pig likes it.' Unfortunately, history is littered with examples of failed attempts to sidestep or neutralize strongman leaders by invoking ethical and political principles that are readily trampled on by violence. Fighting strongman leaders, on the other hand, may play to their strengths, which include blackmail, bullying, calumniation, innuendo and so forth.

The second characteristic of strongman leaders is their passionate character and their appeal to their followers' passions. Like demagogues throughout history, strongman leaders eschew reasoned debate and argument in favour of a direct appeal to passions. As 'men of the people' opposed to the elites, strongman leaders are 'passionate' leaders, emoting and shouting. Their eyes, their faces, their voices, their entire physique radiate emotion. They share their followers' emotions, articulate them and lend them legitimacy and currency. They dismiss complexities and subtleties in favour of direct and simple explanations and solutions. These are often in the form of slogans and catchphrases which they repeat endlessly, in recent times through social media postings. Their explanations and promises hardly stand up to scrutiny, but they play to their followers' anxieties, ignorance and prejudices. Anxiety, fear and resentment are par excellence emotions to which strongman leaders pander, turning them into anger and rage at being cheated, dispossessed and marginalized. Using passion in place of reasoned argument, strongman leaders are able to redefine boundaries, boundaries of what is civil and what is outrageous, boundaries of what is ethical and corrupt, boundaries of who and what belongs to 'Us' and who and what is the 'Other'. By castigating the Other as parasitical or exploitative, strongman leaders rally their supporters and create a level of unity that often defies differences in wealth, status and power.[5]

In addition to regular recourse to violence and arousing powerful emotions, strongman leaders create a personality cult that is generally at odds with democratic politics. They use the techniques of political propaganda not merely to spread their message but to maintain a constant and permanent presence in the public's eye.[6] In addition to conventional techniques of mass communication, today's strongman leaders use tweets and other postings on social media to create a 24/7 bond with their followers. Who would dispute the standing of Donald Trump as the King Frog of tweeters? The strongman's images, their pouting lips, bulging eyes and every other feature of the physiognomy – doctored and enhanced, of course – saturate the visual landscapes online as well as in the more conventional press and television media.

Strongman leaders make constant pronouncements and keep themselves at the centre of publicity with whatever means. They are seen and heard almost ceaselessly. In this way, they readily come to be viewed, at least by their followers, as charismatic in Max Weber's classic conception.[7] Weber argued that, unlike impersonal bureaucratic authority, charismatic authority is distinctly personal. While he did not use the term 'personality cult', a term whose first political use is attributed to Karl Marx,[8] he viewed charisma as a political phenomenon that sets the leader apart from his (rarely her) predecessors and the institutions through which he (rarely she) comes to assume a leadership position. In this way, the political realm comes to be dominated by the personality of the individual leader that eclipses everything else, including existing institutions and rules. Followers not only experience such a leader as if he (rarely she) is a personal acquaintance with whom they have an individual bond, but they are constantly preoccupied with his (rarely her) every utterance and action, and often surround him (rarely her) with an entire tissue of narratives and stories akin to myths.

Charisma has little to do with any objective qualities and talents of the leader themselves, apart from an undoubted talent in communication. Charisma has all to do with how the followers see them, which reflects their own desires, needs and insecurities. In certain circumstances, a clown or a donkey may come to be viewed as charismatic. Indeed, the frogs' tale suggests that briefly even the log was seen as charismatic because of the splash it made. More routinely, a ridiculously protruding chin, an absurd moustache, a pouting mouth, a flabby chest and all kinds of individual characteristics can be seen as marking the charismatic apart as an individual of exceptional qualities and powers.

The frogs and Zeus: The allure of power and the responsibilities of the sovereign

What accounts for the strongman's irresistible attraction to his followers? Undoubtedly part of his appeal is the appeal of all bullies: the mesmerizing effect of violence and the desire to be on the side of the strong, especially in times of insecurity and strife. The strongman's promise is to stand up for his followers, to protect them, to fight and defeat their enemies. The desire to be represented by a strong champion cannot be underestimated – even democratic parties, after all, will agonize over which potential leader is best able to defeat the opposition.

The strongman's promise, however, goes well beyond what any democratic politician would dream of. His is truly a Faustian deal which says: 'Support me unconditionally and I will protect you from all outsiders and foes; I will clean our land of parasites and undesirables. I will unite us against the common foe; I will bring back the glories of the past; I will stand up for you against the local elites and established interests. *I will relieve you of fear.*' In this way, when a twelve-year-old girl in December 2016 told presidential candidate Donald Trump at a rally in North Carolina, 'I'm scared. What are you going to do to protect this country?', he instantly replied, 'You know what, darlin'? You're not going to be scared anymore. *They're* going to be scared.'[9]

The need for protection is one that runs deep in most humans. We all spend a long period as infants relying on our parents to fulfil our every need. Throughout this period, we build a variety of anxieties. Will I be abandoned? Will I retain the love of my parents or carers? Will I ever be able to stand on my own two feet? We also develop various defences to address these anxieties, many of which consist of elevating the parents to godlike status. They are all-powerful and all-knowing to protect us; they are all-loving to support us; they are our true and legitimate parents, so they have our real interests at heart; they are even immortal so that we will never miss them.[10] In later life, when we find ourselves needy and dependent, we may project onto figures of authority, such as teachers, therapists but also bosses and politicians, the same godlike qualities that shrouded our parents during our early years. It is they who come to be experienced as omnipotent, omniscient, all-loving, all-giving, legitimate, ever-present and so forth in order to meet our anxieties and aspirations. In this way, a strongman's promise to relieve his followers of fear, to fight for them by means fair and foul just as their enemies are doing, becomes irresistible to many people when they feel frightened and exposed.

Yet, in Aesop's original fable as well as in all subsequent variants, protection is not the reason why the frogs plead for a strong leader. What they seem to crave is a leader who he will resolve their disagreements and relieve them of the anarchy that prevails among them and the resulting 'factious discontent'.[11] The strongman they desire is one who will resolve internal disputes, a bringer of peace and maybe a bringer of justice – less a commander and more a lawgiver or a referee.

Disenchantment with democracy is something that brings Aesop's fable very close to our times. The ability of democratic institutions and governments to address today's pressing issues is being questioned across many countries and continents. The standing of democracy itself as an unassailable political value is now seriously challenged. For example, a 2022 survey published by the UK Onward think tank (which is aligned to the 'moderate wing' of the Conservative Party), based on a sample of more than 8,000 respondents, found an alarming rejection of democracy from all segments of society but especially younger people. A remarkable 61 per cent of 18–34s surveyed agreed that 'having a strong leader who does not have to bother with parliament and elections would be a good way of governing this country' while 46 per cent agreed that 'having the army rule would be a good way of governing this country'. This compared to 29 per cent and 13 per cent for over-55s, respectively. Fully a quarter (26 per cent) of 18–34s thought democracy is a bad way of governing this country.[12]

The frogs' demand for a strong leader is motivated, in the first place, by their frustration with a democracy that has descended into anarchy. They appeal to Zeus as subjects of a supreme sovereign requesting that he act to prevent a Hobbesian descent to a 'war of all against all' where the life of each individual ends up being 'solitary, poor, nasty, brutish, and short'. Zeus, however, misreads their demand as stemming from vanity rather than their desire for order and fairness. He addresses their demand by sending King Log who makes a splash but shows no interest in resolving differences or disagreements. The frogs are impressed at first by the splash which they read as a token of the new leader's power. It is only when they return with a request for a leader capable of leading that Zeus decides to 'teach them a lesson' which reflects his own annoyance rather than the unreasonableness of the frogs' demand.

Or is Zeus trying to teach *us* the lesson, since the poor frogs are no longer alive to appreciate it? If so, Zeus' lesson is that, in times of uncertainty, confusion and chaos,[13] a strong leader, even an authoritarian or tyrannical one, is desired as someone who will restore order. Yet, such a leader thrives precisely on chaos and disorder. Far from bringing peace and stability, such a leader is more likely to exacerbate the disorder and turn it violent, too.

This reading of our story shifts the responsibility for the carnage away from the frogs themselves onto Zeus, an intolerant and mean god, or a sovereign who fails in his duty of maintaining the social contract, protecting his or her subjects and establishing a legitimate system of law. All the same, it is hard to exempt the frogs from all charges of vanity. Frogs after all are frogs. They are the one fixed element in a narrative that can be told in many ways. The stork can easily be replaced by a water serpent or a heron without altering the essence of the story. Zeus can be changed into any god capable of granting favours and teaching lessons. Even the log can be substituted by any object capable of making a big splash. The one constant in the story is the frogs. Try telling the story by replacing the frogs with cats or dogs or sheep and the story immediately crumbles into nonsense. Even replacing them with mice or little chicks which are rather more easily edible by a larger animal hardly preserves the gist of the original. So, what is it about frogs that gives the story its signature and meaning?

Frogs: Myths and archetypes

Frogs feature in many of the world's folklores and mythologies. Aesop himself tells several stories with frogs, including the one about the frog who inflated himself to become like an ox with a predictable outcome.[14] Another of his fables has the frogs complaining to Zeus about a prospective marriage of the Sun liable to 'propagate a race of fire' that would soon dry up all their pools.[15] In Egyptian mythology frogs are symbols of fertility and life, as they are in Greek mythology, where they also feature as noisy, licentious, vain and foolish. The Grimm brothers and central European folklore frequently cast the frog as an ugly creature capable of transforming himself into a prince or another being of beauty. Carl Jung refers to frogs in numerous passages of his *Red Book*, often to denote the impersonal and unthinking multitudes, while the 'son of the frog' is a leader who represents their spiritual but futile quest to rise mystically above the confines of their pond.[16] In all of these ways, frogs, while seemingly simple and foolish, are creatures rich and complex in the symbolism they carry. In our story, too, the frogs, despite their reasonable desire for order, feature as foolish and vain creatures. Why else would they even briefly be taken in by the splash of King Log?

In our times, it is hard to resist the view of the frogs' anarchic multitude as epitomizing the cacophony of social media, where each individual seeks to make their voice heard while struggling to rise above the general buzz. They find themselves trapped. They want every voice to be heard – free speech is of great importance to them. And yet, when every voice is heard, no voice is heard, beyond maybe a split second when it rises above the others which will eventually choke it. They want a ruler who will somehow adjudicate among them without sacrificing their liberty to do as they please, to say what they want and to croak as they like. If we identify and sympathize with the frogs in the story it may be that we admire their love of freedom and their determination to make their individual voices heard, while trapped in a cacophony of empty noise. But beyond their desire for someone to referee their disputes, beyond their 'annoyance with the anarchy in which they lived', the frogs' craving for a strong leader could be the result of unrealized ambition and injured pride. They have been unable to rise in the hierarchy of creatures above the status of modest and anonymous inhabitants of an ordinary pond, as per Jung's concept. A strong leader may not only sort out the disputes among them, but also enable them to rise in the hierarchy or, who knows, maybe help them all to turn into princes.

This brings us back to the strongman and his allure. Beyond the riveting effect of his willingness to use violence against their enemies, much of the strongman's magnetism lies in his promise to repair the injured pride and the ailing narcissism of his followers. Most strongmen today will do this by promising to revive the glories of the past, a mythical past produced and sustained by nostalgia. It is not accidental that nostalgia plays a big part in the repertoire of strongman leaders from Mussolini's ambitions to return Italy to its Roman glories to Trump's promise to 'make America great again' and Putin's dream of restoring Greater Russia. Nostalgia is a powerful political emotion. It spawns narratives of a 'golden age', a time in the past constructed variously as heroic, romantic, happy, free and communal. This is a past constructed in such a way as to cast the present as impoverished, lacklustre and lacking. As a political emotion, nostalgia can be viewed as the flip side of the ideology of progress. When faith in a better future fades, people are liable to seek solace in nostalgia for the past.

Now, the frogs, as a race, are unlikely to hark back to a great and glorious past. They can, however, crave for a leader whose greatness will rub off on them and elevate them above their current unimpressive status. The leader they crave can nourish their narcissism through his own ambitions and dreams. As a salesman of dreams, the strongman may offer a variety of promises that readily seduce his followers. The leader's dreams become their own dreams of greatness. His very personality can act as the bedrock on which a new collective identity can be built, a confident, unafraid, ambitious and *communal* identity that erases internal squabbling and focuses the followers' energy on realizing this greatness. This is where Zeus decides to intervene and crush their ambition. He cannot allow them to harbour dreams above their station in life. He defends the natural order of things and preserves the status quo.

The pond: Bickering while the water is getting warmer

What then are we to conclude about the meanings of our story in post-truth times, when sanctimonious moralizing has gone out of fashion as have linear narratives with obvious messages? Are we to see the frogs as foolish creatures punished for their vanity? Or, are they freedom-lovers who end up as martyrs to their cause? Or, are they reasonable petitioners in quest of a law that would enable them to live in peace with each other? Is Zeus an uncaring lord unwilling to exercise his part of the social contract? Or, is he a sadistic god always ready to defend the status quo? Is this an unfair world where the powerless and weak get tormented *pour encourager les autres*? Or, is it a world where one day some frog colony in a different pond may have dreams that meet with a different outcome? May some frogs' chorus at some point sing together in solidarity? Could such a chorus even, as per Aristophanes, end up mocking the power of the gods themselves?

While these and several other meanings surface and fade away from Aesop's fable, our current anxieties may invite yet a different reading. Could the frogs, in their quest for a leader, have failed to notice that the world is not standing still? Could they have failed to look after the pond that feeds and sustains them? Could they be bickering and pleading with Zeus while their pond is getting warmer? Could they be so captivated by their troubles that they have failed to notice a mortal threat to their survival, one that threatens one and all, from which no strongman will save them?

This may trigger memories of a different story, a story about a single frog. According to this story, a frog who accidentally falls into a pot of boiling water will instantly jump out to save herself. By contrast, a frog who finds herself in a pot of pleasantly warm water that is gradually getting hotter will stay in the water until she boils to death. The accuracy of this tale has been conclusively refuted by no less an authority than the curator of reptiles and amphibians at the Smithsonian National Museum of Natural History[17] in Washington DC, but its popularity endures. This qualifies it as an urban myth, a plausible, entertaining, often macabre, if inaccurate, story. The story features in Al Gore's film, *An Inconvenient Truth* (2006), and has been widely used by environmentalists to alert us to the dangers of climate change. It is also used by politicians and other commentators to warn of some creeping danger that goes unnoticed. This danger may be environmental, but it can equally be social or political, such as the growth of violence and crime or the erosion of privacy and other civil freedoms. It is the same phenomenon alluded to in the famous poem attributed to pastor Martin Niemöller, according to which, 'First they came for the Socialists, and I did not speak out – Because I was not a Socialist ...'[18]

The enduring popularity of the urban myth of the boiling frog may attest to something deeper. It may highlight a general human tendency to disregard gradual changes in favour of the here and now. Its popularity may equally be the result of living in times inundated by continuous warnings and scares and an alarmist climate of phobias and paranoias. Each day a new scare or a new moral panic surfaces, often apocalyptic in its scope, as if a thousand Cassandras warn us about a million risks or a thousand boys cry wolf at every opportunity, as per another famous Aesop fable. We live in a society where many of us experience acute vulnerability, where terrorism, crime, technology, migration and a whole raft of political and cultural developments appear to threaten our way of life, our assumptions and our values. In such a society, conspiracy theories proliferate, and it becomes difficult to tell truth from paranoid fantasy, real conspiracy from conspiracy theory, real threat from imaginary threat. Science itself is drawn in, sometimes to dispel some untruths, sometimes accused of propagating them as part of a conspiracy.

In this cacophony of scares and conspiracies, magnified by social and traditional mass media, it is easy to see ourselves as suffering from the same malaise as those frogs who, in their distress, turned to Zeus. Their fate suggests that appealing to a strong leader for certainty, order and comfort may be less wise than learning to live with uncertainty, disorder and malaise or acting in concert to address dangers that threaten the well-being of all of us.

6

Odysseus and Nausicaa: Encounters with the Uprooted Other

Shipwrecked, Odysseus finds himself fighting the waves for two days and two nights. Finally, he is washed up on dry land, naked, starving and desperate. Exhausted, he falls asleep.

When he wakes up, he sees a group of young women playing a game of ball. They catch sight of him, and they all scatter in fear of the wild man – all except for one of them, the princess Nausicaa who steps forward to meet the stranger. She is fascinated by him and wants to hear what he has to say.

Odysseus addresses her with words that bridge the gap between himself, the helpless, homeless mariner, and the princess in her comfort and security. She will offer him shelter at the palace of her parents, the king and queen of the Phaeacians. They will receive him with kindness and hospitality. In exchange, they will receive from Odysseus one of the most fabled narratives in all literature, the story of his adventures at sea since he and his fellow Greeks sacked the city of Troy.

Nausicaa will find herself irresistibly drawn to Odysseus, but he is resolved to continue his onward journey to his homeland. Odysseus and Nausicaa will part from each other – he on his way to Ithaca where he will soon discover that more trials await him. And she? We will never know Nausicaa's future, but we can be certain that she will weave her own tales of her life-changing meeting with the shipwrecked stranger.[1]

The world of the *Odyssey*

The world of the *Odyssey* could not be further apart from our own world. It is a world of heroes and heroines, gods and goddesses, witches and monsters, a world created by an illiterate poet or, more likely, several of them.[2] It is a world with no formal laws and no documents. Its information storage capacities go no further than individual memories. There is no cash and its economy is to a large measure based on barter, gift and plunder relations.

The *Odyssey* is the second of two vast epic poems attributed to Homer, believed to have been composed around the second half of the eighth century BCE. It was part of an oral tradition and probably underwent many modifications and embellishments before it was committed to the written word, some centuries later. The earlier poem, the *Iliad*, is a narrative which combines epic and tragic qualities. It describes a phase of the Trojan War, a long and brutal conflict that saw armies from mainland Greece attack the fortified citadel of Troy and its allies in Asia Minor. It recounts the events that followed the dispute between Agamemnon and Achilles, two of its Greek protagonists, and its tragic consequences. The universe of the *Iliad* is heroic, aristocratic and almost static. Friends are friends and foes are foes; this makes the disputes among friends powerful drives in the story. War is depicted in all its savagery, in spite of which it is conducted according to certain rules of etiquette and honour.

The *Odyssey* narrates the journey of Odysseus and his followers on their way home to Ithaca, following the fall of Troy and the defeat of the Trojans. The *Odyssey*'s universe is very different from that of the *Iliad*. It is a world in constant flux, dominated by images of the wine-coloured sea, the waves, the wind and the salt, much as the *Iliad* is full of images of the land, bitterly contested and blood-soaked. It is a great seafaring adventure, a journey through storms and shipwrecks, punctuated by meetings with strange creatures and people, a journey full of dangers but also a journey of unpredictable wonders, boons and discoveries. The *Odyssey*'s world is a remarkably interconnected and cosmopolitan world, reflecting the world before what has become known as the Late Bronze Age collapse. This saw the collapse of every single major civilization in the eastern Mediterranean and the Middle East in a short period of time around the middle of the twelfth century BCE.[3] The *Odyssey*'s world is a world of people moving across land and sea, people meeting strangers and telling stories to each other, people offering and receiving hospitality, exchanging gifts, eating and drinking together. It is a world where, in spite of sudden bursts of violence, people do business with others, different from themselves. They routinely try to resolve their differences with negotiation, discussion and diplomacy rather than brute force.[4]

This is the world that Odysseus and his comrades in twelve ships navigate on their way back to Ithaca. The word used by the Greeks to describe their journey is *nostos*, a word well known to us from the term 'nostalgia', which originally referred to a painful yearning for one's homeland and home.[5] A *nostos* is a journey with a task, but without a mission. Unlike the journeys of other seafaring heroes like Iason, Theseus and Orestes, Odysseus' wanderings are not in pursuit of a noble deed, a homeland or vision. His is neither a band of rescuers nor one of refugees. Still less is Odysseus' journey a voyage of exploration, discovery or pilgrimage. Unlike the expedition to Troy, it is not a raid, nor a conquest. The journey of Odysseus and his companions is a homecoming, a homecoming after a long and cruel war of plunder, slaughter and destruction and all its dehumanizing consequences. It is a journey drawn towards the centre, Ithaca, the home and the marital bed, against forces of resistance. Its psychological motive is nostalgia, a yearning for home, for a barren land, no matter how poorly it compares with the wonders that are discovered along the way. Organizationally, we may say straightaway that the *Odyssey* is a disastrous journey, since Odysseus alone among his crew will ever set foot on Ithaca again.

But the *Odyssey* is not only a journey. The second half of the poem takes place in Ithaca herself. On his return, Odysseus discovers a gang of suitors installed in his palace, eating and drinking what remains of his wealth, harassing his wife Penelope, and plotting the death of his young son Telemachus. During his twenty-year absence, the land is ravaged, the city decayed and nothing is as he left it. With rightful despair, he might have exclaimed, paraphrasing a famous line, *Chez moi le deluge!* But Odysseus is not one given to despair. While experiencing powerful emotions of rage, pity and self-pity, he remains a practical man with a new task at hand, to reclaim his rightful position as the king of the land and punish the suitors.

Odysseus conceals his identity and sets about testing the ground, finding those who have remained loyal to him during his absence, as he masterminds the destruction of the suitors and his return to the throne. In a series of powerful if perplexing encounters, he reveals his identity to different people: his son, the loyal shepherds, the old servant woman Euricleia, the suitors, and finally his wife and his father. Through these recognition scenes, it emerges that the warrior's homecoming after twenty years away is no easy task, but a dangerous, confusing and painful event which requires much versatility and courage to accomplish.

The conclusion of the *Odyssey* lacks the *Iliad*'s tragic closure and suggests many more adventures and suffering to come. Odysseus has slain the suitors and is reunited with Penelope, but it is clear that much work needs to be done to restore peace and prosperity in his realm. The dead suitors' families set upon him and his loyal followers. A battle erupts and only Athena's divine intervention restores the peace, a peace which is too tentative and built on too much injustice and suffering to last. It will take much work of truth and reconciliation to bring back justice and peace.

The *Odyssey*'s narrative structure is a source of endless fascination. Unlike the *Iliad* which takes place in serial time with occasional flashbacks, the *Odyssey* involves numerous interwoven narratives developed by many storytellers for the benefit of many listeners, some of whom are themselves parts of these stories. There is a profusion of stories within the story, and even stories within stories within the story – the very idea of a central narrative becomes blurred. There are many flashbacks and a few flashes forward, many narrations, many storytellers and many listeners. Thus, we learn about the fall of Troy, second hand, from the stories told by Nestor, Menelaus and Helen to Telemachus, Odysseus' son, and third hand from the songs of the blind bard Demodocus (Homer's self-portrait of his younger self, perhaps) to the Phaeacian court. We learn about the deaths of Achilles and Agamemnon through their own narrations, when Odysseus meets them during his visit to the underworld.

Most importantly, we learn the majority of the seafaring adventures from Odysseus himself, as he recounts them to his hosts, the king and queen of Phaeacia, the parents of the princess Nausicaa. This allows both for poetic embellishments and for dazzling changes of pace, where leisurely narrative and lengthy digressions give way to paroxysms of narrative activity. This is far more unpredictable than the *Iliad*'s majestic movement from dispute to crisis to misfortune to tragic resolution. Yet, the *Odyssey*'s structure is very active and self-generating and a far cry from the passive sequence of successive adventures to which it is reduced in children's and cartoon renderings. Its characters, far more than those of other epics, are storytellers and story-listeners in their own rights, performing their stories to each other, embellishing them, omitting vital details, and placing themselves into each other's stories. Within this structure, Odysseus himself emerges first and foremost as a man with a story for every occasion, the master storyteller.[6]

Odysseus: A man of many skills, many turns, many faces

Who is Odysseus, the story's central character? Odysseus is one of the most widely discussed, explored, and parodied literary characters. He probably equals Don Juan and Faust in popularity and notoriety, surfacing among others in the works of Sophocles, Euripides, Plato, the Stoics, Virgil, Ovid, Dante, Shakespeare, Tennyson, Joyce, Seferis and Kazantzakis. He is a character capable of remarkable transformations from hero to villain, displaying extremes of courage and malice, eliciting equally admiration and vilification.[7] The character is already familiar to readers of the *Odyssey* through his participation in the *Iliad*, where he is a major character, even if he never overshadows the towering presences of Agamemnon, Achilles and Hector. Already in the *Iliad*, we are familiar with his central qualities. He is the most versatile of characters, the embodiment of practical intelligence, the source of countless stratagems and ruses, a compelling and persuasive speaker. His bravery, never in question, is always tempered by prudence and he appears to lack the trademark narcissism of other Iliadic heroes. Unlike them, he is not surrounded by coteries of flatterers and admirers, his self-confidence is such that he needs no friend or others to approve of him, and he never acts in order merely to prove a point. He is a solitary individual, thoroughly mature, and needs no human to hold his hand – although gods frequently come to his assistance, especially in the *Odyssey* where he and Athena form an inseparable team.

Odysseus is feared by foes. His fellow Greeks respect him and fear him in equal measure. They certainly show little sign of love for him. They recognize him as indispensable for success in the military campaign and, in a famous incident, which is not part of the *Iliad*, reward him with the armour of the dead Achilles much to the dismay of Ajax, who subsequently lapses into madness and kills himself. Already in the *Iliad*, he is described as *polymetis*, a man of many skills. This is one of several epithets used for Odysseus that include the prefix *poly*, i.e. multiple. He is referred to as *polytropos*, a man of many turns, as *polymechanos*, a man of many devices, and as *polytlas*, a man who can endure much suffering. Unlike Achilles, Agamemnon or Diomedes, men who rely on their valour and reputation to see them through, Odysseus is a man of many wiles, who uses different means in different situations – he uses gentleness, persuasion, silence, planning and improvisation more often than brute force, although he does not hesitate to use this when the circumstances call for it.

Unlike other characters whose epic stature depends on winning in the grand manner, Odysseus generally displays an economy of effort, content to achieve his objectives with minimal fuss or drama. For this reason, he possesses the qualities of self-control and self-discipline to a remarkable degree, knowing when to stay silent, when to engage an opponent and when to seek to outmanoeuvre him. Above all, he thinks before he talks and thinks before he acts, in a manner that brings that famous reproach from Achilles: 'Hateful as the gates of Hades is that man, who hides one thing in his mind, but says another.'[8] In contrast to the brusque directness of Achilles, Agamemnon and the others, Odysseus is oblique, indirect and subtle – or, to use a different language, he is deceitful, dishonest and cold-blooded. Still, numerous commentators have observed a gentler side to his character, one that sees him emotionally deeply attached to his wife and his son, but also one that one that makes him especially attractive to women – qualities that are inconspicuous in most of the other warrior-heroes.

The core qualities of Odysseus – his resourcefulness, remorselessness and self-control, his seductiveness and ruthlessness – come into their own in the *Odyssey*. Faced with the unpredictability of the high seas, its monsters, its gods and its enchantresses, Odysseus proves infinitely adaptable. He is decisive when impetuosity is required and gentle when moderation is called for. Faced with adversity, he proves himself a model of survival, using every device and wile to overcome it.

Unlike so many of today's managers, Odysseus never complains of inadequate resources. He is a master of 'bricolage', making do with whatever resources are available to him, capable of redefining useless materials into useful ones and of redefining his objective in line with the resources available. Trapped with his companions in the cave by the murderous giant Polyphemus, the Cyclops who has already brutally killed and cannibalized several of his companions, Odysseus knows that the cave's opening is blocked by an unmoveable rock, so killing the Cyclops will lead to their own inevitable death. Faced with this task, he will use what is at hand, a flask of wine to get the Cyclops drunk and a stake fashioned out of a log lying idly about the cave, sharpened, hardened and heated, to blind the giant. Note, too, the ruse involving his name. By paraphrasing his own name, from Odysseus to Oudeis, meaning 'Nobody', he prepares for his escape, when the blinded giant calls for assistance from his kinsmen. When blinding the Cyclops, he has not yet hatched a plan of how to escape from the cave, though his Oudeis deception prepares the ground, by keeping the Cyclops' kinsmen away. He then uses the Cyclops' own strength as his resource for removing the mighty rock. The Cyclops must open the cave to let his sheep go out to graze, but he is smart enough to seek to stop Odysseus and his comrades escape by guarding the opening. It is then that Odysseus devises the plan's next stage, famously tying his surviving comrades under the bellies of the Cyclops' sheep so that they can escape unharmed.[9]

In using his resourcefulness, his practical intelligence, Odysseus is no gentleman. No means is too immoral or undignified for him. He lies, disguises himself, deceives and bullies to achieve his aims; and in all this he never displays any guilt or moral qualms. He continuously transgresses all kinds of boundaries, geographical, social and moral ones. Everything about Odysseus marks him as a boundary transgressor, from the Wooden Horse ruse which so cruelly broke the defences of the Trojan citadel to the escape from the cave of the Cyclops. He alone among mortals will cross the ultimate boundary, passing through the hated gates of Hades, meeting the ghosts of his dead friends, relatives and enemies, and come out not only unscathed, but also with fresh resources with which to face an uncertain future. In this, too, he proves himself a schemer whose ruses and deceptions invite a mixture of admiration and horror. His utter remorselessness is evidence of his unshakeable self-belief but belies not a little of the psychopath. This comes to the surface when he murders every one of the 108 unarmed suitors and rounds up all the female servants who had served them, forcing them to clean the blood off the floor of his hall before having them massacred in cold blood.

The crossing of boundaries through deception is one of the recurring themes in the *Odyssey*. Deception is despised by Achilles in the *Iliad*, though lesser heroes find much to admire in it. Like us, the Greeks had an ambivalent attitude to it. Yet, unlike us, they seemed to relish it as a kind of virtuosity in its own right. Their gods, too, were prone to deception. As a young child, Hermes stole his brother Apollo's cattle, earning not censure but much admiration from the other gods. Athena, too, routinely practises deception in both the *Odyssey* and the *Iliad*, as do several other gods. In one of the *Odyssey*'s most famous passages, Odysseus, shortly after his arrival in Ithaca, tries to deceive the goddess Athena who has come to help him in the guise of a young shepherd. He spins an elaborate tale about being a fugitive from his native Crete where he, supposedly, murdered a prince who had sought to rob him of his Trojan spoils. Athena listens attentively to Odysseus' fib, and then changes her appearance to that of a magnificent tall woman, smiles knowingly at him, touches him gently on the cheek and says:

> You clever rascal! So duplicitous,
> so talented at lying! You love fiction
> and tricks so deeply, you refuse to stop
> even in your own land. Yes, both of us
> are smart. No man can plan and talk like you,
> and I am known among the gods for insight
> and craftiness. You failed to recognize me:
> I am Athena, child of Zeus. I always
> stand near you and take care of you, in all
> your hardships.[10]

In this remarkable passage, not only does Athena, a goddess, bracket herself with a mortal, but does so in acknowledgement of their shared mastery of deception. The Greeks found much to admire in deception, even when it was not perpetrated for the public good or even in pursuit of narrow self-interest. In fact, the Greeks of old seemed to appreciate deception for its own sake – for the hell of it. And hence, a snatched victory, an undeserved victory, is as sweet, if not sweeter, than one earned with courage and blood.[11] What Greeks scorned is the trickster who fails. Deception, in this way, was a test of character – when successful, at its best, it trumps sheer force. At its worst, failed deception, like a called bluff, reveals the trickster for a fool. In this way, Odysseus is prone to trump the guiles of lesser tricksters.

Deception is the product of the combination of three key of Odysseus' qualities: resourcefulness, remorselessness and courage. To these, we must add the quality that uniquely sets Odysseus apart from all other Homeric characters, his almost super-human capacity for self-control, under extreme conditions of provocation. This, remember, is a society based on shame rather than guilt. Insult is the medium through which the chief currency, honour, is traded. For a man of valour and honour, anger, manifested in direct retaliation, far from being censured, is a means of gaining respect. Yet, on innumerable occasions, Odysseus tempers anger and other emotions, controlling his immediate impulses. Blinding the Cyclops to ensure their escape from the cave means taming his impulse to kill him while asleep. Likewise, after he arrives in Ithaca, when confronted with the storm in his own home, he tempers his craving for instant revenge, engages in a series of elaborate disguises and deceptions to test the loyalty of those he left behind, before planning and executing the suitors' downfall. Can anyone imagine Achilles or Agamemnon sparing the sword for a disguise? His attempt to deceive his own wife Penelope as to his identity, by pretending he is a traveller and disguising himself in rags, has often been criticized as cruel and unworthy of a true hero. Yet, might Agamemnon's brutal end in the hands of his wife and her lover not have been a warning to him?

Odysseus is truly a Protean character. Yet, for all his transformations, his wanderings, his sufferings and his conquests, there is little sign that Odysseus fundamentally changes as a person. Neither his mind nor his body change in any fundamental way. This may be part of the Homeric universe in which a person's identity is not problematic in a psychological sense, although it may be problematic in the forensic sense. The nature of a person does not change either through their actions or through their experiences. Odysseus' overall qualities are unchanged, even if we sense an increasing propensity towards suspiciousness and sentimentality, along with his courage, improvisation, flexibility and cunning, and his less attractive qualities of lying, bullying and immorality.

The *Odyssey*'s other characters are by no means derivative or uninteresting. There are powerful female presences in Princess Nausicaa (as we shall see presently), Helen (previously of Troy, now back in Sparta, who makes an impressive and enigmatic appearance), the nymph Calypso, the sorceress Circe, the Phaeacian queen Arete and, above all, the goddess Athena. And what of Penelope, Odysseus' long-suffering wife waiting for her husband's return? There was a time when she was seen as a slightly passive character, out of line with the feminine ideals of our times. At times moody and depressed, she seems to be deceived by Odysseus' disguises. Yet, in recent times, commentators have discovered a different Penelope in the text, with much more to admire than female constancy, obedience and sound housekeeping.[12] Like Odysseus, she displays an excellent ability of reading situations, she is a cunning schemer in her own way, as shown by her stratagems to keep the suitors at a distance, she has fortitude, and she is as good at defending boundaries as is Odysseus at prising them apart. Far from being tricked by Odysseus' disguise as a beggar, she is aware of his true identity from early on. It is for this reason that she risks the challenge of the twelve axes, which without Odysseus' presence might have seen her a hostage to fortune. Far from being a passive victim, waiting to be saved by her noble husband, still less the spoils of the struggle, Penelope is the perfect match for Odysseus – prudent, resourceful, a complete survivor. Both are skilled crisis managers and know when to stand and fight and when to deploy different means to achieve their ends.[13]

The final reunion of Penelope and Odysseus is a poetic masterstroke. In it she turns the tables on him, affecting to test his identity (she is not one to be tricked by any impostor pretending to be her husband) when in fact she is testing his feelings, prior to reopening her heart to him. Only then are the two reunited as husband and wife, as lovers, as storytellers and story-listeners, as in Homer's words, 'The two in their room enjoyed the delights of love, then pleased one another with recounting what had befallen each.'[14]

Yet no sooner have they been reunited in love that, true to their nature, they plan for the immediate future, how to face the angry families of the suitors the following day. They also discuss the longer-term future, as Odysseus tells Penelope Teiresias' strange prophesy – according to which there will be more travels and sorrows ahead and a peaceful death in old age.

As traveller in perilous seas and storyteller, as trickster, schemer and bully, as a lover and a family man, as a leader of men and a reader of situations, Odysseus has woven his way easily into stories past and present. As inhabitants of a perilous world engaged in our own travels through life, Odysseus speaks to us directly across the ages. He can inspire us and infuriate us, he can seduce us and repel us. Maybe he can also teach us how to handle difficult situations and how to survive different ordeals and challenges. Let us now meet him as he emerges shipwrecked, naked and lost in a foreign land.

Meeting the shipwrecked Other

The encounter between Nausicaa and Odysseus is one of the *Odyssey's* most famous scenes, serving as a timeless archetype of the encounter between the privileged and the deprived. It starkly contrasts those who enjoy domestic stability and routine with the uprooted and impoverished Other. This poignant meeting readily evokes images of refugees, arriving in hundreds or thousands on the shores of Lesbos, Lampedusa, or Dover, and invites us to reflect on the subject of the uprooted Other as an object of fear and ridicule but also of compassion and hospitality.

Picture the scene. After sailing for twenty days on a raft, Odysseus' fragile vessel is smashed to pieces by a storm. He battles the waves for two days. At last, he reaches a rocky and forbidding island summoning every ounce of strength to drag himself onto solid ground. A true castaway, he finds himself stripped of everything, naked, starved, utterly depleted. The resourcefulness of his subtle mind is his sole remaining possession. Exhausted, he fashions a makeshift bed using a pile of olive leaves; he then falls into a deep sleep.

As dawn breaks, Odysseus awakes to the sound of joyful laughter and spirited shouts from a group of young women who, of all things, are playing a game of ball. It is a scene of peaceful domesticity for a man who has confronted man-eating Cyclops, monstrous sea creatures, devious enchantresses and has even ventured to the depths of the underworld. A seasoned warrior, he has fought a ten-year war and has spent another ten years sailing the oceans on the homeward journey. He is now faced with a different challenge – how to approach the young maidens and plead for hospitality and help. This is how Homer describes the scene:

Odysseus emerged from the bushes.
He broke off a leafy branch from the undergrowth

And held it before him to cover himself.
A weathered mountain lion steps into a clearing,
The wind and rain have let up, and he's hunting
Cattle, sheep, or wild deer, but is hungry enough
To jump the stone walls of the animal pens.
So Odysseus advanced upon these ringleted girls,
Naked as he was. What choice did he have?
He was a frightening sight, disfigured with brine,
And the girls fluttered off to the jutting beaches.
Only Alcinous' daughter stayed.[15]

What a scene, as the mountain lion meets the carefree virgin! Her companions have fled as if they had encountered a ghost or maybe like a group of carefree tourists suddenly meeting a refugee washed up on a Greek beach. In these circumstances, Odysseus 'pondered'[16] how to best approach the princess, what words to use to seek help and whether to touch her knees in supplication or to keep his distance. Instead of telling a fake story about his origins and identity as he did in numerous other encounters, he instead chose to deliver a long blessing, dressed in plentiful if skilful compliments which concluded with a little paean to marital bliss and domesticity:

My lady, pity me.
Battered and wrecked, I come to you, you first –
and I know no one else in this whole country.
Show me the town, give me some rags to wear,
if you brought any clothes when you came here.
So may the gods grant all your heart's desires,
a home and husband, somebody like-minded.
For nothing could be better than when two
live in one house, their minds in harmony.[17]

Moved, Nausicaa develops more than a passing interest in the stranger. She feels pity and compassion, and offers him food, clothes and information, advising him how to seek hospitality from her parents, the queen and king of the Phaeacians.

Hospitality is as important in the *Odyssey* as courage is in the *Iliad*. Throughout Odysseus' journey, he seeks, receives and is refused hospitality by various hosts reflecting their character and values. Hospitality, or *xenia* in Greek, involved reciprocal relations between hosts and guests – a sacred obligation by hosts to offer food, shelter and much else to their guests, and a concomitant obligation of the guests to receive hospitality with gratitude and respect. Some characters in the *Odyssey*, notably the Cyclops Polyphemus and Circe, violate the sacred codes of hospitality as do the suitors who abuse Penelope's generosity. Other hosts, like kings Nestor and Menelaus, exemplify the ideal of generous hospitality, providing their guests with shelter, abundant feasts and gifts. Nobody, however, matches the unbounded hospitality offered to Odysseus by the Phaeacians, the model of a civilized, urbane and well-run society. To this royal family, Odysseus will eventually recount his adventures, with us the readers eavesdropping on his tales before he is despatched to Ithaca on a Phaeacian vessel with noble gifts.

What made hospitality such a sovereign value in Homeric society? Undoubtedly the absence of alternative accommodation, inns, restaurants and hotels, for travellers were an important economic factor. Hospitality was essential for upholding a trading economy that reached far and wide and meant that the person receiving hospitality one day could be offering hospitality the next. In addition, hospitality was a way of showcasing a host's wealth, status and sophistication, an opportunity for making friends and extending social and economic networks. These economic reasons were compounded by firmly held religious beliefs that a person appearing in the guise of a beggar or a stranger could be a god in disguise. There were countless examples of divine retribution against those who, unknowingly, slighted such divine visitations. When meeting strangers, characters in the *Odyssey* often inquire whether indeed they have met a god – Odysseus, for example, on meeting Nausicaa wonders aloud whether he has not met the goddess Artemis, and Nausicaa's father, Alcinous, on meeting Odysseus asks whether he might not be one of the immortals.

Maybe the most surprising but persistent feature of ancient hospitality was that strangers were not asked for their name or purpose until well after they had been fed and sheltered. It is in this light that we must understand how Odysseus does not reveal his identity to his hosts until he has been truly welcomed in the court and has been moved to tears by the bard's recitation of the fall of Troy, an event of which he was the protagonist. His own story of his seafaring adventures that hold the Phaeacians in a trance comes as the culmination of an elaborate ritual of give and take, recognition and respect.

Odysseus will depart from the island on the Phaeacian boat laden with gifts and will arrive in Ithaca without further misadventures. He will leave Nausicaa behind having ensured what some may cynically view as a free ride back home. But such a view would do injustice to Nausicaa and her family as well as to Odysseus. They part, as they met, with a blessing:

> And there stood Nausicaa as he passed. Beside a column
> that propped the sturdy roof she paused, endowed
> by the gods with all her beauty, gazing at
> Odysseus right before her eyes. Wonderstruck,
> she hailed her guest with a winning flight of words:
> 'Farewell, my friend! And when you are at home,
> home in your own land, remember me at times.

Mainly to me you owe the gift of life.'
Odysseus rose to the moment deftly, gently:
'Nausicaa, daughter of generous King Alcinous,
may Zeus the Thunderer, Hera's husband, grant it so,
that I travel home and see the dawn of my return.
Even at home I'll pray to you as a deathless goddess
all my days to come. You saved my life, dear girl.'[18]

Some commentators have felt a little cheated by this scene. A marvellous love affair between Odysseus and Nausicaa never materializes. I disagree. What would another conquest by Odysseus – to add to those of the nymph Calypso and the enchantress Circe – achieve? In narrative terms, very little besides augmenting his reputation as a reckless seducer and diminishing Nausicaa's reputation as a gullible victim. Instead, their curt, sad parting has qualities seen by no less an authority than Nietzsche as sublime: 'One ought to depart from life,' he wrote, 'as Odysseus departed from Nausicaa – blessing it rather than in love with it.'[19]

Blessings, like those that open and close the short interlude when the lives of Odysseus and Nausicaa come together, are not common in the world we inhabit. Blessings have now lost their religious qualities. Instead, the word 'blessing' has come to signify either tacit approval or an unexpected boon; in the latter case, it is often accompanied by 'in disguise'. Odysseus delivers a kind of benediction that in contemporary contexts could appear tawdry and unconvincing. Just try to imagine one of today's armies of refugees emerging from the sea, meeting a local person in their familiar surroundings and addressing them with a blessing.

Odysseus blessings may seem a little old-fashioned but are neither tawdry nor unconvincing. What they achieve is to bridge the age gap, the culture gap and the gender gap that separate the shipwrecked warrior from the gentle maiden whose biggest adventure to date has been a picnic with her girlfriends. This narrative achievement does not come easy. Homer himself felt compelled to oil the encounter with ample doses of divine intervention by Athena, who helps transform a chance encounter into a memorable turning point in the story. Odysseus does not simply rely on Athena's intervention to touch Nausicaa's heart. He is the epitome of that ancient Greek saying attributed to Aesop, 'Along with Athena, move your own hand.' His performance shows the effort and ingenuity that it takes for narrative to build relations across differences and to overcome the mistrust and fear of the unknown stranger, the man who comes from a different universe, the Other. In Nausicaa, we meet a woman who is willing to stand and listen with sensitivity, curiosity and generosity, unlike her friends, who, terrified, run away. It is her willingness to listen that allows Odysseus' voice to be heard and for their stories to come together. Instead of shutting her ears and running away at the prospect of a troublemaker entering her life, Nausicaa stands and listens to the Other's voice, the Other's story. And it is the poet's narrative accomplishment, too, that all this is achieved without appearing contrived or artificial.

Contemporary encounters with the Other

Today we are deeply conscious of the importance of narrative. Narrative gives meaning to experiences, events and characters. Narrative can turn defeat into victory, suffering into heroism and joy into folly. It can turn a hero into a villain and a moment of shame into one of pride. It can turn someone washed up by the sea in a foreign land into 'a person like us' a fellow man or fellow woman in need of help or, conversely, into an Other – a fraud, a parasite, or just flotsam, human debris to be got rid of. People arriving uninvited and seeking to cross borders without the proper papers can be cast in different narratives. They can be seen as vulnerable individuals in need of protection and care, as victims of criminal gangs who exploit their despair with fake promises, as fraudsters with an eye to the riches afforded by our social services, or even invaders intent on supplanting our culture and our values.[20] 'Our' – the word has now entered our own narrative, a narrative that becomes a narrative of 'our' encounter with the Other.

With the melodies of Nausicaa's encounter still lingering in our mind, let us move to a different scene. You will be familiar with this or similar scenes from social media, the 24/7 news bulletins or newspaper reports.

On 6 June 1993, I was visiting New York when the city awakened to news that a shipwreck had been sighted not far off Rockaway beach. A group of desperate men and women were seen swimming ashore. Within minutes the police, the coastguard, the immigration services, the media with pundits and the public had gathered at the scene. Ten of those shipwrecked drowned; approximately three hundred made it to the land.

In the next few hours, an immense organizational machinery was mobilized to 'welcome' the shipwrecked. A few of them, crafty heirs of Odysseus, managed to slip through this machinery. Subsequently, police with dogs captured five of them in the borough of Queens. Twenty were never accounted for. As for the remaining 282 'illegal aliens' as they had become by nightfall, they were handcuffed and sent to different prisons scattered across the United States.

Since the shipwreck, many people spoke about the survivors or on their behalf; here are some of the media headlines:

- SMUGGLED TO NEW YORK: THE SCENE: WAVES OF PANIC YIELD TO ELATION OF REFUGEES – *New York Times* 7-6-93

- ALIEN-SMUGGLING SHIP RUNS AGROUND;
  HUNDREDS OF CHINESE SWIM ONTO NY BEACH; 7
  DIE IN FRIGID OCEAN – *Washington Post* 7-6-93
- A SEA OF VOICES, ALL YELLING – *Sun Sentinel* (Fort
  Lauderdale) *New York Daily News* 7-6-93
- SMUGGLED TO NEW YORK: 7 DIE AS CROWDED
  IMMIGRANT SHIP GROUNDS OFF QUEENS; ONE
  FAILED VOYAGE ILLUSTRATES FLOW OF CHINESE
  IMMIGRATION – *New York Times* 7-6-93
- 7 ALIENS DIE IN QUEENS; SURFSHIP FOUNDERS,
  DISGORGES 250 ILLEGAL CHINESE IMMIGRANTS
  – *The Record* 7-6-93
- TIDAL WAVE OF HUMAN FLOTSAM ON A
  DESPERATE VENTURE WEST – *Lloyd's List* 9-6-93
- STOP THE FLOW OF HUMAN CARGO – *Seattle Post*
  8-6-93
- SEND THEM BACK – *New York Post* editorial 9-6-93

Having survived 112 days in the darkness of the rust bucket *Golden Venture*, on a single toilet and a bowl of rice daily, the 282 'registered' ones will experience a long incarceration and many of them a forced repatriation to China. Many will seek political asylum as victims of China's one-child policy, and a few will be offered refugee status on humanitarian grounds. Despairing of the dreadful conditions at the detention centres, several will opt for voluntary repatriation. Their subsequent story could be described as an *Odyssey* in its own right, of the Kafkaesque rather than Homeric variety.

Several human rights organizations took up their cause. The story emerged that they came from the Fujian province of China and had each paid about $30,000 to human traffickers. Two of these traffickers were notorious members of Asian gangs operating in New York. They were subsequently tried and convicted. The migrants might have ended working as indentured workers in Chinatown. Instead, most of them spent more than three years incarcerated as 'non-criminal aliens', before being freed through a curious twist, typical of the narcissistic sentimentality of the Clinton years. In February 1997, more than three years after the *Golden Venture* shipwreck, House Representative Bill Goodling of York, Pennsylvania, the site of the prison in which many of the *Golden Venture* refugees had been kept, showed Clinton some of the artwork the prisoners had produced – intricate folded-paper sculptures of caged eagles and other symbols. 'That sure is beautiful,' Clinton told the congressman. 'That's what you do when you are in prison for three and a half years,' Goodling responded. Moved, the US president signed the papers for the release of the prisoners – not their 'naturalization', the Chinese migrants would still have to prove to the authorities that they were fleeing political persecution.

I do not wish to use the incident to draw any moralistic conclusions. Cruelty and the defence of borders were features of Homer's universe as they continue to be today. Forced migrations, ethnic cleansings and escape from persecution and war have marked human history as well as human storytelling, ancient and recent. What else were the Israelites' Exodus from Egypt, Aeneas' escape from the burning citadel of Troy, or the Holy Family's flight to Egypt to evade Herod's Massacre of the Innocents? It is telling, however, to contrast the voice of Odysseus speaking to Nausicaa and the 'voices' of the screaming Chinese in the moonlight that alerted New Yorkers to the shipwreck. These voices are lost as soon as they are washed ashore. Like Odysseus, the Chinese refugees, hungry, cold and covered in brine, emerge from the hostile sea. Unlike him, they will meet no Nausicaa to listen to them. Instead, they will face a plexus of organizations, police, immigration services, criminal justice systems and even refugee charities, which are all interested in labelling, classifying and 'processing' them. Each of these organizations will seek to incorporate them into their own narratives and respond accordingly. The refugees' own stories are not relevant, they are not part of the narratives which will engulf and swallow them faster than the angry sea. Are they 'deserving' political refugees from Communism or 'undeserving' economic migrants? Are they survivors or victims of criminal people-traffickers? Are they criminals themselves? Within a matter of hours, their Otherness has been appropriated, classified and organized into our narratives of Otherness – they have become 'illegal aliens', defined by their lack of suitable papers and their failed attempt to deceive our legal system. All else is immaterial.

In the 1990s, the *Golden Venture* incident had an almost exotic quality. At the time, few of us in the West were interested in who the people who served us in Chinatown restaurants were and how they got themselves there. Western nations had not faced the mass dislocations of people caused by the wars and the crises that followed the terrorist attacks of 9/11. Since then, encounters with the uprooted Other, whether referred to as refugee, economic migrant, asylum seeker or whatever, have become much more regular. Frozen and clinging on the undercarriage of aeroplanes, suffocated in containers, crammed in precarious boats in seas that have not changed since the days of Odysseus – these are people whose images we encounter regularly in our daily lives. Sometimes, especially when they end in tragedy, their plight moves us. As individuals and in groups, we may display hospitality, as did several American families that offered to host the victims of the *Golden Venture* tragedy. In the recent past, numerous communities in different countries have helped support and resettle refugees from wars in Ukraine and elsewhere. Even at the institutional level, countries like Sweden and Germany welcomed refugees and organized extensive resettlement programmes.[21] Out of the attention of Western media, countries like Turkey, Colombia, Pakistan, Uganda and Jordan have hosted[22] millions of people escaping war, political repression and hunger.[23] None of these dislocations of people has been easy and many of the politicians who welcomed migrants in their countries have paid a heavy political price.

If there is one issue that Nausicaa's encounter with Odysseus highlights it is that meeting the uprooted Other is not easy. A magnificent fifth-century BCE amphora now in Munich's Staatliche Antikensammlungen depicts the scene. Between a palpably startled Odysseus who is holding a pathetic branch to hide his nakedness and a coy-looking Nausicaa and her friends who are fleeing in terror stands the massively authoritative figure of Athena ready to facilitate the contact between the shipwrecked sailor and the princess. Meeting the uprooted Other is harder in our times when there is no Athena to facilitate the encounter. Even when the uprooted Others are allowed to stay in a new country, it can take years before they can rebuild their lives and much longer, sometimes several generations, before they are accepted as an integral and legitimate part of 'us'.

There is one more question that Odysseus' encounter with Nausicaa, or should it be Nausicaa's encounter with Odysseus, raises – who in this encounter is We and who is the Other? Are we seeing Odysseus through Nausicaa's eyes or Nausicaa through Odysseus' eyes? We have referred to Odysseus as the Other by virtue of his being uprooted, helpless and destitute, by contrast to Nausicaa's comfortable immersion in her domestic routines. This, however, flies in the face of Odysseus being the protagonist of the *Odyssey*, someone long cast as the archetypal heroic Westerner who travels and triumphs, through whose eyes the entire narrative unfolds. Like Robinson Crusoe in a different narrative, is it not Odysseus who defines the characters and the events in the plot? Could Nausicaa in her erotic exoticism not be the real Other in the narrative? In our times when we have learnt to mistrust fixed meanings and interpretations, these are valid and probing questions that fire our imaginations since they can never be settled conclusively. They are questions prompted by mythological thinking that help us delve more deeply into our own conundrums and the powerful emotions that stir us when we come face to face with the outsider, the stranger.

Epilogue

The Greek language has given us the word 'xenophobia', the fear of the stranger. It has also given us the less commonly used word 'philoxenia'. This is often understood as offering hospitality to a stranger. In the princess Nausicaa, we have a wonderful example of a philoxenia which goes well beyond giving food and shelter to Odysseus. It means listening, understanding, communicating and being prepared to form a relation that unsettles comfort and routine. Philoxenia means being open to a stranger, being interested in meeting and learning from the encounter. It also means overcoming the inner resistances that create an aversion to the stranger. Nausicaa's young friends, on the other hand, the ones who flee in horror on seeing the naked stranger, are examples of visceral xenophobia, a fear that quickly turns into repulsion and avoidance.

While philoxenia endures in our times, xenophobia is becoming ever more apparent. Increasing population movements across countries and continents resulting from war, famine and climate change trigger fears, some of which are primal – fears of being invaded, replaced and swamped even in countries with long traditions of hospitality and openness to refugees. Ever stricter frontier controls are introduced between countries, even in the European Union that had sought to eradicate them. The United Kingdom opted for Brexit under the slogan of regaining control of its borders. Physical walls are rising in many parts of the world, separating countries from their neighbours. Visas and passport controls are becoming ever stricter. The Covid-19 epidemic made the crossing of frontiers yet more difficult, even for those equipped with the right pieces of paper.

We are now erecting ever more borders in our societies, more enclosures aimed at keeping strangers outside, and these borders are patrolled ever more vigilantly. As modern Greek filmmaker and celebrant of Odysseus, Theo Angelopoulos, put it:

> We are creating borders, around ever smaller areas. Soon I will have borders right outside my own front door. I will have a border all around my house and in no time at all I will be a state all unto myself. Me![24]

Such borders are not just physical obstacles. They are obstacles to communication, to learning, to enjoying the uncomfortable pleasures that come from meeting the Other and discovering how much unites us across cultures and territories.

7

Narcissus and Echo: A Culture of Narcissism or a Culture of Echoes?

The water stirs, the image of the beloved disappears . . .

Narcissus was a young man, a huntsman, famed the world over not for his hunting skills but for his beauty. Boys and girls fell in love with him in droves, but he spurned them all, leaving them broken-hearted.

Most devastated among them was the mountain nymph, Echo. The poor girl had been a chatterbox but had now lost her own voice and could only repeat what others said. This is how Hera had punished her for concealing some of her husband Zeus' frolics with other mountain nymphs. But another goddess, maybe Artemis or Aphrodite, took pity on Echo and decided to punish Narcissus for leaving her broken-hearted.

One day he caught sight of his own image in the crystal-clear water of a pond. At once he fell in love with what he saw, his own reflection. But every time he reached out to touch the object of his love, the water stirred, and the image disappeared. He died by drowning in the spring water. Others say that he used a dagger given to him by another spurned lover. Yet others believe that he just wasted away on the water's edge. In his place, all that was left was a solitary flower of great beauty and grace.

And Echo? She never forgave Narcissus. But still in love with him, she wandered off in the forests mourning his death as she gradually withered away. Eventually there was nothing left of her but furtive whispers heard by the passers-by in canyons and ravines, echoing their own words. Like Narcissus, she was consumed by love that could not be consummated. The object of her infatuation was blind to her presence and deaf to her pleas.

We meet Narcissus every day. We meet him in the street, we meet him at work, we meet him on holiday. We meet him at home among our family and friends. In moments of candid introspection, we may meet him in ourselves. In fact, we meet so many Narcissi that we lose track of them. How then can we be sure that when we see someone looking at their image in a mirror, taking a selfie on their phone, or posting a picture on Facebook, we have met the real Narcissus? For one thing, Narcissus does not return our look. He is lost in himself. Like his mythical counterpart, he barely registers our existence. In his presence, we become invisible just like Echo, the poor nymph whose love for him left her repeating the words of others with no voice of her own. Nar-cis-sus, Nar-cis-sus.

The story of Narcissus, some argue,[1] has become the dominant myth or our times. Our love for Narcissus has supplanted other loves: our love for tragic Oedipus, for wise Athena, for heroic Achilles, for mighty Heracles and for long-suffering Sisyphus, even our love for beautiful but boring characters like Adonis. Today we are mesmerized by Narcissus, the radiant youth who loses himself in self-admiration. Narcissism has long ceased to be the guarded secret of psychoanalysts and psychiatrists, entering easily into our daily conversations, political commentaries and constant chatter in print and online. It is an indispensable part of different discussions of culture, politics, the arts, media, consumption, to say nothing of mental health and self-healing. Amazon currently lists over 8,000 books with the word 'narcissism' in the title, ranging from self-help manuals to grand pronouncements about the 'narcissism epidemic'.

It is ironic then that while Narcissus was unwilling to have conversations with anyone, narcissism, the condition named after him, easily slips into so many conversations. It surfaces readily whenever we start talking about a person or a situation that reeks of grandiosity, self-obsession and entitlement. It seems to capture to perfection our current preoccupation with image, our own as well as that of every brand we consume, our fears of losing our looks and our independence, and our difficulties in forming lasting relations with others.

Narcissus becomes a Narcissist

How did Narcissus turn narcissist? This was largely thanks to Sigmund Freud, as even his many critics will acknowledge. Freud was someone who knew his ancient myths well. At the turn of the twentieth century, he made Oedipus the centrepiece of his psychology arguing that every child goes through a phase when they reach out for their mother as the object of their absolute infatuation and view their father as a dangerous rival. Freud encountered the term 'narcissism' in about 1910 in the work of physician Havelock Ellis and psychiatrist Paul Näcke. He quickly realized the power of the myth of Narcissus in highlighting the importance of self-love, of love directed at oneself.

Freud's theory of narcissism went through several revisions, but the core idea remained the same – just as our love can reach out to different people, different groups and different objects in the world, it can also turn inwards, adopting our own ego as its object. There is nothing abnormal or pathological about this. We all direct part of our love towards ourselves. Only when this happens at the expense of our ability to create meaningful relations with others or to find interests beyond ourselves, only then does narcissism become the cause of different psychological disorders. The exact opposite, the inability to find anything to love in our self, also leads to disorders – perennially low self-esteem, inability to stand up to others, and an excessive proneness to guilt and shame.

The introduction of narcissism in Freud's psychology came with two realizations. First, that our individual ego can no longer be seen solely as an active agent seeking to enhance our well-being and promote the achievement of our aims in life. Instead, it must also be seen as craving love and trying to attract love towards itself. 'Look at me! I am special, I am unique, I deserve love!' our ego appears to be saying not only to the world out there but also to the unconscious parts of our own mental personality, as it seeks to draw interest and attention to itself.

The other realization was that self-love *precedes* love for other people or for different objects of the outer world. As a new-born baby, we each have no inkling what kind of world we have come into. All we are aware of is an undifferentiated universe, a big cocoon which engulfs us. This universe sometimes frustrates us and sometimes fulfils us. This is the moment when what Freud described as 'his Majesty the baby'[2] takes it for granted that they are the centre of the universe. This early or primary narcissism will be rudely disrupted as we begin to discover, each in our distinct way, that mother and father are not there purely for our benefit and that a large part of the wider world is indifferent or hostile to us.

Memories of this grandiose self linger on in later life when we try to recreate something of the glowing comfort of primary narcissism.

We want to find ourselves once again at the centre of a loving world. To this end, we try to attract love towards our ego which has now matured and established itself as a conscious, thinking part of our mental personality. Those of us who were only-children and enjoyed the doting and exclusive love of our parents in early life are liable to develop particularly strong narcissistic desires in later life, especially if our parents were permissive and lenient. In its efforts to make itself lovable, our ego will then create an idealized version of itself, an ego-ideal, to which it seeks to channel love. This ideal-ego is an amalgam of idealized images, phantasies and wishes which we carry with us, against which our ego measures itself. The closer our ego gets to its ideal the more narcissistic self-love it attracts to itself.

The ego-ideal, then, emerges as a wishful phantasy of ourselves, as we would like to be, in order to become once more the centre of an admiring and loving world:

> What individuals project as their ideal is the substitute for the lost narcissism of their childhood in which they were their own ideal … To this ideal ego is now directed the self-love which the real ego enjoyed in childhood. The narcissism seems to be now displaced on to this new ideal ego, which, like the infantile ego, deems itself the possessor of all perfections.[3]

In attempting to draw love to our ego we may follow loosely two paths – the first claims: 'Admire me for what I have achieved!' and the second: 'Admire me for being so beautiful!' The first is achievement narcissism. It prompts us to excel in any sphere of social activity, such as business, sport, the arts, politics or science. The other, image narcissism, drives us to make ourselves beautiful and admired for our appearance, which may include any number of accessories and trimmings.[4]

Both kinds of narcissism are important in our times. Achievement narcissism may drive us to work relentlessly, building our careers and competing in a race to the top, a race that has few winners and leaves many of us licking our wounds. Image narcissism, for its part, is tied to the culture of celebrity, of social media 'likes' and every conceivable type of consumption that promises to improve our physical appearance or our general attractiveness. Whether it is a facial cream that promises to return our skin to pristine youthfulness or a fashionable tourist destination from where we can post exuberant selfies, consumerism has myriads of ways of feeding the culture of narcissism that we inhabit. There are times when image and achievement narcissism merge into one, as when we spend long hours in the gym working hard to build the perfect body for ourselves. Unlike Narcissus, our mythical model, drawing love to ourselves does not come easy. It requires work, discipline and money.

The societies we inhabit exacerbate our narcissistic cravings by inflicting constant blows to our narcissism. Small family sizes, more permissive child-rearing techniques and a constant preoccupation among the middle classes about their kids' brilliance encourage the belief in many children that they are special and deserve success and admiration. Parents project onto their children their own narcissism, turning them into fixtures of their own ego-ideals and hoping that they will realize all the dreams that they were unable to realize for themselves. Yet, our societies pitch us in constant competition with each other from a very early age. In this competition, we often find ourselves failing or succeeding but only fleetingly and with great effort. Others appear constantly to be more successful, more attractive, more in control of their lives.

Even more damaging for our narcissism is the immense impersonality that engulfs most of us living in Western societies, the crushing isolation that seems to threaten us and other people's general indifference to us. Living in large cities, surrounded by millions of unfamiliar faces, we must learn to live as unknowns in the midst of unknowns. Impersonality is a fundamental affront to our narcissism. From being unique members of a family, a clan or a group, urban life consigns us to the status of cogs, dispensable and replaceable. In compensation, we seek to develop identities of our own, to distinguish ourselves from the crowd, to establish our own individuality and uniqueness. This is how identity, discovering our unique voice, writing our own life narrative, becomes a 'project' for many of us, something we constantly strive towards and agonize over.[5]

One clever way that our narcissism has discovered for boosting itself is by incorporating into the ego-ideal the qualities and perfections we attribute to the groups and organizations we identify with. Identifying with a nation enables our narcissism to relish its moments of historical glory, its military, cultural and scientific achievements, its sporting successes, the long-standing traditions and symbols that set it apart from other nations. We may not personally have accomplished very much, but our shared heritage, our collective ideals and myths, make us as part of a larger entity, the nation, going back into the centuries and turn into nourishment for our narcissism.

In our times, support for narcissism has come from two formidable sources, two substantial machines for boosting narcissism, or more precisely for providing consolations for the numerous blows that its impersonality inflicts on it, rampant consumerism and grandiose organizations. Each of these offers the promise of enriching our ideal egos and restoring us in the midst of an admiring audience. Consumerism with its cornucopia of offerings, clothes, accessories and every imaginable beautifying accoutrement promises to enhance our image. Some of the opulence of the glamorous logos on offer may rub off onto us and enrich our self-image. Alternatively, we may find ourselves working for a successful, powerful organization, a tech company, an advertising agency, a university, preferably one with a recognizable brand name. Some of its power and prestige rub off onto us. Both of these sources of consolation, consumerism and glamorous employment, however, may provide more fuel to our narcissism without assuaging it.

A culture of narcissism: 'Shop till you drop'

Contemporary consumerism is a near-perfect companion to our ailing narcissism. Consumerism is defined in many different ways, but its principal purpose is simple – to replace 'her majesty the baby' with 'her majesty the consumer':

> The consumer is now a god-like figure, before whom markets and politicians alike bow. Everywhere it seems, the consumer is triumphant. Consumers are said to dictate production; to fuel innovation; to be creating new service sectors in advanced economies; to be driving modern politics; to have it in their power to save the environment and protect the future of the planet.[6]

Over the past hundred years or so, consumerism has displaced many other spheres of human activity as a major source of meaning, identity and value. Along the way, the meaning of the word 'consume' has shifted from the objects that are used up or dissipated in the process of consumption to the human needs that are fulfilled by the process. Consumption for mere survival has been replaced by consumption as the royal path to the good life, fulfilment and success. Along with mass production, the twentieth century signalled the rise of mass consumption, the quest by ever-widening masses of population for a better life through consumption of more and better goods and services.[7]

Towards the end of the twentieth century, mass consumption underwent a vital transformation, partly made possible by new technologies that allowed the production of highly differentiated products. Consumers were called to exercise ever-increasing choices on how to spend their money in a huge proliferation of differentiated goods, brands and services. These enabled consumers, or at least some of them, to experiment with different identities and different lifestyles. Without abandoning their craving for material goods, consumers turned to images, spectacles and experiences as the primary means of creating attractive identities for themselves. Even when buying material objects, like cars, clothes or mobile phones, it is the power of the brand that makes them desirable rather than their actual uses, each product triggering off a fantasy of enjoyment and fulfilment.

Consumerism spawns an infinite array of dreams, of ideals and of models which we can embrace as we seek to make ourselves attractive. We are each cast in the role of a sovereign choice-maker in what has been described as a menu society,[8] a society that presents us with a bewildering variety of options, a society where the right to choose becomes the bedrock of our freedom. As we discussed in Chapter 3, aspects of life that previous generations viewed as matters of birth, fate and social rank now turn into arenas for the exercise of choice. Choice informs every good and service we consume – our clothes, our diets, our leisure activities and so forth. Choice also informs our occupation, our partners and friends, the shape of our body, our gender and so forth. These choices open up infinite possibilities of identity construction, as we set about appropriating the idealized qualities of commodities, aided and abetted by the propaganda of the advertisers, the makers of dreams. In this way, the world of commodities comes to the rescue of our narcissism. The offerings of consumer capitalism promise to counter our fears of being left behind, of growing old and ugly.

The freedom of choice is one we defend vehemently since it is essential in propping up our narcissism. The goods and images we consume become, at least temporarily, parts of our identity, boosting our self-image and self-esteem. But choice, as we saw in Chapter 3, also creates burdens and anxieties. Have we made the right choices? Have we missed out on hidden possibilities? Can our choices be reversed, if they prove unsuccessful?

A chronic insecurity pervades many of our consumer choices, exacerbated by the comparisons we keep making with those around us. Why do so many of the objects that we truly desire lie beyond what we can afford? Why is our glance always drawn to those better looking, more glamorous than ourselves? Why does somebody always seem to be ahead of us in the fashion stakes or the popularity stakes? Consumer capitalism creates new needs and insecurities in us faster than most of us can satisfy them. Yesterday's cherished object or thrilling experience soon loses its allure and another one assumes its place as a target of desire. We discard commodities constantly even as we clutter our homes with unwanted objects many of which were once, however briefly, props for our narcissism.

Several authors have commented on the addictive quality of contemporary consumption – while temporarily appeasing our narcissism, consumer culture creates long-term dissatisfaction, dependency and meaninglessness. Or as Lasch has put it:

> 'Shop till you drop.' Like exercise, [shopping] often seems to present itself as a form of therapy, designed to restore a sense of wholeness and well-being after long hours of unrewarding work. 'I feel like hell and I go out for a run, and before I know it, everything's OK.' Shopping serves the same purpose: 'It hardly matters what I buy, I just get a kick out of buying. It's like that first whiff of cocaine. It's euphoric and I just get higher and higher as I buy.'[9]

One of the consequences of consumerism is that we often end up treating other people as accessories to our own success, as props for our own popularity. And conversely, we find ourselves as accessories to somebody else's popularity. Searching for a partner in online dating services becomes akin to shopping for a better accessory to enhance our image. Relations with others, with friends and lovers, become nervous and transitory, until we or they discover better or more popular ones. The same social pressures that emphasize the importance of being special and unique can also flatten most of us to the level of mundane ordinariness.

Grandiose organizations: Glass palaces or glass cages?

The grandiose self finds the world of mass consumption mesmerizing but also frustrating. There is another sphere, however, where the grandiose self may seek fulfilment – the world of work, of money and careers. This is a sphere where reputations can be forged, where palpable signs of success are evident for all to see and admire. A simple job will not do, of course. It does not impress other people, nor does it live up to the exorbitant criteria of success demanded by the grandiose self. What is needed is a start-up business success or, more commonly, a stellar career in a prestigious organization or, better still, in a series of prestigious organizations.

In pursuing a career, we must be seen to be making active choices and not be tied down as cogs on a machine. We must appear to be independent and free, doing something creative, using our imagination, the full range of our creative abilities, our unique talents. To this end, we must not commit our loyalty and freedom to any one employer but must always keep our options open. We must be constantly on the lookout for better options to move our careers ahead and enhance our image. To this end, we assiduously learn to cultivate networks and constantly adjust our life stories to meet the demands of prospective employers. The simple listing of our accomplishments in a résumé turns into the arduous art of creating different life narratives to suit the requirements of each moment. If at the height of capitalist modernity, success in the workplace was deemed to be the product of hard work and loyalty to a single employer, in our times, we succeed by being on the move and grasping each opportunity as it presents itself by placing ourselves in the right place at the right time. In this way the grandiose self hopes to benefit from the grandiosity of the organizations which provide employment.[10]

Grandiosity, of course, is hardly a new phenomenon. Pyramids, mighty fortresses, grand temples, monuments and palaces are all testaments to grandiosity across continents through many centuries. In old myths, grandiosity often featured as hubris inviting divine retribution, as the story of the Tower of Babel illustrates. What is unique about the grandiosity of our age is the generalized attempt by virtually every organization to claim uniqueness and specialness. What was once a dangerous quality of conquerors and potentates now suffuses the culture of most organizations.

Grandiosity colonizes every domain of social and economic activity, private and public, businesses, NGOs, universities, hospitals and so forth. Nearly every organization, from the largest to the smallest, routinely claims to be a 'World Leader', 'No. 1', 'Cutting Edge' and suchlike, or at least to aspire at being these things.[11] 'We are ranked top for our playing activities' proclaims a huge banner in the little primary school in my neighbourhood. A branding mentality becomes dominant as different brands constantly strive to outdo each other with ever more outrageous promises and claims. Just as every organization proclaims itself to be unique and special, so, too, do individuals by turning themselves into brands and learning how to sell themselves. A branding and marketing orientation dominates most aspects of human life, even as the uniqueness of each is only visible to the eye trained in taking in infinitesimal differences.[12]

One of the areas where organizational grandiosity is most visible is in two types of building that have transformed Western cities in the last fifty years – office towers and shopping malls. These modern cathedrals of work and consumption now dwarf the real cathedrals, like the once mighty St Paul's whose stature in the London skyline diminishes with every passing year. The signature material of these buildings (and many others besides) is glass, just as concrete was the signature material of a previous era. Concrete is a substance which solidifies forever into a rigid and unchanging mass. Glass, too, may be solid, but its defining property is optical rather than static – its ability to allow light to pass through it, even as it reflects, distorts or refracts it. It is a substance which generates changing images, a substance whose mere presence attests that what it encases is worthy of attention.

Today's glass buildings, with their wide-open spaces and imposing atriums, transform all those inside them – workers, customers, visitors – into members of a cast. They all become part of a brand on show. For those working in open-plan offices, in boutiques and shops, in bars and restaurants, the constant exposure to the public eye creates a distinct ambivalence. On the one hand, they enjoy the narcissistic thrill of being part of a winning team or brand. On the other, they feel constantly exposed, their looks, their performance and their personality under constant scrutiny. The customers and visitors, for their part, are engaged in a game of spotting the latest trends and fashions, assessing themselves against each other. They have no choice but to observe, to judge, to compare, to desire, to choose and to buy.

The ethos of grandiosity has led to a fundamental re-evaluation of the function of management in today's organizations. Instead of focusing single-mindedly on efficient production and rational administration, management today seeks to bewitch their stakeholders with the fantastic, the alluring, the magical. Managers are increasingly preoccupied with the shaping of corporate image, spinning fantasies and appealing to emotions.[13] It is natural therefore that management, especially in top positions, attracts highly narcissistic individuals, attractive and imaginative people with great flair in communicating their ideas and relishing the limelight.[14] They can inspire their followers, employees, customers, shareholders and other stakeholders with their visions and promises.

Narcissistic leaders are liable to become ever more concerned with public relations, celebrations and ceremonies, opulent buildings and grandiose projects, losing track of the organizational 'nuts and bolts', the machinery necessary to ensure the successful running of an organization. These leaders easily lapse to hubris, preoccupied with preserving the corporate image at all costs, cutting corners in anything that does not directly enhance their organization's profile and believing themselves to be special. Such leaders may gradually lose touch with reality altogether – their vision becomes a reality, whether it has been realized or not, a delusional reality to be sure but one they live in and one they force onto their followers. In this way, the leaders' narcissism can function effectively as a force inspiring and uniting the followers but regularly brings about an organization's decay and disintegration.

One of the abiding images of the capitalist organization at the outset of the twentieth century was provided by Max Weber, the founder of the theory of bureaucracy. Weber described bureaucracy as an iron cage where rigid hierarchies and rules that claim to represent rationality constrict people into ever tighter compartments, turning everyone into a cog on large, impersonal machines.[15] The glittering sites of today's capitalism – the glass towers, the shopping malls and other cathedrals of consumption – suggest a different metaphor, that of a glass cage, which entraps those inside it by exposing them to constant scrutiny to the eye of the customer, the fellow employee, the manager. Glass cages with their emphasis on display and image offer a powerful illusion of transparency. Are they cages at all, or are they glass palaces housing those privileged to work and live in them? To those outside the glass palaces, they look glamorous, full of successful people and enticing objects. Those denied access, through their lack of resources, mobility, looks or whatever, feel truly excluded. And those inside them feel anxious that maybe one day they, too, will be refused entry.

Narcissism in a post-truth world

When historian Christopher Lasch published his book, *The Culture of Narcissism*,[16] in 1979, it became an instant bestseller. At the time, there were no mobile phones, personal computers with small monochrome screens were several years away, and photography was still in its now forgotten Neanderthal/Kodak days. Yet, his book prophetically critiqued a culture of narcissism as a culture worshipping the power of image, the production and consumption of which dominated the 'me generation' of baby-boomers. Lasch also astutely noted how the proliferation of images undermines our sense of reality, blurring the boundaries between fact and fantasy. His book may have gone in and out of fashion several times since then, but the hegemony of image has exploded, supported by every kind of technology introduced since, reaching a kind of apotheosis in our own post-truth times.

If there is one idea that energizes the concept of post-truth, it is the idea that even when we know that an image is doctored and fake, we still find it irresistible. And this is what makes the myth of Narcissus, the youth eternally drawn to his own image, so seductive. This is why narcissism has spilled out of the clinical domain and overtaken virtually every other psychoanalytic idea in popularity. Its success is due to its ability to match nearly anything we like or dislike about ourselves and our culture. Narcissism is popular because it can be flexibly used, responding to any projection, wish and desire. Narcissism has long ceased to be a medical disorder, much as the compilers of successive editions of the *Diagnostic and Statistical Manual of Mental Disorders* (DSM) have tried to pin it down to different definitions. Instead, it has become itself a mirage, a word that reverberates in our post-truth echo chambers.

And yet, there is one jarring aspect of the myth of Narcissus that refuses to capitulate to a profusion of interpretations and projections. Narcissus needed no audience and relied on no beautifying accessories. He needed no Photoshop, no 'likes', and he never belonged to an organization or a cabal, prestigious or otherwise. Even after his demise, unlike other unfortunate characters in Greek mythology, he did not turn into a star until he was appropriated by our culture which worships him and vilifies him, envies him and celebrates him. He didn't need company and didn't want anyone to tell him that he was special and unique. He didn't have an identity project nor did he struggle to discover his voice, something denied to poor Echo. All he wanted was to touch the beautiful image he was seeing in the calm water of the spring. We are drawn to Narcissus as Narcissus was drawn to himself, but we are not drawn to his solitude or his quietness. Unlike Narcissus, we need external stimulation to divert our boredom. We crave action and entertainment. We watch movies. We look at our phones every few minutes, we search social media for new likes, we want news, we want stories. We want music every minute of the day.

All this is virtually the opposite of what Narcissus craved and what he did. Instead of identifying with Narcissus, we are drawn to him as a compensation for what we lack. Ours is a culture of narcissistic deficits, which makes the odd leader, CEO or celebrity with a narcissistic surplus truly stand out. By contrast, most of us are survivors, licking our narcissistic wounds, underappreciated and sidestepped. Lost in our impersonal cities and our impersonal workplaces, we seek solace in our equally impersonal cathedrals of consumption and our pathetic social media self-promotions. In seeking to emulate Narcissus, we risk becoming more like the shrivelled carcass and subjectless voice of poor Echo. If there is one lesson that the ancient myth of Narcissus tells us, it is that ours is not a culture of narcissism so much as a culture of echoes.

8

The Trojan War and the Argonautic Expedition: Heroic Missions, Leadership and Hubris

Quest for glory and loot: The Trojan War

A golden apple bearing the inscription 'For the Fairest One' appears at a feast of the gods. Three goddesses want it. They appeal to Zeus. He declines to make a choice, but says: 'Go to Paris, a fine young prince with a sharp eye for beauty and ask him to judge who should have the apple.' Hera, Athena and Aphrodite, for they are the three goddesses, appear at once in front of Paris, the prince of Troy who is peacefully grazing his sheep on Mount Ida. They dazzle him with their beauty and each tries to entice him with promises of gifts.

'Give the apple to me,' says Hera, 'and I will make you a fabulously rich king and the founder of a dynasty that will rule Europe and Asia for centuries.'

'Give the apple to me,' says Athena, 'and I will make you a wise ruler, victorious in war and celebrated for all eternity.'

Aphrodite is coy. She smiles, she looks at Paris sideways and says, 'Give the apple to me and I will give you the love of the world's most beautiful woman.'

Paris, the romantic, does not hesitate for a single second. He awards the golden apple to Aphrodite. Trouble. The world's most beautiful woman is already married, to the king of Sparta, Menelaus. No problem for Aphrodite. A quick visit by Paris to Sparta, a well-aimed arrow from Eros, Helen falls madly in love with the handsome stranger and the two of them elope to Troy.

A very angry king of Sparta calls Agamemnon, his brother, the mighty king of Mycenae, and the most powerful man in Greece. 'The Trojan has insulted me, he has insulted all of Hellas. We must get Helen back, we must teach these Trojans a lesson.' Before long, Agamemnon gathers an army including every Greek king and hero of the times and launches an armada of a thousand ships to conquer Troy.

What follows is a series of many adventures, much fighting, and a lot of bloodshed. After nine years of war between the Greeks and the Trojans, Agamemnon falls out with his greatest champion, Achilles. Over a woman, as it happens. Achilles refuses to fight. He withdraws along with his troops, the Myrmidons, and broods in his tent, as the Trojans get the upper hand on the battlefield. They venture closer and closer to the Greeks' ships and their own great hero, Hector, threatens to set them ablaze. In despair, the Greeks and Agamemnon himself beg Achilles to return to the battlefield. He refuses to fight, but allows his beloved Patroclus to rejoin the battlefield ahead of the Myrmidons.

After various exploits, Patroclus is killed by Hector. Deranged by his anger and his grief, Achilles re-enters the battlefield killing mercilessly all who stand in his way. He eventually kills Hector and drags the body of his defeated enemy behind his chariot around the citadel of Troy, *spreading desolation and despair among the Trojans. Then, in the dead of the night, he receives an unexpected visit from King Priam, ruler of Troy and father of Hector. He has arrived at the enemy camp laden with gifts and begs Achilles to return the body of his son to him for a proper funeral. In a moment of deep emotion, the two enemies, Achilles and Priam, are reconciled. As they relive their lives now as father and son, they come to recognize the tragedy of war. Achilles returns the body of Hector to Priam and they agree on a ceasefire to bury their dead with appropriate rites.*

Thus does Homer's Iliad *end. But the war has not ended. Many more warriors will die on both sides, including Paris and Achilles himself. Eventually the Greeks will sack Troy. Following the advice of canny Odysseus, they build a large wooden horse in which Odysseus and some of their best warriors hide. The rest of their army pretends to depart, leaving the horse behind as a gift to their enemies. Oblivious to various warnings, the Trojans take the horse into their citadel, even demolishing a part of the fortress in order to drag it inside. While the Trojans rejoice in what they take to be a great victory, Odysseus and his comrades, under the guise of darkness, creep out of the horse's belly. They open the city gates and the rest of the Greek army, having returned from their hiding, pour into the city. They kill, they burn, they plunder. They commit many atrocities. A smouldering pile of rubble is left where a great city and its famed citadel once stood.*

The Greek chieftains, those who survived the ten long years of war, laden with looted Trojan gold and enslaved Trojan women, set off for the return journey to their Greek motherlands. Most of them will have a bad end. Agamemnon will be murdered by his wife and her lover upon returning to Mycenae. Menelaus and Helen will eventually find their way back to Sparta, apparently reconciled, but how can a couple be reconciled after what they have been through? Odysseus will wonder the seas for ten years, enduring many trials before returning to his country,

Ithaca, where more troubles are waiting for him. A band of Trojan survivors, under the leadership of Aeneas, son of Aphrodite, will escape the massacre of Troy and, in their ships, will seek refuge elsewhere. They will eventually find a home in a new country, Italy, not without more fighting and strife. Fighting and strife between the Greeks and their Asian neighbours will hardly ever cease in the coming millennia. And it all started with a golden apple.

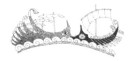

Quest for glory, adventure and justice: The Argonauts' expedition

'Go and fetch the Golden Fleece, young man, and when you bring it back you can have the throne that I have usurped from your father.' This is what Pelias, King of Iolcus, said to Iason,[1] the rightful heir of the throne of Iolcus. The fleece of the Golden Ram was in Colchis, a distant kingdom at the furthest end of the Black Sea, in the shadow of the Caucasus, ruled by King Aeetes. It was guarded by a dragon breathing fire. Eager for fame, adventure and justice (in that order), Iason naturally accepted the challenge.

Seizing the Golden Fleece and bringing it back to Greece was not a simple matter. It required organization, starting with the building of a ship, capable of sailing in the harshest of seas and, not least, crossing the dreaded Clashing Rocks at the entrance to the Black Sea. Iason commissioned Argus, a famed shipwright, to built the 'Argo', a fifty-oared ship. Helped by the goddess Athena, Argus built the swiftest and most famous ship in Greek mythology.

Seizing the Golden Fleece also required recruiting a workforce to sail the Argo and to support the young hero in his venture. Iason put out a call and was immediately rewarded with backing from every major hero in Greece. Nobody wanted to be left out of an adventure that would resound through the ages. More than fifty of them joined Iason, including sons of gods and sons of heroes, mortals and immortals. Among them, we can recognize Orpheus, legendary musician; Castor and Polydeuces, the eternal twins; Theseus, the hero of Athens; Atalanta, the legendary huntress; and Greece's greatest hero, Heracles.

The sea journey of the Argo and the Argonauts has been told by several authors in competing versions. During their voyage, the Argonauts visited most places in the known universe, from Libya and Crete to the Danube and the furthest reaches of the Black Sea. They met many strange creatures, friendly and hostile, they fought many battles, they tamed many beasts and overcame many obstacles.

When they eventually reached Colchis, Iason moored the Argo in a hidden bay and called a war council. Accompanied by a few handsome Argonauts, he then made his way to the palace of King Aeetes. Along the way, local people looked admiringly at the young foreigners – could they be gods descending from Mount Olympus, they were wondering? King Aeetes, by contrast, received Iason and his companions coolly. No Greek was meant to sail through the Clashing Rocks and survive the journey. Still, the king offered to surrender the Golden Fleece to Iason, if Iason would complete certain labours that Aeetes claimed he had completed himself. He was to yoke two ferocious bulls with feet of bronze and flames shooting out of their mouths. He was then to plough a large field and sow the furrows with the teeth of a dragon. From these teeth, an army of warriors would spring, and Iason was to fight and defeat them. If he succeeded, he could take the Golden Fleece back to Greece.

Iason was undaunted, but he would surely have met his end had he not suddenly acquired a new ally, the princess Medea. Medea was the daughter of King Aeetes and priestess of the ancient goddess Hecate, goddess of the arts of sorcery. She was dark, determined and dangerous.

While Iason was talking to Aeetes, Hera and Athena had been holding a council of their own, trying to work out how they could help him achieve the impossible tasks he faced. They recruited the help of Aphrodite, so all three goddesses who would later argue over the Golden Apple worked together. Aphrodite used her influence on Eros (Cupid), the amorous little god of infatuation, who targeted one of his arrows at Medea. At once, she fell in love with Iason.

Medea, the granddaughter of Sun god Helios, was famed for her sorcery. She offered to put her magic at the service of Iason, on one condition. He should marry her. Little knowing what he was agreeing to, Iason consented. She then smeared his body with a balm that made him invulnerable for a day. She also advised him how to deal with the army of warriors. Thus prepared, Iason was able to harness the fearsome bulls to the yoke, plough the field and sow the dragon's teeth. When the warriors sprang out of the earth, armed to the teeth and ready to exterminate him, he threw a large rock in their midst, whereupon they turned against each other and started fighting until none of them was left alive.

Aeetes did not keep his promise to let Iason have the Golden Fleece. Instead, he planned to have him killed. Medea, once again, stepped in. In the middle of the night, she took Iason to the grove sacred to Ares where the Golden Fleece was guarded by the dragon. Using her magic, she put the monster to sleep, while Iason seized the Golden Fleece. Together with the other Argonauts, they set sail back to Greece.

The Argonauts' return journey to Greece was long and hazardous and called for ever more outrageous magical interventions from Medea, not least killing and dismembering her own brother, Apsyrtus. Once they arrived back in Iolcus, King Pelias, needless to say, refused to honour his promise and return the throne to Iason. Medea contrived a particularly gruesome end for him. She impressed everyone in Iolcus with one of her party tricks, her ability to make the old young again. She cut an old ram into pieces and placed it in her magic cauldron, filled with a special liquor. After some incantations, the ram jumped out of the cauldron in the prime of youth. She then offered to do the same for King Pelias and persuaded his daughters to cut down their father and put the pieces of his body in the cauldron. He was never seen again.

Following this deed, things did not work out for Iason. Terrified by Medea, the people of Iolcus gave the throne to Acastus, Pelias' son, and chased Iason and Medea, now his wife, out of the city. After many wanderings, Iason and Medea ended up in Corinth. There they lived for many years and had several children, nobody knows exactly how many. What is certain is that at some stage Iason got sick of Medea. Was it her sorcery? Did he suspect her of planning to murder king Creon of Corinth as she had several other kings and princes? Was she, a barbarian foreigner, an obstacle to his political ambitions? Nobody knows. What is certain is that Iason decided to end it with Medea and marry the sweet daughter of Creon, Creusa, also known as Glauce.

Medea's revenge was terrifying. Pretending to accept Iason's decision, she dispatched a wedding gift to Glauce – a golden crown and a magnificent white robe. As soon as the young princess put them on, she was consumed by flames and so, too, was her father, King Creon, and all of their guests. They all died in excruciating pain. Only Iason managed to escape, jumping out of a window. Enraged by the murder of their king, the Corinthians seized the children of Iason and Medea and stoned them to death. According to a different version invented by Euripides, Medea herself killed her children.[2]

There are many stories of what happened to Medea after the death of the children, some happy, some sad, some outrageous. For Iason, the end was tragic. Like Oedipus and Bellerophon, he wandered homeless from city to city, overwhelmed by his misfortunes. Eventually he came to rest under the Argo, which was now standing as a shrine to Poseidon. A piece *of masonry suddenly dropped from the hulk of the great ship. It struck Iason on the head, killing him instantly.*

Missions and campaigns

Greek myths of the heroic type[3] tend to centre on a central character in a personal quest or a journey with a mission. The mission usually aims to right a wrong, to meet a challenge or to prove a point. There are even missions just for the hell of it. Above all, the mission is intended as the hero's path to glory, the foundation of an immortal reputation and an immortal story. Greek myths exist in different variants and some characters jump from one story to the next. The protagonist of each story, however, is usually set apart from the other characters, his (or more rarely her) decisions, actions and trials defining the central plot.

There are, however, some myths, like the Trojan War and the Argonautic Expedition, that involve large casts of interacting characters, complex organized activities and many different plot turns. These epics, apart from their literary qualities, are useful for the study of leadership, organization and strategy, all core topics in management theory and practice today. This is one of the reasons I have selected to look closely into these two myths. The other reason is, of course, that since my earliest childhood they have both been important parts of my own life. These epics have attracted a great deal of commentary, analysis and adaptation. They have inspired different artistic and literary movements, including those of neoclassicists, romantics, modernists and postcolonials. Across the ages, they have fuelled powerful emotions, not least nostalgia for the heroic age. According to Plutarch, Alexander the Great carried a copy of the *Iliad*, annotated by his tutor Aristotle, throughout his own campaigns.

My own discussion is more modest, limited to considering them as complex campaigns and identifying some features they share with the challenges facing large-scale campaigns today in the military, political and business fields. I will focus on some of the features accounting for the success and failure of such campaigns. These include the building of successful coalitions, the qualities of leadership, the different resources necessary for success, including technology, information and personal qualities like courage and guile. I will also signal some of the intrinsic dangers that afflict all campaigns like those stemming from a leader's character flaws.

The Trojan War started ostensibly to right a wrong, the kidnapping of a Greek queen. So, too, did the Argonauts' expedition, to establish Iason in his rightful throne, the one that Pelias had usurped from him. The quest for glory and adventure is common to both myths as is the building of an alliance, necessary for the success of the mission. The gathering of the heroes, each carefully named in the epics, is part of the preparation. They include friends, relatives, like-minded heroes and other parties that have suffered injury or insult. They all want a share of the adventure and the glory promised by the expedition. Alliances also include different gods and goddesses, some of whom may support the expedition for reasons of their own. Athena and Hera support the Greeks in the Trojan War due to their injured pride; Hera supports Iason in her wish to see the impostor Pelias punished; Athena supports him the way she supports nearly all adventurous, brave and handsome young heroes in their quest for glory.

Building an alliance is central for the success of any mission, but alliances involve conflicts and disagreements. Maintaining an alliance requires much effort and work. There are big egos to placate, there are insecurities to respect, there are diverging interests and priorities, hence alliances are fraught with potential conflicts. A large part of the *Iliad* is devoted to the conflict among Greeks themselves, prompted by the quarrel between Achilles and Agamemnon. The Argonauts' expedition may give the impression of a happy few, a band of brothers, but there are numerous tensions and conflicts among them, not least those over whether Atalanta, a woman(!), should join the crew. Heracles in all variants of the myth drops out, for one reason or another, precipitating different conflicts and disagreements. The management of an alliance of diverse personalities and interests is therefore one of the first essentials facing a leader of heroic missions in these Greek myths.

Two campaigns, two flawed leaders

The two campaigns, the assault of Troy and the quest for the Golden Fleece, were led by two famous characters, Agamemnon and Iason, as different from each other as can be, yet both marked by some critical flaws of character. Agamemnon is a seasoned warrior, a bull of a man, the leader of the largest Greek kingdom; Iason is a young man, barely out of adolescence, handsome, charming, modest and hesitant. They both boast noble lineage. Agamemnon is the grandson of Pelops, who gave his name to the Peloponnese, and great-grandson of Tantalus, famous for the punishment inflicted on him by the gods. The curse of the House of Atreus (his father) hangs over him and the rest of his family who are immersed in an ongoing miasma of murders and other atrocities. Iason's lineage links him all the way back to Prometheus. Like Agamemnon's, his family history is tarnished with numerous crimes and punishments, not least that inflicted on his famous great-uncle, Sisyphus.

Both Agamemnon and Iason enjoy legitimacy as leaders of their expeditions. Agamemnon is the ruler of the largest kingdom in Greece, contributor of the greatest force assaulting Troy, and undisputed holder the sceptre of power, a cult object given to him by Zeus himself. He is also a brave fighter in his own right. In the *Iliad*, he is accorded an *aristeia*,[4] a passage of nearly 200 lines in book XI which portrays a warrior at the apex of his glory when he becomes invincible, wreaking havoc among his enemies and filling his followers with courage. On the battlefield he is certainly no coward. His is one of the three names that his army want to see come out of the helmet as their champion to fight Hector in a duel in book VII. Away from the battlefield, however, Agamemnon's character is full of flaws. He is arrogant, impetuous and thirsting for glory, including its more earthly and mundane forms – obsequious respect, flattery and the lion's share of all valuable resources, especially loot. He is hugely boastful and is quick to humiliate his opponents in words and deeds. He routinely insults others, including some of his chief champions – Achilles, Odysseus and Diomedes.

Two of Agamemnon's most telling qualities as a leader are his unwillingness to take responsibility for his actions, consistently blaming the gods for the different disasters that afflict the campaign, and his sudden and total collapse when the campaign reaches its nadir and the Trojans are threatening to burn the Greek ships. In book IX of the *Iliad*, the Greek soldiers are fleeing the enemy in 'panic and fear', when Agamemnon calls a general council of war. At the council he is seen shedding profuse tears which Homer likens to a spring running down the face of a rock, as if to highlight the contrast between a leader who crumbles under pressure and the rock. Overwhelmed by anxiety, Agamemnon blames the gods for all the misfortunes that have hit his army and, in blind panic, urges them to return to Greece. The sight of a leader paralysed by fear must have been devastating for the morale of all his followers and it takes the supreme skill of Diomedes (whom Agamemnon had insulted in an earlier council of war) and Nestor to steady the ship and form a plan to placate Achilles, re-engage him in the hostilities and turn the tide against the common foe.[5]

Ancient audiences would have been aware of two subsequent developments against which to judge Agamemnon – the successful conclusion of the Trojan War and his dismal death at the hands of his wife and her lover. The fall of Troy earned Agamemnon undisputed credit. Yet, even at the moment of his supreme glory, as the Greek conquerors prepare to return home, he acted with a 'child-like foolishness'. As we learn from old Nestor in book III of the *Odyssey*, he awarded himself the war's prime booty, the Trojan princess Cassandra, sacrilegiously seized while a supplicant in Athena's temple.[6] The already angered Athena will do him no further favours. And then, there is his end, what the Greeks called *kakos nostos*, or 'bad homecoming'. Murdered by his wife and her lover 'like an ox at feeding time', Agamemnon's death was the very opposite of a glorious death on the battlefield, the epitome of a bad end for a warrior. It is not accidental that Agamemnon's death enters so many recesses of Greek mythology, epitomizing something unspeakably awful and terrifying.[7]

In most regards, Iason is the opposite of Agamemnon. Against Agamemnon's bombast, Iason strikes us as modest, gentle and willing to listen to others. Several commentators have described him as a gentleman and at least one as a 'dude'.[8] As a leader, he often asks for advice, he takes votes and, finding himself at the head of a dream team of talent, he delegates decisions and tasks to his followers. The most compelling portrait of Iason as a young man is provided by Pindar in his celebrated *Fourth Pythian Ode*, written in 462 BCE. A piece of lyrical poetry in contrast to the Homeric epics, it portrays Iason is glowing colours. When he arrives at Iolcus to reclaim his father's throne, he visits a marketplace crowded with people. They look at him admiringly and wonder whether this stranger may not be Apollo himself or Ares. He responds to Pelias' rude welcome ('Do not befoul your story with most hateful lies') with grace; he generously offers his usurper uncle all the possessions he has stolen from his father but demands his rightful throne. The poet repeatedly refers to Iason's genial voice, his 'gentle words' and his surpassing beauty. In every regard, Iason is the personification of youthful grace and charm.

The other poet who offers a detailed portrait of Iason is Apollonius of Rhodes in his *Argonautica*, a poem in four parts written in the third century BCE when Apollonius, a scholar with deep knowledge of earlier literature, lived in Alexandria. This poem, often unfavourably compared to Homer's epics, presents Iason as a kind of anti-hero, who confesses his anxieties, is often insecure, hesitant and mistake-prone. He speaks little and fights even less. Dealing with conflict, he favours diplomacy over force and cunning; dealing with awkward situations, he favours tact, a rare quality among Greek heroes, over bluster. His diplomacy and his tact are frequently successful. Yet, from the moment that Medea enters the plot in the work's third part, she completely overshadows him with the force of her personality as well as her range of stratagems and ploys. She takes the initiative in most critical moments using a formidable array of devices and magic, pushing Iason to the margins. Iason can therefore be seen as a hero with two characters, before Medea and after Medea. Before Medea, he is a likeable fellow, with determination, an open mind and a thirst for adventure. He can solve problems, mostly in a diplomatic rather than a heroic way. Once he has met Medea, he becomes increasingly dependent on her for the challenges facing him and his crew. His dependence on Medea will ensure the success of the expedition but will later come to haunt him.

In spite of this increasing dependence on Medea, at no point in the expedition does Iason lose the loyalty of the other Argonauts, a major accomplishment. Throughout a voyage of nearly 10,000 miles, he displays a quality towards them that is conspicuously absent in Agamemnon – pastoral care.[9] He takes his responsibilities as a leader very seriously and he cares for his crew in a far more mature way than does Odysseus during his own homecoming. He keeps them informed at every stage, consults with them and is concerned with their well-being. In short, Iason is a caring leader, even if he is not a particularly commanding presence. It is telling that he is frequently referred to by Apollonius as *amechanos* ('resourceless' or 'clueless'), the opposite of *polymechanos,* the man 'with a solution for everything', one of the common attributes of Odysseus and one that could easily apply to Medea. While Iason is no Odysseus, it is good to remember that not one of Odysseus' comrades made it back to Ithaca, whereas all but two[10] of the Argonauts returned to their homes in Greece alive. (Admittedly several of them were immortal!)

Still. Iason gets into a terrible mess with Medea and his end is hardly better than Agamemnon's. If we follow Euripides in his *Medea,* Iason turns into a virtual monster, spurning the woman to whom he owes everything and without whom he would have amounted to little. But Euripides, cunning genius that he is, is able to turn everything upside down and can hardly be trusted. He turns a woman who has massacred her brother, betrayed her country and is about to kill her children into a feminist icon, a woman whose stand against male oppression resounds across the ages.[11] And he turns Iason into an abhorrent male chauvinist, an ungrateful man and a thoroughly contemptible character.[12] Even without Euripides' chicanery, however, Iason's end is an unhappy one, as he eventually gets tired or terrified of Medea's sorcery and her blood-curdling personality, and seeks happiness in a nice domestic arrangement that he will never attain.

Two campaigns and two flawed leaders. Two campaigns that achieved their objectives, two successful campaigns, and yet two campaigns that left behind a trail of suffering, pain and trouble. Two leaders who can hardly serve as models for today's leadership aspirants but who, through their successes and trials, can offer some insights into the challenges facing expedition leaders across the ages.

Machines and other resources, technical, narrative and emotional

In addition to leadership, successful campaigns in Greek mythology called for different instruments and resources.[13] These could be technical tools or inventions, like the wings that allowed Daedalus and Icarus to escape from the Labyrinth or the wooden horse that enabled the Greeks to enter and conquer Troy's impregnable citadel. They could be magical or supernatural tools, like many of the balms, potions and incantations deployed by Medea in meeting the challenges thrown in the path of Iason and his crew. They could also be critical pieces of information or knowledge that enable a hero to overcome a seemingly impossible obstacle. Iason was advised by Phineus, a blind king he had helped during his travels,[14] how to successfully navigate the Argo through the Clashing Rocks, just as the sorceress Circe advised Odysseus how to navigate successfully the Sirens' rock. In addition to information, stories could be useful resources for the success of a mission. They pointed out earlier failures and successes, providing warnings and encouragements. This is what accorded respect to old men, like King Nestor in the *Iliad* and the *Odyssey* whose stories of past trials, in spite of being long-winded, offered guidance on how to handle current challenges.

Some tools used by the heroes are very simple and opportunistic. Odysseus blinds the Cyclops with a log that he has spotted lying idle in the cave where he and his comrades are trapped. Iason uses a heavy rock to turn the warrior army against each other. Other tools, like the Trojan Horse, are complex contrivances that required much ingenuity and work to make. Many of these resources are given to the male protagonists by women who love them. Ariadne offers Theseus a ball of thread with which he will find his way out of the Labyrinth once he has killed the Minotaur. Medea is the peerless champion among heroes' lovers, one who provides a prodigious range of resources to Iason at every stage of the expedition.

In addition to having the right information and the right material resources, the success of heroic missions calls for emotional resources. Chief among these, of course, is courage, a *sine qua non* of every Greek hero and every hero in every mythology. Courage, or *andreia* (literally 'manliness') in Greek, is the essential fuel of heroic deeds; without it, there is no heroism. Physical strength and bravery in battle are routine qualities of Greek heroes, but so, too, are the willingness to risk not only their lives but also their reputations in pursuit of their mission and their perseverance in adversity. Heracles is celebrated equally for his superhuman strength as for his fortitude in enduring terrible ordeals. Courage also meant standing up to public opinion and powerful opponents in defence of what is right.

Courage does not necessarily mean fearlessness, although some heroes were celebrated for being fearless. Instead, it is a willingness to put up a fight even when the odds are stacked against the protagonist, even when he has good reason to feel frightened. An extreme case of this type of courage is provided by Hector who, against the entreaties of his parents and following a long inner debate, leaves the safety of Troy's walls to meet Achilles, a bloodthirsty foe whose fury, since the death of his beloved Patroclus, has turned into a killing machine. Hector has no delusions. He knows that his chances of victory at this stage of the war are negligible. Still, he opts to fight an enemy deranged by hate because retreating in the face of such a foe would be more damaging to the cause of his people than a brave death.

In the heroic age, courage meant putting the interest of a cause or a mission above personal interests and appearing to do so. Leaders of such missions, like Hector, Iason and Agamemnon, were particularly fearful of being accused of cowardice and therefore needed to display courage almost constantly. Someone who claims the right to lead others must risk harm to themselves in the interest a communal mission.[15] Even so, putting the public good above all else was not a necessary condition for courage. Nobody accused Achilles of cowardice when, in defence of his own reputation and pride, he withdrew to his tent and refused to fight the enemies of his side. He, by contrast, recognizes the extraordinary courage of King Priam, an old man with little physical strength left in him, when he throws himself at Achilles' feet, entreating him to render him the body of his son. Priam's demand is motivated not by self-interest or pride, not even by paternal love, but by the need to observe the funeral rites for a dead hero demanded by timeless laws.

Courage can be displayed by the old as much as by the young, by the physically weak as well as by the physically strong. In spite of its ubiquity, however, courage alone is not enough to guarantee the success of heroic missions. This regularly requires guile or cunning and its natural expression, deception.[16] Deception is to guile what strength is to courage. With less force, guile frequently achieves better results. In the heroic grammar, courage brings glory while cunning brings success. Failure of courage brings the ignominy of cowardice; failure of cunning brings the ridicule for foolishness. The Greeks' admiration for guile was almost unlimited and several of their heroes demonstrated it to a greater or lesser extent. Cunning is, of course, the calling card of Odysseus and, among his many successful deceptions, none competes with the wooden horse that finally prised open the gates of Troy.

Some heroes, like Achilles and Hector, would hardly lower themselves to rely on deception – their aristocratic demeanour protected them from stooping so low. Iason may not use deception directly but discovers in Medea a supreme champion of the craft. Most Greek heroes routinely resorted to it to achieve their objectives, individual or collective. And so, too, did nearly all Greek gods and goddesses, who frequently deceived the mortals but also each other. The gods would sometimes deceive the mortals for a particular purpose, like revenge, but would also do so purely for their amusement as is made plain in the expression 'man is the plaything of the gods'.[17] Concerned that Hector may succumb to fear and seek safety behind Troy's walls, Athena assumes the form of his brother Deiphobus and offers his support in confronting Achilles. But once Hector engages in the duel, Deiphobus magically vanishes, whereupon Hector realizes that the gods have abandoned him to his fate. Gods also deceived each other, sometimes blatantly. One of the most shocking examples occurs in book XIV of the *Iliad* when Hera seeks to gain an advantage for the Greeks by seducing Zeus and then lulling him into a deep sleep. Emboldened by Poseidon, the Greeks quickly gain the upper hand until Zeus wakes up and the scales swing the other way.

Guile and deception seek to achieve with greater economy of effort what force cannot achieve or achieves at costs that are self-defeating. They are tactical rather than strategic resources, inexorably linked to surprise. Deception means springing a surprise on your opponent, catching them unprepared. Very often, deception means 'Act friendly and plan the downfall of your adversary', 'Strike your opponent at their weakest point', 'Redefine the game in order to win' and above all 'Test and transgress boundaries'. This is what made Hermes, the trickster god of deception, a very popular deity among the ancients. His name generates two important words that we use today, the word 'hermeneutics', the squeezing of hidden meaning out of an opaque text, and the word 'hermetic', an impregnable boundary which guile alone is capable of breeching. One of Hermes' epithets was *dolios* or 'master of deceit', which made him protector of thieves, travellers, tradespeople and all who cross boundaries, including moral ones. As the master of extricating himself from 'hermetically' tight situations, he is a model for heroes ancient and modern, from Odysseus to Figaro and James Bond, shrewd improvisers rather than master strategists.[18]

Atē, hubris and phronesis

The success of epic campaigns in Greek mythology relies more on opportunism than on careful planning, on divine help and sudden quirks of luck than on careful calculation. What stands out are the many plans and stratagems used by the protagonists including the gods, rather than any overall *strategy*. Strategies are bound to be tested not least by the caprices of the gods, as well as the dangers and temptations that lure the protagonists away from their missions. In addition to external factors, heroic missions are threatened by inner factors, the protagonists' own flaws. Some of these result from divine interventions, others are outcomes of their own weaknesses, such as pride or recklessness. Divine interventions and individual flaws are often indistinguishable, but their result is the same – trouble.

One of the commonest ways of explaining the troubles of Homeric man is *atē*.[19] The heroes of the *Iliad* themselves as well as the poem's author accepted that human beings are liable to be seized by moments of temporary madness, or *atē*, which result in self-harming behaviour. Atē (Delusion) was a goddess, daughter of Eris (Discord), her of the golden apple. Like her mother, Atē was a goddess of mischief, but also a goddess of delusion and recklessness. Her special skill was in blinding her victims and causing them to act against character and against their own interest. Atē was held responsible for the extreme mood variations that characterize many Homeric heroes, notably Agamemnon and Achilles.

The entire plot of the *Iliad* is set in motion by the *atē* that seized Agamemnon when he insulted Achilles, his greatest champion, by snatching Briseis from him. This is how Agamemnon himself explains his behaviour and its disastrous effect on the campaign, offering apologies, Briseis and generous gifts by way of atonement. Later, when following Patroclus' death, the two foes are reconciled, Agamemnon seeks to expiate himself for insulting Achilles with these words:

> Many times did the Achaeans speak this charge against me,
> and kept faulting me; but it is not I who am to blame,
> but Zeus and Fate and the Fury who walks in darkness,
> they who in the assembly cast savage Delusion [Atē], in my mind
> on that day when, on my own authority, I took away Achilles'
>   prize.
> But what could I do? God accomplishes all things to fulfilment –
> the elder daughter of Zeus is Delusion [Atē], who infatuates all
>   men,
> ruinous one. Her feet are soft; for they do not touch upon the
>   earth,
> but she walks over the heads of men
> tripping up mankind; so she has trammelled other men
> before me.[20]

Atē afflicted many of the characters of the *Iliad* in an almost arbitrary manner, in large matters and small. Achilles himself is not immune to Atē, when he refuses Agamemnon's apology, his offer to return Briseis and the generous gifts by way of compensation – a refusal which will result in the death of his beloved Patroclus. This is pointed out to Achilles by his friend and mentor Phoenix,[21] and Achilles recognizes it when he speaks to his mother Thetis.[22] At least in its early incarnations in Homer, *atē* is not a divine retribution but something more anarchic and unpredictable. The gods themselves are liable to *atē*, as we learn from Agamemnon's lips, when in self-justification of the madness that seized him, he tells the story of how Zeus, holding Atē accountable for his own blindness to Hera's trickery, threw her out of Olympus and consigned her, Atē, to live among the mortals.

The gods may have been liable to *atē*, but they are not susceptible to hubris.[23] This is a unique privilege of humans and one that afflicts most heroes at some point in their lives. Like *atē*, hubris represents a suspension of rational judgement. But, unlike *atē*, it can manifest itself over a prolonged period of time. Dodds defined it as 'arrogance in word or deed or even thought'.[24] It is an attitude of excessive pride, overconfidence, invulnerability and grandiosity that often afflicts mortals, especially after a great success or achievement. Hubris is, by its nature, sacrilegious. It offends a god whose wrath brings about retribution, nemesis. This generally results in the complete downfall of the man or woman guilty of hubris, a downfall often out of proportion with the magnitude of the hubris itself. In extreme cases of hubris, an individual claims to be the equal of or even better than a god in some regard. For example, Arachne, a Lydian maiden and expert weaver, boasted that her skill was greater than that of the goddess Athena. She challenged Athena to a contest and wove a tapestry of such magnificence that the goddess could find no fault in it at all. Angered, Athena tore Arachne's work to shreds and struck her repeatedly. Overwhelmed with shame, Arachne hanged herself. Athena then took pity on her and turned her into a spider who would spin her webs for all eternity.[25]

One of the most powerful examples of hubris is provided by Aeschylus in his tragedy, *Persians*.[26] This is the only surviving tragedy from classical Greece that deals with an actual historical event rather than an ancient myth – Xerxes' massive but disastrous campaign against Greece in 480 BCE, just eight years prior to the first performance of Aeschylus' play. The drama takes place in the Persian capital Susa in front of a royal palace as news of the crushing defeat of Xerxes' army reaches the city. It involves a chorus of Persian elders as well as Xerxes' mother Atossa, the ghost of his dead father Darius, and a messenger who brings news of the disaster of the Persian army and navy. At last, Xerxes himself arrives onstage in torn robes, defeated and devastated:

> You see me here, alas, a sad
> and useless wretch who has become
> an evil presence for my race
> and for my native land.[27]

The play is undoubtedly a celebration of the Greeks' victory and an illustration of the clash between two cultures, Greek and barbarian. Aeschylus himself had fought in the earlier battle against the Persians at Marathon in 490 BCE and may have been present at the sea battle of Salamis in 480 BCE. In spite of its celebratory qualities, the play offers a sympathetic portrait of the defeated Persians and the horrors that follow a crushing defeat.

At the heart of the drama is Xerxes' hubris, the cause of the debacle. This is attributed by Aeschylus, first, to the gods, and only secondarily to the valour, unity and cunning of the Greeks. The ghost of Xerxes' father Darius[28] explicitly states that he offended the gods with his arrogance (831), while the elders of the chorus attribute it to Atē:

> Alas! Alas, you spirits above,
> you bring us such disaster,
> so unforeseen and yet so clear to see,
> as if the goddess of folly, Atē,
> had glanced at us in this calamity.[29]

So, what was precisely the nature of Xerxes hubris? Amassing an army and a navy of an unprecedented scale, bridging the Hellespont to enable his army to cross into Europe, desecrating many of the Greeks' holy sites, reducing the whole of Athens to rubble (which Aeschylus' audiences would have known all too well) – these were testaments to his hubris. As the ghost of Darius says,

> He wished to check the sacred Hellespont
> by tying it down with chains, just like a slave,
> and that holy river, too, the Bosporus.[30]

These deeds demonstrated Xerxes' disdain for the Delphic injunctions, 'Nothing to Excess' (*Mēden Agan*) and 'Moderation is Best' (*Metron Ariston*). But maybe the most insulting aspect of his demeanour to the gods was his claim of being their equal (*isotheos*), as stated by the chorus early on in the drama.[31] This was a terrible presumption, as every Greek would have known, and one that would amply justify why the gods turned against him.[32]

Great campaigns carry great risks. The Greeks were careful to preface the start of such campaigns with copious entreaties to the divine – soothsaying, prayers and sacrifices – none of which Xerxes troubled himself to undertake. Agamemnon and Iason did not neglect such observances; unlike Xerxes' campaign, theirs were successful. Yet, neither Agamemnon not Iason was impervious to hubris and they both ended up paying the price. Agamemnon's character structure and a whole catalogue of deeds – the brutal dismissal of the supplicant Chryses, his claim to prefer the captive Chryseïs to his own wife, the reckless insult of Achilles, the appropriation of loot sacrilegiously seized as well as his almost continuous boasting – make him an archetype of hubris and account for his eventual downfall.

Iason's hubris is more difficult to discern. The breech of his marital vows and the rejection of the woman to whom he owes nearly everything, someone who left her family and country to follow him in exile, appear hubristic to us. At least the way he is portrayed by Euripides, Iason is a thoroughly loathsome character. Still, abandoning a woman who helps a hero would not have unduly troubled ancient Athenians, accustomed as they were to great heroes like Odysseus and Theseus, abandoning the women who helped them. Moreover, Medea's terrifying nature and her escalating levels of sorcery and cruelty would be seen as factors mitigating her abandonment. Besides, she was a foreign, indeed a barbarian woman, something that again would have counted against her for a Greek audience. Putting aside Euripides' hostile picture of him, Iason's hubris may have been to believe that he could tame a dangerous woman, a woman of fearsome will, a greater intelligence than his, with a huge array of magical powers at her disposal. He made himself entirely dependent on her and meekly colluded in her sorcery. His hubris would then be that he cut a deal with someone far smarter and more ruthless than himself, ending up by paying the consequence of such a deal.

Atē and hubris were perennial risks of any campaign. A measure of protection against them could be offered by phronesis, or 'practical wisdom'. A key virtue in Aristotle's ethics, phronesis is the ability to make sensible judgements in complex, real-life situations that cannot be solved using technical or philosophical knowledge. Phronesis can mitigate hubris and moderate *atē* by fostering self-awareness, self-control (*sophrosyne*), humility and respect for the divine (*eusebeia*). It is a kind of wisdom that recognizes one's own limitations and is mindful of the potential consequences of one's actions, protecting individuals and especially leaders from overestimating their abilities and making rash or arrogant decisions that lead to hubris.

Recognizing unpredictability and uncertainty in human affairs, the voice of phronesis is soft and subtle, rather than authoritative and dogmatic. One of its core aspects is the ability to read situations accurately. It means taking in the big picture without losing sight of the details. It means distinguishing between routine situations and situations that pose special threats or offer unexpected opportunities. It means filtering out noise, without ignoring small warning signs of imminent danger or disaster. In the complex world of politics, business or economics, no two situations are ever identical even if they share many characteristics. Instead of seeking a general approach or a strategy to address different challenges and crises, phronesis recommends different approaches in different situations. Some situations call for courage and decisive action, others for caution and patience, others for cunning and subterfuge and still others for diplomacy, tact and dialogue. Recognizing the unique qualities of each situation means avoiding universals. It will be noted that the injunctions *Mēden Agan* and *Metron Ariston are* universals – phronesis may indicate that in exceptional situations they, too, may need to be suspended.

In contrast to other types of wisdom, phronesis does not aim at abstract or eternal generalizations. It is pragmatic, down to earth. Theorizing different intellectual virtues as a philosopher, Aristotle distinguished phronesis from four other intellectual virtues: wisdom (*sophia*), science (*episteme*), practical skill (*techne*) and intuitive intelligence (*nous*). While he cast wisdom at the summit of these virtues, he saw phronesis as the essential intellectual virtue of successful political and other leaders,[33] offering Pericles, the democratic leader of Athens during its Golden Age, as his chief example. In the Homeric epics, Odysseus offers numerous examples of phronesis, while the old king Nestor is regularly seen as its quintessence. Beyond these heroes, however, phronesis is the domain of the goddess Athena who also embodies every kind of intellectual virtue, from wisdom to handicraft, and let us not forget, just and judicious warfare, too.

Phronesis will never provide a full protection against error and failure. Pericles himself, Aristotle's exemplar, launched the Peloponnesian War that would eventually bring ruin not only to his own state but to virtually the entire classical Greek world. Human beings are fallible creatures, and the world is too full of unexpected events like the terrible plague that hit Athens in the second year of the Peloponnesian War that killed many of her citizens including Pericles. All that phronesis can do is to forestall some of the worst disasters brought about by wilful blindness, excessive confidence and the corrupting effects of power.

Atē, hubris in our times

The mythical campaigns led by Agamemnon and Iason, full of stratagems and ploys as they are, are not great toolkits for strategy, whether in the military, the political, the business or any other domain. They certainly offer none of the codified recommendations of Sun Tzu's *Art of War* or Machiavelli's *The Prince*. Strategists with an interest in ancient Greece would do better to look at the works of historians Thucydides and Xenophon than those of poets, like Homer, Pindar and Apollonius. Even so, the work of these poets has much of relevance to our complex and fast-moving world, when plans and strategies tend to become rapidly obsolete. *Atē* and hubris continue to afflict many leaders, causing avoidable disasters and suffering. Understanding them can help forestall some avoidable misfortunes.

Unlike the Greeks, we cannot accept the religious dimensions of these phenomena. There is no goddess Atē in our pantheon and no guaranteed divine retribution against excessive pride and confidence. Psychologically, however, both *atē* and hubris can be widely observed in our time. *Atē* is generally evoked when a person has a 'moment of madness' or presses 'the self-destruct button', observed regularly in public life. Consider the following examples:

- A successful entrepreneur in the jewellery industry makes a statement during a speech to a large audience describing one of his company's most successful products as 'total crap'. The value of his company collapses overnight by £500 million forcing the closure of nearly three hundred shops, a total financial restructuring and rebranding, and his own dismissal.

- A world-famous and universally admired footballer is coming to the end of a glorious career. He is playing his last football match as his country's captain in the sport's most prestigious event, the World Cup final. In extra time, following a provocation, he headbutts an opponent and is dismissed from the game. His side goes on to lose the match.

- In the midst of history's worst oil spill and one of the worst ever environmental catastrophes, the CEO of the company responsible for the spill tells a reporter: 'There's no one who wants this thing over more than I do, I'd like my life back.' A short while later he is forced to resign.

- A presidential candidate describes 'half' of her opponent's supporters 'as a basket of deplorables . . . racist, sexist, homophobic, xenophobic, Islamophobic'. Her opponent and his supporters reappropriate the 'deplorables' moniker with dire consequences for her campaign.

- An actor about to receive an Academy award walks across the stage and slaps another actor across the face, ostensibly due to an insulting comment the latter had made about his wife. He is forced to resign from the Academy and banned from its events for ten years.

Another type of moment of madness takes the form of Freudian slips or minor errors. These either reveal an individual's unconscious wishes which are contrary to their expressed ones or are seen by others as doing precisely this. When former president George W. Bush, instigator of the 2003 invasion of Iraq, denounced Putin's and Russia's 'wholly unjustified and brutal invasion of Iraq' (instead of 'Ukraine' which is what he had meant to say), even without recourse to psychoanalysis, it was immediately read as an acknowledgement of his own guilt for a campaign that had gone seriously wrong.

Moments of madness do not seize only people in positions of high visibility. Whether as gaffes, as Freudian slips or as serious errors of judgement, they are part of our everyday life. Once we grasp the idea of *atē*, we may be surprised how common it is. We regularly witness examples when a person speaks out of line or behaves out of character in ways that are perplexing even to themselves. Individuals known for their anti-racist attitudes will suddenly spout a racist expletive; individuals known for their financial prudence will throw all their resources in a doomed project; others will ruin their family's lives in short-lived, impulsive affairs; yet others, known as perfectly peaceful individuals, will in a moment of madness engage in some extraordinary act of violence or self-harm.[34]

Our modern minds generally attribute such moments of madness to some kind of 'intoxication', brought about by anger, pride, alcohol, carelessness, frustration, stress or some such. The ancient Greeks would have been satisfied to know that this is something that afflicts most people from time to time, some more, some less, sometimes as a result of a nasty and cruel goddess deciding to have some fun, sometimes for other reasons or for no reason at all. We, on the contrary, seek reasons. We want to know *why* people, including people in high positions, but also our relatives, our friends and even ourselves, are seized by such moments of madness. In this, we are maybe displaying our inability to rid ourselves of our rationalist assumptions that view people, at least those we consider 'normal', as being generally calm, rational and coherent, an assumption that might have perplexed people living in other cultures.

If moments of *atē* are a regular phenomenon in our times – a kind of regular occurrence of irregularity – so, too, are cases of hubris at the individual or collective levels, low and high. Some individuals afflicted by hubris appear, for a time, to get away with all sorts of immoral or illegal behaviour from sexual harassment to financial offences and other crimes including murder. Developing a sense of invulnerability, such individuals take ever greater risks, until at least some of them are eventually caught to general surprise. Inevitably, political, military and business leaders are most susceptible to hubris – figures like Richard Nixon, George W. Bush, Margaret Thatcher and Tony Blair being prime examples, committing grave errors as a result of their belief in their infallibility, exaggerated pride, overwhelming self-confidence and contempt for others.[35] Likewise, numerous business leaders, like Robert Maxwell, Carlos Ghosn, Dennis Kozlowski and Conrad Black, were brought down by hubris, while others, like Steve Jobs and Jack Welch, became increasingly hubris-prone in the later stages of their careers without ever meeting their full nemesis.

In addition to individual examples, hubris can afflict organizations and their managers collectively. Two common forms of organizational hubris are the hubris of total control and the hubris of grandiosity. The former imagines a world that can be completely controlled, not by brute force as Xerxes thought, but by calculation. The hubris of control is part of the mindset of the modern bureaucratic manager, who measures, calculates, plans and standardizes everything in the interest of efficiency and order. Management, since its early days when it persuaded universities to accept it as a scientific discipline, is a profession particularly prone to this kind of hubris epitomized in the statement of those high priests of consulting, McKinsey and Co.: 'Anything can be counted, and anything that you can count you can manage.'[36]

Faith in measuring and controlling everything flies in the face of the messiness, unpredictability and chaos that most managers encounter in their daily lives.[37] It is a fantasy expressing a deep-seated wish to live in a world that operates with the precision of a well-oiled machine. The follies stemming from this fantasy are easy to see at the personal, organizational and national levels. It places short-term measurable objectives above long-term desirable goals; it makes no allowances for exceptional cases or situations; it ignores personal and emotional factors that shape what goes on inside every organization; it is notoriously averse to change and adaptation; and it results in slow decline or sudden collapse as happened to numerous companies like Kodak to Blockbuster Videos, that remained wilfully blind to the effects of the digital revolution. The hubris of bean counters is to imagine a world made up of beans and nothing else, a world where those who produce most beans automatically get to the top.

The hubris of total control through calculation meets, in our times, another management hubris, one that we have already encountered in the previous chapter, the hubris of organizational grandiosity. Huge resources are devoted to marketing and branding aimed at enhancing every organization's image. This preoccupation with image and hype reflects the widespread narcissism of our times and has been seen as one of the factors responsible for some major organizational failures, ranging from NASA's Challenger disaster to the well-publicized Enron and Lehman Brothers scandals.[38]

If the hubris of total control imagines a world that can be ordered, measured and managed, the hubris of grandiosity imagines a world where facts cease to count, and everything succumbs to the power of image. Image is raised above substance as we learn to be seduced by it, even when we know that it is fake. Reality melts away under the heat of illusion and real-life events are obliterated by what Daniel Boorstin named, with great prescience in 1961, long before the advent of post-truth, 'pseudo-events'. These events are the products of mass and social media, generating popular images that immediately grab the attention of the public far more than pressing actual events. 'We risk being the first people in history,' Boorstin wrote, 'to have been able to make their illusions so vivid, so persuasive, so "realistic" that they can live in them.'[39] We seem to lose ourselves in the world of shimmering images, pretending that the constraints of glum reality have ceased to apply. Yet, confronting the hubris of grandiosity, glum reality and unpleasant facts have a habit of visiting us from time to time. These visits can be painful, as few things match the devastation left behind by powerful illusions when they are finally smashed.

Management and business are not the only professions given to hubris. Scientific hubris, with chief champion Victor Frankenstein and his monstrous creation, is one that we encounter regularly when scientists appear to 'play God' in fields such as genetics, biotechnology and artificial intelligence. Nor are natural scientists the only ones prone to hubris. Economics can provide several examples of confident predictions and assessments that proved deeply misguided, not least 'the great moderation' of the early 2000s, when many economists proclaimed that the global economy had entered an era of permanent stability and low inflation. And with the benefit of hindsight, can we not regard the 'end of history' thesis that proclaimed the definitive triumph of free-market capitalism and liberal democracy as the final stage of political and economic development as hubristic?

Hubris pervades many parts of modern life. What is notable is how long it can take for hubris to meet its reckoning, or how frequently it seems to evade it altogether. While individuals such as Xerxes were brought down by their hubris, there are many tyrants who die peacefully in comfortable beds despite their monstrous actions. For every serial criminal or abuser caught and punished, there may be several who are discovered posthumously or never at all.[40] Hubris is not a constant in a mathematical equation where the unknowns to be determined are the time it takes for nemesis to strike and for the severity of the chastisement.[41] Hubris is itself a variable, something that waxes and wanes, that is mitigated or exacerbated, that can be shared and diluted or concentrated and distilled. Much as we may like to see every culprit of hubris chastised, we must live with the uncomfortable knowledge that such an implacable sense of justice which many of us expect of the divine was not a major characteristic of the Greek gods.

Conclusion

The Trojan War and the Argonauts' expedition, two epics of Greek mythology, offer vivid illustrations of the factors behind successful campaigns. Setting up a strong coalition, attracting diverse talents, improvising the right stratagems in unexpected circumstances – these are all essential for success. In the epic tradition, these myths focus on the characters and failings of leaders – complex, three-dimensional characters – rather than the experiences of the followers, the workaday foot soldiers. They celebrate large gestures, honour and sacrifice, valour and endurance, but they also recognize cunning and prudence. Deception is a major feature in these epics – knowing when and how to deceive an opponent but also how to outsmart their opponents' attempts at deception. Knowing who to trust and whose promises to believe, whose flattery to avoid, and how to seek the right information and the necessary resources are all features of successful campaigns.

These two epics also illustrate some of the common ills that afflict great campaigns. These result from internal squabbles and fights, from failure to observe time-honoured ceremonies, from underestimating the qualities of opponents, and from becoming excessively dependent on a single individual or resource. Some of the most spectacular failures in these epics result from moments of leadership madness or blindness, from *atē* and hubris – often products of excessive pride and confidence.

What lessons do we learn from these epics about forestalling such ills? 'Don't pick fights you can't win', 'Don't insult unnecessarily your opponent or indeed your strongest champion', 'Don't lose your temper and say or do things you will regret', 'Try to treat your followers with some respect and recognize they have needs of their own', 'Avoid treating others, including your opponents and your followers, as idiots', 'If you make a mistake, try not to compound it, by pretending it didn't happen'. Few would disagree with any of these which, in truth, are not very original. Reading Homer, or Apollonius or Pindar, will not make you a great general. Nor will it necessarily make you a better person, nor conversely, as Plato believed, will it lure you into intemperance and immorality.

Reading these authors is likely to fire your imagination and excite your emotions, sometimes in overwhelming ways. You may feel tears welling in your eyes as you read of the Trojan king Priam touching the knees and kissing the hands of the man who killed his son, the implacable Achilles. You may recoil in shock as Iason and Medea kill her brother Apsyrtus in cold blood and throw his dismembered body in the sea. You may relish the tender family scene of Hector, his wife and their baby son, the baby startled by his father's 'bronze encased face and the horsehair plume on his helmet'.[42] You may celebrate Odysseus' cunning, admire Diomedes' valour. You may be repulsed by the duplicity of King Pelias or the brutality of many of the lead characters. You may decide to rewrite these myths from a different angle, as many have done in the past, not least Euripides and Ovid. You may choose, like many fine contemporary authors are doing, to retell the stories from the perspective of some of their underappreciated and maybe underrated female characters – Penelope, Briseis, Circe or Cassandra;[43] or indeed from the perspective of the ordinary foot soldier Thersites, who stands as a target of ridicule in the *Iliad*.

In our times of great change, dislocation and turbulence, the warfare heroics may have lost some of their appeal; instead, we may be drawn to some of the more ambiguous, dark and paradoxical aspects of these tales, the moral dilemmas facing the protagonists, the choices and decisions they make, and the outcomes of these choices and decisions. We are certainly drawn to the complexities of the leading characters – where Achilles is not just a fighting machine, Iason is not just an adventurous young man, Helen is not just a pretty face, and Medea is not just an evil witch. But we are also drawn to those silent and hidden presences of characters whose true feelings and actions we never get to hear about. We are drawn to the passions and caprices of the gods, so powerful and yet so vulnerable. We are drawn to those moments when individuals seized by extraordinary forces reach beyond themselves and become capable of great and terrible deeds, when fortune and misfortune strike, at times with a perfect sense of justice, at others with terrifying arbitrariness.

How we make these experiences part of our own lives will differ. Some of us may seek 'lessons' and there are some lessons to take away from the Greek epics. Many will read them for entertainment and escape from the mundane realities of everyday life. But for some of us, reading these epics may be transformative. Sooner or later, we will look at the world and at each other with fresh eyes. Some of us may even look at our own selves with fresh eyes and may discover things about ourselves that we do not know or that do not please us.

9

Odysseus and the Sirens: Songs, Noise and Silence

During his long return journey to Ithaca after the Trojan War, Odysseus and his crew sailed past the rock of the Sirens, whose sweet and powerful song lured mariners to their death. The Sirens were strange creatures with heads of women and bodies of birds. Their craggy rock was littered with the dead and decomposing bodies of sailors who had been unable to resist them.

Forewarned by the enchantress Circe, Odysseus blocked the ears of his shipmates with beeswax to stop them hearing the Sirens' song. He himself, however, longed to hear it, so he had himself tied to the ship's mast and ordered his fellows to 'tie him even harder' if they saw him struggling to release himself as the Sirens' bewitching sounds reached his ears.

In this way, they sailed safely past a hazard that had caused the deaths of all who had previously been exposed to it.

The story of the Sirens has intrigued many commentators over the centuries, from Cicero to Dante and from Adorno to Seferis. Sirens are still part of everyday life, describing in many languages devices emitting excruciating noises to warn of imminent danger. Sirens are regular features of city life as ambulances, police cars and fire engines alert us to the constant private crises and dramas played out near us but out of sight. Sirens also warn of imminent public dangers, such as fire, flood or aerial bombardment. A siren is an instant trigger of anxiety.

The encounter of Odysseus with the Sirens features twice in Homer's *Odyssey,* as the hero recounts his adventures to the royal court of the Phaeacians, whose princess Nausicaa we met in Chapter 6. We first hear about the Sirens from the mouth of Circe, the sorceress who initially turned Odysseus' crew into pigs, and who is now prepared to help them on their homeward journey. She warns Odysseus of his imminent meeting with the Sirens and of the deadly threat that their beguiling song poses to sailors, drawing them towards the rocks where they meet their ruin. As figures of danger, Sirens pose a mortal threat to family life by seducing men and driving them to their demise. Aren't women seducing married men away from their families occasionally still referred to as sirens? In Homer's story, the Sirens seek to wreck Odysseus' homeward journey to be reunited with Penelope and Telemachus and see his beloved country once again.

A little later in the *Odyssey,* Odysseus describes what actually happened in his encounter with the Sirens which essentially dramatizes the earlier account, while adding the honeyed words with which the Sirens seek to tempt him:

'Come here,' they sang, 'renowned Odysseus, pride of the Achaeans and listen to our two voices. No one ever sailed past us without pausing to hear the sweetness of our song. He who listens will go on his way not only charmed, but wiser, for we know all the ills that the gods laid upon the Argives and Trojans before Troy, and can tell you everything that is going to happen over the whole world.' They sang these words most beautifully, and as I longed to hear them further, I indicated by frowning to my men that they should set me free. But they quickened their stroke, and Eurylochus and Perimedes bound me with still stronger bonds till we had got away from the Sirens' voices. Then my men took the wax from their ears and unbound me.[1]

This is the last we hear of the Sirens in the *Odyssey*.

It is a dazzling story, a story that enchants most people who hear it. It is a story of temptation, a constant theme in the *Odyssey* as various forces conspire to deflect Odysseus and his comrades from their destination. It is a story of seduction, one to which Odysseus only partially succumbs without having to pay the price, thanks to Circe's advice rather than to his own cunning as he readily admits. There are no mishaps, no recalcitrant fellows (as there are in several other episodes of the *Odyssey*) unblocking their ears or catching a sound from the Sirens which would lead to their death. Odysseus' pleasure is incomplete, since he never gets to hear what the Sirens would tell him, but it is a non-addictive pleasure. There is no lingering desire to return to the Sirens to hear the rest of their song once he and his comrades are out of harm's way.

Homer's story contains some ambiguities about the Sirens and their song. Who are the Sirens? Undoubtedly, they represent a primal force that destroys humans and especially family life. They stop sailors from ever returning to their homes, from *nostos*. They are instruments of an ugly death for their victims who die unmourned and unburied. About the Sirens' motives and purposes we know nothing – they are forces of nature, without motive or purpose.[2] As to the content of their song, Homer is unambiguous. They seek to tempt Odysseus with flattery and with the promise of information that Odysseus craves, information about the fates of Agamemnon, Menelaus and his other comrades-in-arms, and also about his wife, his son and his parents whom he hasn't seen for years. Nor is there any ambiguity over the quality of the Sirens' song – it is 'sweet as honey'. It would not stretch Homer's story to read the sweet song that leads sailors to their ruin as an allegory of the promises made by populist leaders who seduce their followers with their sweet rhetoric and offering easy solutions to complex problems.

What of Odysseus? As in his meeting with Nausicaa, he displays practical intelligence, but in his meeting with the Sirens we also encounter his rampant curiosity, for the sake of which he is prepared to submit himself to the humiliation of the lowest slave. His thirst for new experience, however, is coupled with caution and indifference to how others may regard him. He treats his followers with haughty legerdemain inviting none of them to share his experience – in the incident of the Sirens, as elsewhere, he stands aloof and separate. Undoubtedly Odysseus cares for his followers but in critical moments of their long journey, his inclination is to order them or keep them in the dark about the risks facing them.[3] Not surprisingly, his followers never fully trust him.[4] On the final stretch of their journey, with Ithaca in their sights and with Odysseus asleep on the deck, his followers open the ox-hide bag that the wind-god Aeolus has gifted Odysseus, the one containing unfavourable winds, which allowed the light westerlies to blow the ship gently homewards. Ignorant of the gift's true nature, the followers suspect it contains a treasure that Odysseus intends to keep for himself alone. Opening the bag instantly unleashes the furious winds that sends their ship to the bottom of the sea and all of them, Odysseus apart, to their deaths.

Homer's account of Odysseus sailing past the Sirens' rock is ingenious and short. It is full of meaning but it allows different audiences to make their own sense of those Sirens, be seduced by them and/or resist them. Over the centuries, the incident lent itself to many different interpretations. Cicero saw Odysseus as a man thirsting after knowledge.[5] This view was shared by Dante who had no access to Homer's original but only knew about the character from Virgil's consistently hostile portrait. Early Christians saw in Odysseus Christ resisting temptation and then dying on the cross. Montaigne, more conventionally, saw Odysseus as tempted by flattery, a fatal flaw of most Homeric heroes but, I suspect, not Odysseus. Horkheimer and Adorno, in *The Dialectic of the Enlightenment*, present Odysseus as the archetypal capitalist who can savour half-pleasures – the full pleasures will always elude him – while denying his comrades any pleasure whatsoever and getting them to row for him. For these authors, Odysseus is the calculating and rational enlightenment man, dominated by the reality principle at whose behest he dominates those around him, just as capitalists dominate their workers.[6] In a rather different interpretation, George Seferis, in his exalted poem 'Foreign Land', sees the Sirens as part of the superhuman forces that stand in the way of Odysseus, a man in exile, who wrestles with the world he inhabits in body and soul.[7]

Kafka's Ulysses

One of the most surprising reinventions of Odysseus' encounter with the Sirens was offered by Franz Kafka in his short story, 'The Silence of the Sirens'.[8] It was written in October 1917 as the First World War was entering its final phase and the Russian Revolution was about to cast its defining shadow on the decades to come. In Prague, Kafka, deferred from army service for what his employers claimed to be 'crucial government service in the insurance sector', had been diagnosed with tuberculosis, the disease that would kill him seven years later. At this precise moment, Kafka turned his attention to the *Odyssey* with an audacious retelling of the Sirens' story.

Two master storytellers, Homer and Kafka (or should it be Odysseus and Kafka, since it is Odysseus who tells the story of the Sirens in the *Odyssey*?) worked with the same characters across three millennia while inhabiting entirely different narrative and material worlds. Did Kafka's eyes ever catch a sight of the sea any more than Homer's blind ones? Several conversations I had with Kafka experts offered no conclusive answer to this question, but it is certain that he never saw the Mediterranean. Against the *Odyssey*'s open and mobile universe, Kafka's is a highly static world of prisons, doors, rooms, corridors, walls, barriers and boundaries. It is a world of rules and laws, offices, procedures and documents. It is a world of secrets, lies and misunderstandings, not least between author and his readers who are never quite sure if Kafka means what he says and why. This is world of mysteries, many of which remain unresolved.

Unlike Homer's world of named persons,[9] Kafka's world is mostly inhabited by 'nobodies'. Unlike Odysseus who willingly adopts the 'Nobody' moniker in his encounter with the Cyclops to return to his familiar name later, Kafka's characters are doomed to a perpetual nobodyhood. As the protagonist of another of his short stories, 'Excursion into the Mountains', states,

> 'I don't know,' I cried without being heard, 'I do not know, if nobody comes, then nobody comes. I've done nobody any harm, nobody's

done me any harm, but nobody will help me. A pack of nobodies. Yet that isn't all true. Only, that nobody helps me – a pack of nobodies would be rather fine, on the other hand. I'd love to go on an excursion – why not? – with a pack of nobodies. Into the mountains, of course, where else?'[10]

This is a world where things are not what they appear to be to the characters, to us the readers and maybe to the author, too. It is a world of games whose rules nobody fully understands, a world of deceptions and self-deceptions. Here then is the first clue of Kafka's interest in Homer, a fellow storyteller and one whose main hero, Odysseus, has stood as an archetype of deception and transgression. Kafka's world, like Homer's, is a world of deceptions, transgressions and their unpredictable consequences. It is Kafka's fascination with transgression, temptation and seduction that may have drawn him to Odysseus and the Sirens. And it is his extraordinary powers of imagination and narration that enabled him to reinvent the story in the most unlikely way.

Kafka's narrative in 'The Silence of the Sirens', terse like Homer's, opens with a moral, 'Proof that inadequate, even childish measures, may serve to rescue one from peril', and closes with a codicil. The body of the story is made of some five hundred words, in which we hear that Ulysses[11] blocked his own ears with wax and had himself bound to the mast of his ship, knowing that such measures were of little use against the piercing song of the Sirens, yet fully trusting that his little stratagem offered him adequate protection.

The story continues by alerting the reader to a still more powerful and mysterious weapon of the Sirens than their song, their silence. It is with silence that the Sirens meet Ulysses as he sails by, lost in contemplation, his blissful face entirely indifferent to them. As his ship moves on, he briefly notices the Sirens, who soon fade from his sights. The Sirens, for their part, no longer had any desire to allure; all that they wanted was to hold as long as they could the radiance that fell from Ulysses' great eyes. If the Sirens had possessed consciousness they would have been annihilated at that moment. But they remained as they had been; all that had happened was that Ulysses had escaped them.[12]

In the cryptic codicil which acknowledges that 'here the human understanding is beyond its depth', the reader is told that guileful Ulysses might have been aware of everything and merely played along, his pretence 'a sort of shield' against fate.

Kafka's retelling of the story is so audacious that it undoubtedly leaves us momentarily speechless. At the heart of this reimagining of the Homeric text lie two disappearances and two metamorphoses. Gone are Circe and her warning and gone, too, are Odysseus' companions, those hardworking nobodies tied to the oar. This leaves the limelight on the two protagonists, Ulysses and the Sirens, who undergo dramatic transformations, Ulysses from an active character to a passive one, the Sirens from noisy creatures to silent ones.

Like Homer's tale, this is a tale of temptation and seduction, but the temptation here becomes a test of wits between Ulysses and the Sirens. If Odysseus' triumph in Homer's original was not good enough, Kafka augments it. While Homer's Odysseus is kicking and screaming to be let loose, Kafka's Ulysses is the model of placidity. Enraptured in his self-contained cocoon, Kafka's Ulysses is indifferent to the Sirens. They, unlike their Homeric counterparts, are entranced by the radiance of his eyes, by his very indifference and self-containment. Engrossed in Ulysses as he sails past their rugged rockface, they feel a swelling of desire, the early onslaught of passion. In this way, Kafka turns Homer's forces of nature into women with desires, though not, in the quote above, with consciousness. They remain silent.

We, the readers, easily overlook the total disappearance of Ulysses' companions, those pesky 'nobodies', from Kafka's narrative. More importantly, however, we the readers, along with several commentators, may be deceived into overlooking the crucial fact that in Kafka's story Ulysses *blocks his own ears*, not those of his companions. How remarkable that Kafka, that master of veils to match Parrhasios, turns Ulysses, that Ciceronian model of universal curiosity, into one of zen-like detachment. Could this be one of the 'little tricks' that Kafka enjoyed playing on the readers 'when he got to work on legends', as Walter Benjamin suspected?[13]

A game of misperceptions

Kafka's story is a game of misperceptions – Ulysses misperceives, the Sirens misperceive, and we the readers are tempted to misperceive, thinking that Kafka is misperceiving. But is he misperceiving or is he just pretending to misperceive? Kafka had considerable knowledge of the Greek language and mythology, and this radical twist of Homer's tale could hardly have been an oversight on his part. Why then does Ulysses, in Kafka's telling, plug his own ears instead of those of his fellows? This single act, so atypical of the Homeric hero, transforms him instantly into a character who seduces Kafka along with his readers, a figure oblivious to feminine temptation, serenely pursuing his own journey. Homer's Odysseus, ever speaking, ever listening, ever seeing, ever active, becomes a passive hero, a Ulysses cocooned in his own head, whose passivity turns him into an object of desire for those silent Sirens.

Kafka's text, like Homer's, may seduce us the readers, but for entirely different reasons. Rather than his cunning, his industriousness and, maybe less attractively for our times, his heroic and brutal qualities, we are here seduced by Ulysses' self-containment, serenity, indeed his narcissism. We are seduced by his ability to sail blissfully, unharmed through a sea of *silent killers*, not unlike the coronavirus that wrought havoc across the globe in our times.

Seduced by a text that is mysterious and opaque, we are likely to miss the trick that Kafka has played on us – that of turning a story of a dangerous, noisy and musical encounter into a story of silent and invisible danger. Heroics have no answers to the dangers facing Kafka's Ulysses, unlike those facing his Homeric counterpart. Ulysses is here reduced to a solitary presence. He can turn to no Athena to protect him from the dangers of the silent Sirens. All that he needs is a bubble of isolation in which to lock himself. This he achieves by blocking his ears, or, as Kafka's casually mentions in the codicil, maybe not:

> Ulysses, it is said, was so full of guile, was such a fox, that not even the goddess of fate could pierce his armour. Perhaps he had really noticed, although here the human understanding is beyond its depths, that the Sirens were silent, and opposed the afore-mentioned pretence to them and the gods merely as a sort of shield.[14]

The Sirens: Silent portents of death

Leaving Ulysses in his armour that nothing could pierce, we now turn to the Sirens and their muteness. Why are Kafka's Sirens silent and why is their silence more deadly than their song? These are questions that have preoccupied several commentators.[15] Walter Benjamin, a keen early interpreter and admirer of Kafka,[16] argued that the Sirens fall silent 'because for Kafka music and singing are an expression or at least a token of escape, a token of hope which comes to us from the intermediate world – at once unfinished and commonplace, comforting and silly'.[17]

This muteness of the Sirens as evidence of the loss of hope is in line with Adorno's dismissal of recorded music as the ultimate degradation of modern culture.[18] Recorded music represents, in this view, the self-alienation of music, where production turns into reproduction, part of the general tendency for spectacle and simulation that replace the 'real' thing. The Sirens' silence may then be seen as a by-product of a culture in which people lock themselves in their headphone cocoons of sounds furnished by the culture industry, seeking escape from the very regime of commodities that lies at the root of their alienation. The silence of the Sirens stands for a culture that denies music its critical and subversive potential, turning it into the latest opium of the people.

Interesting as this interpretation is, it flies in the face of Sirens as seductive portents of *death*. It also clashes with Kafka's notorious lack of musicality (a quality he shared with Freud), as reported by Max Brod, one that finds some support in Kafka's own admission that 'the essence of my unmusicalness consists in my inability to enjoy music connectedly, it only now and then has an effect on me, and how seldom it is a musical one.'[19] While Kafka's unmusicality has been the subject of some debate, it seems unlikely that he would choose to muffle his Sirens in acknowledgement of the musical decadence of his times, although admittedly it may account for his unwillingness to equate seductiveness with sweet song.

A different explanation for the Sirens' muteness is provided by Renata Salecl who sees it as the result of their transformation from inert, if brutal, forces of nature into human subjects.[20] The Sirens fall silent once the gaze of Ulysses has turned them into living women with desires and passions. Their silence is proof that they are no longer forces of nature oblivious to human laws. Instead, they are now subjects in their own rights, women with desires for the Other, the Other who remains indifferent to them. One may risk saying that their silence mirrors the silence of a young woman at a party who fails to attract the attention of someone whom she desires. Compelling as this interpretation is, it opens up another mystery: why should the silence of the Sirens be 'even more fatal' than their song?

Death, Nirvana and silence

Written during the First World War, a more tempting approach is to see the Sirens' silence as the silence of death. As Freud observed in his famous essay, 'Beyond the pleasure principle', written shortly after that war, in contrast to noisy Eros, death works silently and invisibly seeking to return all life to inorganic inertia.[21] In this view, silence, exemplified by the silence of Cordelia in Shakespeare's *King Lear*, is the symbol as well as the portent of death.[22] Death in this conception represents in the first place a primal longing for peace, a return to a state of Nirvana from which all tensions and stresses are removed, a deep sleep from which we never wake. It is only later and in response to the different vagaries of life that the death instinct assumes violent, aggressive and destructive forms.

The connection between Ulysses, the muteness of the Sirens and the peaceful state of Nirvana is captured poetically by Goliarda Sapienza in her novel 'Appuntamento a Positano', Positano frequently being associated with the Sirens' rock:

> Running under the bright sun, as I arrive out of breath at the beach with the pebbles, I understand why the legend says that this is exactly where Ulysses had his encounter with the Sirens. It is simple, their song is nothing other than the silence I hear just now, the silence from bullets that follow each other in space, the silence of the voiceless and serene wandering of the souls in the endless meadow of non-existence.[23]

The Sirens' muteness here stands for the silence of non-existence, the complete opposite of the constant noise of everyday life. This is what many of us experienced during the Covid-19 pandemic, when public spaces, offices and factories, restaurants, theatres and sports venues, places of worship fell silent. Only, instead of a blissful respite from the din of everyday life most people experienced increased levels of fear and anxiety. Some of this anxiety was doubtless the result of massive uncertainties over the future, jobs, health and so forth, which affected different groups of people differently. Some of it, however, would have been the result of boredom. Deprived of our usual entertainments and diversions, we sought to fill the void that threatened to overwhelm us by gluing ourselves to our different screens, phones, computers, television. It was there that we sought and found the noise we craved, created by constantly screaming news and opinions and the whirling cacophony of social media. Far from bringing bliss the way it did to Kafka's Ulysses, silence for most of us brought the terror of permanent listlessness and boredom.

Silence is dangerous because it is unbearable, especially when it is forced on us by isolation and loneliness which leave us alone with our dark fantasies and fears that threaten to overwhelm us. 'All of humanity's problems stem from a person's inability to sit quietly in a room alone,' claimed Pascal in 1645. Sitting in a room mostly on our own is precisely what the pandemic forced on many of us. It deprived us of our usual defences in noisy social interactions, a deprivation for which the second line of defence, hooking ourselves online and on-media, offered only partial diversion. Depriving us of our customary noisy opiates, the arrival of the coronavirus Covid-19 unleashed some of our darkest fears. As a germ that discriminated only on the most arbitrary and flimsy grounds, the virus awakened fears of being left to die alone and forgotten, unloved, uncared for and unmourned. Unlike Ulysses and his Homeric predecessor, Odysseus, we would then vanish leaving no trace, sinking to the level of those Kafkaesque 'nobodies' or the sailors whose bones lined up the rocks of the Homeric Sirens. This is a silence from which our clamorous universe of spectacles and sounds failed to protect us.

Yet, Kafka's Ulysses with his blissful defiance in the presence of a silent killer can also provide us with a more positive alternative, a more reassuring archetype for discovering new strength and fortitude in times of darkness. This is the Stoic archetype of 'a patient and enduring hero who knows his lifespan is a sequence of departures which he cannot control, but has to accept'. For the Stoics, Odysseus and his persistent twenty-year-long journey to return home was their model for the *homo viator* or 'itinerant human', each human on his or her own journey through life.[24] In his retelling of the story of Ulysses and the Sirens, Kafka appears to connect with the old Stoic tradition that was inspired by Ulysses' patience, endurance and piety, but above all his self-control.[25] It is known that Zeno of Citium, the founder to the Stoic school and a shipwreck survivor himself, admiringly referred to Odysseus in many of his writings, none of which survive, unlike those of Seneca which reveal the Roman philosopher's deep admiration and identification with Homer's hero.[26]

The Stoic ideal of *homo viator* was exemplified in our times in a blog by Alexandros Karayiannis, written during the early part of the pandemic. This is a time, easily downplayed in the pandemic's aftermath, when anxiety and uncertainty about the magnitude and consequences of the disease were overwhelming. It was a time when individuals died from one day to the next, when hospitals in many countries were stretched to breaking point, and when most of us suddenly found ourselves cocooned in forced home isolation. Karayiannis, an old Greek man, who described himself as a 'retired lawyer and engaged citizen', wrote movingly:

For us old people, our lives have changed little since the epidemic. Even before this evil, we spent most of our time alone, in our homes. We have long been on a waiting list, a list without firm priority exits, labelled 'destiny'. Those of us who are left, are now living out what remains of our lives and our times . . .

I took my afternoon stroll walking on the veranda. The streets below were deserted and silent like a wilderness. On a branch of the plane tree which stretches each year as if to shake hands with me, two sparrows were playfully flirting. It is now getting dark. The unavoidable night is approaching slowly and creeps into the house which is getting dark. Evening phone calls with children and a couple of friends. Then silence. I don't turn on the lights. From where I am sitting, I want to see the part of the night sky that I am entitled to see. If I am lucky, the moon will appear for a short while. The moon with her 'beloved silences', the moon that comforts and soothes me.[27]

The 'beloved silences of the moon' mentioned here is an expression, running back to Virgil, that lies at the heart of 'The Last Station', a poem by George Seferis, the Greek poet who was so fascinated by the character of Odysseus, his ancient ancestor:

Beloved silences of the moon,
A stream of thought,
A way of speaking to
a friend about things
that you confess are hard.[28]

The deep silences brought about by the pandemic left many of us, individually and collectively, traumatized and divided. The period of grievances, traumas and recriminations that followed has thrown many societies into a cauldron of uncertainty and strife. In these circumstances, many people are turning again to the Siren voices of demagogues promising easy answers and wish-fulfilling certitudes. By contrast, Kafka's radiant story, attuned to times of silent killers, quarantines and social isolation, may offer us an alternative way of coping with pain and anxiety, his Ulysses serenely sailing past those dreaded Sirens, a bringer of hope and solace.

Epilogue

Beyond the Strife of Myth and Reason

Readers who have followed me along this journey through Greek myths are likely to be, like me, lovers of myth. They are likely to share Aristotle's view in the epigraph that a lover of myth (*philomythos*) is also a lover of wisdom (*philosophos*). Philosophy, like myth, he believed, seeks to unravel not only the mysteries of the world we live in but also those we harbour in our own souls, even when these are disturbing and unsettling.

We lovers of myth discover wisdom, meaning and comfort in old myths. We realize that many of the troubles we face today have troubled humans for a long time, many of our dilemmas are age-old dilemmas. Myths offer shafts of insight that trigger our imagination in our quest for answers to ageless questions and help us approach these questions with fresh ideas and renewed courage. They give light in times of darkness and hope in times of despondency. They also help us better understand ourselves, some of our deepest fears, some of our craziest fantasies, some of the feelings and desires harboured in our unconscious mind. Myths give licence to certain aspects of our souls that hardly ever surface in our everyday lives. Reflecting on the different chapters of this book, I am sure that readers will be able to identify those myths that spoke most deeply to them, those that drew the strongest emotional responses and, maybe, made them think hardest. If nothing else, I hope that my explorations of Greek myths will encourage readers to engage in their own mythological thinking, drawing wisdom and strength from the myths that speak to them.

Like all lovers, we lovers of myth are prone to idealize the objects of our love. Such idealization can lead us astray. Most Greek myths, like those of other cultures, emerged from a heroic age of dragons slayed and castles stormed in the distant past, before the invention of writing, before there were written records and written laws. Their main interest lies in the struggles of heroic characters, whose dominant motive is the craving for glory and fame, and their ensuing triumphs, errors and sufferings.[1] Greek myths celebrate courage as a cardinal virtue and honour as a sovereign value, often at the expense of other virtues and values, including wisdom, solidarity, humility and justice. Women are frequently cast in lesser roles, as mourning mothers, wives and lovers, as victims to be rescued, as spoils of war to be divided up among the victors, or as beauties waiting to be ravished by a god or a hero and suffering dire consequences as a result. Alternatively, they are cast as sorceresses or enchantresses, dangerous creatures drawing men away from their missions or leading them to perdition. Where, in these myths, are heroines and heroes striving for peace and reconciliation, seeking to live in harmony with each other? Where are heroes and heroines seeking to live in harmony with their natural environment?[2] Myths may contain a great deal of wisdom, but they do not contain *all* human wisdom and they contain much that may not amount to wisdom at all.

Idealizing myths can have another negative consequence, that of raising a particular myth or a range of myths above critical scrutiny, turning it into dogma and ideology. Such myths can then become battlegrounds for religious and other wars. If there is one thing we learn from the myths discussed in this book, it is that, like the oracles of Delphi, Greek myths can give at best equivocal and complex guidance on how to act, how to live our lives. Turning a myth into dogma devalues the myth in question but also corrupts the idea of myth itself. It is not accidental that, in our times, myth is often reduced to describing a supposedly self-evident untruth. This can be a popular untruth ('Five common myths about ageing') or a quasi-scientific untruth ('The deficit myth'). Equally reductively, a myth can be used to describe a widely accepted ideal or a fantasy, like 'meritocracy' or the 'American dream', often held unconsciously and taken for granted. Such fantasies may guide people's actions and thoughts, going largely unchallenged even when they fly in the face of reality in an organization or in society at large.[3] They are hollow ideologies legitimizing the status quo with its injustices and oppressions.

Much as we may love Greek myths and seek inspiration and sustenance in them, we would do well to remember that myths can be dangerous. Plato, one of the most extreme and irksome critics of myth, famously sought to banish the work of poets, even great poets like Homer and the tragedians, from his Republic, viewing them as enemies of reason. 'If you admit the entertaining Muse of ... poetry [in the Republic],' he wrote, 'then instead of law and the shared acceptance of reason as the best guide, the kings of our community will be pleasure and pain.'[4] Plato criticized poets for portraying gods as vindictive, deceitful and immoral.[5] He also castigated the poets' aptitude to draw overwhelming emotions on the part of their protagonists which then infect their audiences.[6] Such emotions, he argued, are inimical to rational discourse and overpower our reasoning faculties.

Plato was especially concerned about the influence of myths on young minds. Identifying with a bloodthirsty Achilles or a deceitful Odysseus may be inspiring for a young man but is unlikely to make him a better human being, let alone a responsible citizen. But he was also concerned about the influence of myths on the rest of us. Shedding tears with Electra may help us offload some of our anxieties but will not scatter our troubles to the winds. Immersing ourselves in the world of myth to the exclusion of all else would turn us into Don Quixotes, marvellous perhaps, but not enlightened citizens. Myths can unleash powerful collective emotions which lead to violence, fuelling wars, revolutions and even genocide. The consequences of the myth of Aryan supremacy are well known to all, as are those of different myths of collective emancipation which have driven wars and revolutions, just and unjust.[7] In our times, cocooning ourselves in the world of myth is just as likely to turn us into inhabitants of a parallel universe dominated by UFOs, conspiracies about the assassination of John F. Kennedy, the machinations of the 'deep state', 'big pharma' and the like.

Plato's misgivings about myth need to be taken seriously. Myth cannot be our *only* guide to truth or to effective action, individual or collective. But banishing it altogether denies the righteous claims of our minds to mythological thinking, leaving us spiritually impoverished and at least partially blind. Plato himself recognized this. In defence of his own god, Reason, he made use of numerous allegories, stories *and* myths. He used existing myths, like that of Phaëthon, but he also invented myths of his own, like that of Atlantis and the story of Er, one of his most enigmatic and drawn-out myths that concludes the *Republic*.[8] Far from rejecting all myth, Plato seemed to recognize that if myth does not contain all wisdom, neither does philosophy offer all that our souls need for their sustenance.[9]

We need *Mythos* as well as *Logos* to flourish as human beings, to live enlightened and just lives. We need myth to fill the spiritual emptiness that threatens us, to lift us above the chaotic flux of mundane, everyday life. We need myth to reconnect us with what is enduring and permanent about being human and living with other humans. We need the kind of myth that does not obliterate our reason but prompts us to question our beliefs and to reflect on our actions, to learn from our failings and to celebrate our successes. We also need reason and her offspring – philosophy, science and practical wisdom – to tackle the complex problems – political, technical and environmental – facing us today. We need reason to dispel various destructive myths and delusions and to defend the distinction between truth and lies. Truth is never easy to establish and cannot always be established conclusively. Certainty cannot be found in science or philosophy. Reason more often than not denies us the seductions of certainty. But giving up the quest for truth in the belief that reality can be moulded to whatever we want it to be, to what is dictated by our fantasies and desires and those we share with like-minded people, leaves us sleepwalking in the realm of delusion and make-believe.

In our post-truth times, both *Mythos* and *Logos* are under assault by pseudo-myth, a character adept at masquerading as circumstances dictate, assuming the shape of slogans, iconic images, conspiracy theories, platitudes and 'common sense'. Pseudo-myths also regularly masquerade as scientific theories in any number of disciplines, including history, biology, physics, medicine, psychology, economics and so forth, and even as proper myths. At heart, they are narratives that inoculate themselves against reason and factual evidence, while hijacking the purposes of true myths by stirring the same emotional strings and appealing to the same spiritual needs. Against such pseudo-myths and those who seek to profit from them, it may be tempting to resort to contrary pseudo-myths. This only compounds the sense that everything is just a story, and any story is as good as the next.

Mythos and *Logos* are also under assault from another quarter – technocratic reason that reduces every aspect of our existence to calculation and profit, the logic of markets and numbers. Every problem becomes a technical problem in search of a fix, a fix that is an opportunity for profit and power. In a roundabout way, technocratic reason conspires with pseudo-myth to create different illusions of meaning and fulfilment, illusions that are short-lived and counterproductive. Selling dreams, creating problems and selling solutions to problems, mostly imaginary, becomes a self-reinforcing vicious spiral of illusions, ostensibly offering solace for the discontents of our times, but ending up reinforcing these discontents.

I hope this book has shown that Greek myths address many of the core questions which are part and parcel of the human condition – our proneness to repeat our errors, our desire for what is unattainable, our simultaneous fascination with and dread of the alien, our awe in front of heroic exploits, our problematic relation with our natural environment, our regular encounters with forces greater than ourselves, our tendency to be seduced by surfaces and images. They also provide vital insights into some of the malaise peculiar to our post-truth times and its pervasive pessimism, our struggles for identity, our tendency to vilify the Other, the craving for powerful leaders, and our frequent inability to distinguish between reality and delusion.

Human life is a constant encounter with mysteries and wonders that take many forms and many shapes. Learning to live with uncertainty and doubt is not an easy task. Taking our cue from Aristotle, we may conclude that we need the combined and often contradictory powers of *Mythos* and *Logos* to face the future with fortitude and wisdom.

Appendix
Plato's Myth of Er

How did Plato seek to support his philosophical arguments with the power of myth? I have paraphrased below the long myth invented by Plato to bring his *Republic* to its majestic conclusion both as a contrast to the myths covered in the main body of this book but also to enable readers to reflect on the kind of myth that Plato invented and endorsed. I have omitted the extensive astronomical sections in which the goddess Ananke (Necessity) and her daughters, the three Fates, preside over the movements of the heavenly spheres in the manner of a spindle and a whorl as well as many of the story's secondary details.

A warrior dies on the battlefield. Only, he is not dead. He is having a near-death experience. His body is untouched by decay, while his soul, temporarily separated from his body, spends eleven days in the realm of the dead. On the twelfth day, Er – this is the warrior's name – returns to life and reports what his soul has witnessed during its journey in the other world.

Er saw souls in terrifying loneliness, souls on the move, souls being judged and sent for a thousand years to heaven or to the underworld.

He saw others consigned to be tormented for all eternity in the depths of Tartarus.

He met souls about to be reincarnated into new bodies and start new lives on earth, men turning into women and women into men, animals into humans and humans into animals. They were all making choices based on their previous lives, knowing little about the consequences of these choices, about what their new lives had in store for them.

The soul of a good man who has spent a thousand years in heaven is now having to choose its next life on earth. Habituated to a life of order, comfort and luxury, he has grown complacent and thoughtless. He chooses to return to earth as a powerful dictator; this way, he can force order and peace on everyone; he can lord it over everyone. In his stupidity and greed, he has failed to notice what fate has decreed for such a man – that, in his next life, he is doomed to eat his own children and commit other unspeakable crimes. He now realizes the consequences of his choice. He beats his chest in despair and blames everybody, the gods, fate and anything rather than himself for what is lying ahead for him. He never learnt to take responsibility for his choices.

Next comes a procession of characters familiar to lovers of myth. They are making choices for their next life on earth, choices that are in turn sad, amusing and astonishing. Orpheus chooses to return to life as a swan, a bird who saves his greatest song for last. Atalanta, the swift-footed heroine, chooses the life of a male athlete for her next life, sure to win more prizes and earn greater praise than she ever did as a woman.

Next come some of the Homeric characters. Epeius, the legendary carpenter renowned for constructing the wooden horse that prised open the gates of Troy, chooses to return as a woman, supreme in arts and crafts. Ajax and Agamemnon, embittered with humanity both, choose to be reborn as a lion and an eagle, respectively. The fool Thersites quickly assumes the form of a monkey.

Last comes Odysseus. By now, there are few options left on the table. He wanders around for a long time looking for a future life and, at last, he finds it. Memories of his past sufferings have quelled all ambitions for glory and adventure. He chooses the life of a character disdained by all who chose before him. He happily chooses the life of a private citizen with no involvement in public affairs.

Having made their choices, the souls are guided across a scorching plain to the River of Forgetfulness whose water they thirstily drink. At once, they forget all about their past lives, all about their years in heaven and the underworld, the choices they made. Like shooting stars, they are then blown in all different directions to start their new lives.

The protagonist of the story is stopped from drinking the water from the river. He suddenly opens his eyes as his soul is reunited with his body. He finds himself about to be burnt on top of a funeral pyre on the battlefield and recounts what he saw to his living comrades.

At the end of the story, Socrates, for it is he who has told this story, turns to his interlocutor, Glaucon, and says: 'This myth has been saved from oblivion and so, too, it can save us – if only we take it to heart, crossing the River of Forgetfulness, acting wisely without polluting our souls with unjust acts and unwise decisions.'

The myth of Er, unlike all the other myths discussed in this book, was not part of an oral tradition, nor of course was it composed in verse. The story is told by Socrates, the *Republic's* main hero as he brings a long dialogue with several interlocutors to its close. Having demonstrated the benefits and rewards enjoyed by a moral person while alive, Socrates then tempts his interlocutor, Glaucon, with a story aimed at demonstrating the far greater rewards that moral people can expect after their death. The story is then beautifully told by Socrates and is full of poetic images and metaphors like that of souls blown like 'shooting stars' to begin their new lives on earth.

As a philosophical myth, the myth of Er is full of tensions and contradictions raising a myriad questions.[1] Are the circumstances of our life determined by our own actions in earlier lives and the choices we made while waiting in limbo? Or are they determined by the Fates and Necessity, who rule with total indifference to our well-being? Why should we be held responsible for choices we made with no knowledge of their consequences? Should we choose a just life because justice is itself a sovereign good or because of the rewards brought about by being just? How can we be 'saved' by a myth whose moral appears to be that the universe, the Fates and God himself are indifferent to our well-being? Are we mere atoms living solitary lives and dying solitary deaths or are we bonded to others, to our communities, parts of a larger cosmos as virtually the whole of the rest of the *Republic* testifies?

It is surely remarkable that Plato chose to end his greatest philosophical work, the very work in which he criticized poets, with a myth of his own whose debt to Homer is obvious. Not only do we encounter several Homeric characters as they wait to be reincarnated, making choices in line with their Homeric pasts, but Er, like Odysseus, ventures into the underworld, makes contact with the souls of dead people in the afterlife, and returns to earth to tell what he saw. To this basic plot, Plato injects various mythological and philosophical motifs of his own, notably the themes of last judgement,[2] of reincarnation, of choice and personal responsibility, of an eternal cycle of birth and rebirth. It is especially telling that Plato uses the word 'myth' in the last paragraph of this work to indicate not just an authoritative tale but a narrative with a plot, capable of stimulating the imagination and raising moral questions, in short arousing mythological thinking. And, most remarkable, we hear from the mouth of Plato's hero,

Socrates, that this myth has the potential to *save* us. In the last resort, salvation may not to be found in the extensive philosophical arguments that precede it – on justice, truth and beauty, the discussions of parts of the psyche, of political classes and leadership – but in distilling the essence of this product of pure imagination.[3] At the end of a long philosophical treatise which proceeds in the Socratic manner with question after question, Plato leaves his readers with a *living* myth that prompts ever more questions.

The story of Er has other qualities that qualify it as a myth. Its central character, Er, as well as the main characters he encounters in the afterlife, are larger than life, commanding a heroic or tragic stature. All the same, the multitude of souls that Er meets as well as the souls' solitude and the ordinariness of their actions – camping, marching, conversing, deliberating and so forth – gives an impersonal character to most of the figures that populate the story. Maybe this is sealed by Odysseus' choice to pursue the life of a private citizen with no further involvement in politics. Is it not surprising that Plato consigns the multitalented hero of the *Odyssey* to the standing of a mere citizen in Kallipolis, his ideal city, while discarding the towering figures of Ajax and Agamemnon to the wild where they can reign among the beasts?

Fascinating as it is, the myth of Er, with its anticipation of Christian theology and its salvationist agenda, seems less in tune with our times than the myths I examined in this book. Saving our souls, discovering the ideal polis, understanding the nature of justice and making wise choices are all themes that resound across the ages. But do they reflect directly the burning issues that engulf us today?

Reading On

Introduction

The study of myth is a complex and diverse subject to which many disciplines have made valuable contributions. Inevitably this introduction highlights my own interests in Greek mythology and its contemporary relevance and has only briefly touched or entirely ignored important dimensions of the study of myth. The meanings of different myths can be the object of detailed and sometimes acrimonious scrutinization by philologists, linguists, historians, archaeologists and other scholars.

Important issues in the study of Greek myths that I have sidestepped include the emergence of new myths across different historical periods and their relation to actual historical events (see, for example, Armstrong 2005); the relation of Greek myths to the myths of other cultures including those of the Egyptians and the Hittites (see, for example, Bachvarova 2015); the relation of myth to scientific knowledge (see, for example Lévi-Strauss 1966, 1978 and Lévy-Bruhl 1923/78); the structure of myths (see, for example Lévi-Strauss 1958/76, 1978); and the relation of myth to spiritual and religious beliefs and rituals (see, for example, Eliade 1963).

This book is certainly neither the first nor the only one to explore the meanings of Greek myths for our times. Several books written by distinguished classicists were written for a wider, non-academic public. Two outstanding such books are Richard Martin's (2016) *Classical Mythology: The Basics* and Richard Buxton's (2022) *The Greek Myths that Shape the Way We Think*, which trace the development of Greek myths (including some I discuss in this book) since antiquity and offer many incisive arguments about their changing meanings and enduring relevance.

There are numerous books that have explored the meanings and symbolism of trees as well as their contribution to the well-being of the planet (Beresford-Kroeger 2010; Hageneder and Harper 2020; Mabey 2007). Richard Powers's (2018) novel, *The Overstory*, provides a magnificent panorama of characters whose lives have been touched by trees and a complex plot in which the struggle to save trees from loggers plays a major part.

The Gaia theory of the earth as a living self-regulating system that can be thought of as an organism in its own right was first proposed by scientist and environmentalist James Lovelock (1979, 2006) and has since enjoyed substantial credibility among environmentalists as well as scientists.

Post-truth and a post-truth society are the topics of numerous books (Ball 2017; D'Ancona 2017; Davis 2017; Gray 2018), many of which discuss the role of the social media in blurring the boundaries between truth and falsehood. Haidt 2022 has provided a very insightful account of the effects of Facebook on American society. He uses the Tower of Babel as a metaphor for the increasing fragmentation of meaning and an inability of people to communicate with others outside their particular echo chambers.

Chapter 1

The story on which this chapter is based is by Pliny the Elder (23/4–79 CE) in his *Natural History*. Pliny's original and highly scholarly account of the story can be found on https://www.perseus.tufts.edu/ hopper/text?doc=Perseus:abo:phi,0978,001:35:36.

Pliny presents the story as an accurate historical record in which he compares the virtues and skills of different celebrated painters of antiquity. Interestingly, he recognizes Parrhasios' proclivity to boasting and arrogance. He wrote:

> Parrhasius was a most prolific artist, but at the same time there was no one who enjoyed the glory conferred upon him by his talent with greater insolence and arrogance. It was in this spirit, that he went so far as to ... declare himself to be the 'prince of painters,' and asserted that in him the art had arrived at perfection. (*Natural History* 36, trans. John Bostock)

Extreme though the case of Wilkomirski may be, it is by no means unique. Belgian-born Misha Defonseca, for example, wrote a similar Holocaust memoir which turned out to be a fake. Rosemarie Pence, who posed as a child Holocaust survivor under the name Hannah, was the subject of a 'biography', *Hannah: From Dachau to the Olympics and Beyond*, published in 2005. It later turned out that her testimonies were entirely fake. A more complex case is presented by *The Painted Bird*, a 1965 novel by Polish-American author Jerzy Kosinski, a novel that creates the impression of being autobiographical without making an explicit claim.

A more nuanced and ambiguous case is presented by another memoir. In *I, Rigoberta Menchú* (1984), Menchú, an indigenous Guatemalan woman later honoured with the Nobel Peace Prize, painted a torrid account of the brutality inflicted on her family and her village by wealthy landowners and the government in trying to drive them off their land. Subsequently, David Stoll, an American anthropologist, while sympathetic to the plight of indigenous Guatemalan people, challenged substantial parts of Menchú's narrative (Stoll 1999). With the help of interviews with numerous villagers, Stoll offered evidence that some of the reported atrocities had not actually happened to Menchú's own family and that many of her claims were inaccurate. Based on this evidence, Stoll challenged Menchú's contention that the Mayan Indians had been enthusiastic recruits to the focista guerrillas. Stoll's arguments have become the topic of an acrimonious and extensive controversy among anthropologists and others.

Max Weber discusses rationalization and the ensuing 'disenchantment of the world' in *The Protestant Ethic and the Spirit of Capitalism*, first published in 1905 (Weber 1958). Many authors have argued that modernity is characterized by unprecedented degrees of rationalization in every sphere of human life, which result in a process of 'disenchantment' – i.e. the elimination of charm, magic and innocent pleasures. Some theorists, however, are currently arguing that late modernity, with its emphasis on spectacle and simulation, has brought about a partial re-enchantment of the world through the different mechanisms of consumption (Ritzer 1999).

Chapter 2

My account of this myth is based entirely on Euripides' tragedy, *Iphigenia in Tauris*. The manuscript text of this tragedy, along with those of eight of her sisters, was discovered accidentally in Byzantine Thessaloniki in the fourteenth century CE by a scholar known as Demetrius Triclinius. Until then, the story was mainly known from textual fragments, from the extended accounts and references made to it by other authors, including Aristotle and Cicero, as well as from numerous pictorial representations in vases, frescoes and reliefs.

The myth of the Greek princess, exiled in a dark foreign land and presiding over even darker cult practices until she is accidentally reunited with her brother and his friend and escapes with them, became a popular topic of dramatists and opera composers in the eighteenth century. Outstanding among them is the tragedy by Goethe and the opera by Gluck, both premiered in 1779.

Since then, the fortunes of the myth have waxed and waned, lying in obscurity for much of the twentieth century. It has recently regained something of its popularity with several performances of the original Euripides drama onstage and online. Several performances of the tragedy can now be found on YouTube. It is worth mentioning one staged by the Royal Holloway University of London Drama Society, adapted and directed by James Shannon: https://www.youtube.com/watch?v=e2lrX84devI.

The recent past has also seen the publication of two major commentaries on Euripides' drama: Poulheria Kyriakou's scholarly treatise (2006) and Edith Hall's magisterial survey (2013) which has provided some of the background material for this chapter.

Postcolonial theory is now a major field of study. A foundational classic in this field is Edward Said's *Orientalism* (1985). Other seminal contributions include Spivak 1988, Agamben 1998 and Mbembe 2003. Several authors have addressed the concept of the 'barbarian' (Cartledge 1993; Hall 1989; Said 1994). There is a huge literature on different constructions of the Other, including women as the Other (de Beauvoir 1953), the Jew as the Other (Friedländer 1997) and the othering of different groups that are racialized – i.e. constructed as belonging to distinct races (Fanon 1967; Memmi 1991).

Othering as an aspect of populism and populist leaders is addressed, among others, by Rosenthal 2018, 2020.

Hans Christian Andersen's short story, *The Shadow*, can be found at http://hca.gilead.org.il/shadow.html. Carl Jung addressed the Shadow in several of his writings (e.g. 1953, 1968/2009). In my own work, I have discussed othering as the shadow of the shadow at http://www.yiannisgabriel.com/2020/11/othering-as-shadow-of-shadow-beyond.html.

Chapter 3

The myth of Phaëthon has come down to us from numerous sources, both Greek and Roman. Aeschylus covered the story in his lost tragedy, *Heliades*. So, too, did Euripides in his tragedy *Phaëthon*, of which substantial fragments amounting to some four hundred lines have survived, providing the base for different debates and attempts to reconstruct the play.

References to the myth are made by numerous commentators, but the two comprehensive accounts that have survived come from Ovid in his *Metamorphoses* and the Greek poet Nonnus of Panopolis who lived in Egypt in the fifth century CE. Such is the power of the story as told by Ovid, however, that most modern retellings take him as their starting point. My own account is mostly based on Ovid, but is also influenced by Edith Hamilton's (2013) and Stephen Fry's (2018) excellent modern retellings.

Phaëthon's story is a potent stimulus for unleashing the artistic imagination. Many artists were inspired by this myth and sought to recreate it in works of literature, music and painting. Dante referred to the story and so, too, did Shakespeare in several of his plays. Several painters from antiquity to Rubens in one of his celebrated masterpieces were inspired to paint it. Lully composed an opera on the theme while Goethe reconstructed a tragedy from the fragments of Euripides' play, a task repeated in our times by at least two other playwrights. Classicists have argued energetically about the plot of Euripides' play, as they have about Ovid's sources.

A flying hero, the intoxication of flying, the impulsiveness of youth, the warnings of old age, the shining palace of gold, the gleaming vehicle, the horses out of control, everything else out of control, the panic of the young man, the entire earth in deadly peril, the desperate measures to limit the damage, the final drop of the hero to his death, the grieving parents, sisters and friends – all these combine to make Phaëthon's story one that pulsates across the ages and across cultures. Indeed, similar stories were told in cultures far and away from the Graeco-Roman world, as far away as ancient Mesopotamia, Germany and Estonia to North America, as shown by James and van der Sluijs 2016. They examined the Phaëthon motif in different mythologies and have attempted a synthesis based on mythological, archaeological and geological evidence.

Various authors have discussed Phaëthon's struggles with identity, including Levita 1965 and Winstanley 2004. Phaëthon is also discussed with great insight by Campbell 1949/88.

Čadková 2023 has discussed an adaptation of the Phaëthon story as a play by Otakar Theer in 1917, as an allegory of rebellion against the bondage of the Czech nation in the Austro-Hungarian monarchy.

Jared Diamond (2005) wrote a sobering account of how societies past and present have been wiped out by environmental collapses, partly brought about by their own actions. Eric Cline (2021) has offered a scholarly and highly provocative account of the collapse that afflicted all societies in the eastern Mediterranean at the end of the Late Bronze Age in which climate change was probably a contributing factor.

Chapter 4

The story of Oedipus emerges from numerous accounts and interpretations, starting with Sophocles' three Theban tragedies and

Seneca's *Oedipus*. Several ancient tragedies sprang from the myth of Oedipus, including Aeschylus' *Seven Against Thebes* and Euripides' *Phoenician Women*.

Freud's account of the Oedipus Complex can be found in many of his writings. Good starting points are the accounts offered in the *Introductory Lectures in Psychology* (1916–17/1973) and *The Ego and the Id* (1923/84). An extensive discussion of feminist critiques of the Oedipus Complex and a qualified defence of it is provided by Mitchell 1975.

Albert Camus's *The Plague* provides one of the most compelling accounts in fiction of the onslaught and aftermath of an epidemic. It makes a fascinating counterpart to Thucydides' account of the plague of Athens in 430 BCE.

Lévi-Strauss, the French anthropologist, has argued powerfully that all versions of the story of Oedipus and all interpretations are part of the same underlying unity, a unity that must be read not linearly, like a story, but vertically, like an orchestral score, with different voices speaking together, in harmony or in counterpoint (Lévi-Strauss 1963).

Robert Parker's (1983) essential study of miasma in Greek tragedy draws extensively on the classic work of anthropologist Arnold van Gennep (1960) and Mary Douglas (1966/2002, 1975) on liminal spaces and the importance of ritual.

Fineman 2014 offers a vivid and readable account of blaming and scapegoating across the centuries. He argues that Western societies have evolved into blame cultures, the attribution of blame a constant obsession, indeed a business, whenever we are confronted with an accident, a calamity or simply a problem.

The concept of miasma in organizations undergoing rapid downsizing was developed in my own work (Gabriel 2012), building on the important insights of Stein 1998, 2001 and Sievers 1994.

Chapter 5

Unlike Homer, Aesop is almost certainly a historical person and the author of many of the famous fables attributed to him, although no written works by him survive and no reliable biography. He probably lived in the second half of the seventh and first half of the sixth centuries BCE. His work is already mentioned by Herodotus in his *Histories*, Plato in his *Phaedo* and Aristotle who, in *On Rhetoric*, recounts the delightful story of the fox and the hedgehog, as supposedly told by Aesop, while defending a corrupt leader who was being tried by the local assembly in Samos. Traditions and depictions of Aesop abound – that he was enslaved, that he was African, that he was ugly, that he was admired by many rich and famous people and was able to buy his freedom.

Aesop's numerous fables emerged from oral traditions that spread from Greece to other parts of the world. Written accounts of them have surfaced across the ages, many of them from Roman sources, starting with the collection by Gaius Julius Phaedrus (*c.* 15 BCE–*c.* 50 CE), who produced the first collection of fables in Latin verse. His is the first account of the story of the 'Frogs who Wanted a King'. The first collection of fables in English was published by William Caxton in 1484. An index of some seven hundred Aesop's fables was compiled by American classicist Ben Edwin Perry – the Perry Index, of which the 'Frogs who Wanted a King' is No. 44. Not all of the fables in the Perry Index can reliably be linked to Aesop.

On the deeper symbolism of frogs in mythological and folkloric traditions, see Pallua 2019, and for a detailed analysis the Grimms' *The Frog King*, see Zipes 2008. Carl Jung discusses the symbolism of frogs and the frog king in several passages of the *Red Book* (2009).

Literature on the strongman has been growing rapidly since the rise of populist leaders in the recent past. Rachman 2022 and Ben-Ghiat 2020 provide insightful accounts of this phenomenon.

Leadership has generated an enormous literature over the centuries. Followership, on the other hand, has been far less popular as a topic of discussion, even as leadership comes to be viewed in relational terms as an asymmetrical process involving leaders and followers. A good starting point for understanding this relation is Freud's *Group psychology and the analysis of the ego* (1921/85), whose arguments are developed by Lindholm 1988. In my own work, I have examined in detail the fantasies that followers build around their leaders and the reasons for the grip of these fantasies (Gabriel 1997, 2015).

The different fears and phobias that characterize risk societies like ours have been examined by, among others, Beck 1992, and, more controversially, Füredi 2006 and Glassner 2018.

Chapter 6

The immense distance that separates us from the world of the *Odyssey* does not hinder the fascination it exercises. On the contrary, it is arguably the most widely known web of Greek myths and the commonest metaphor for any kind of journey, geographical, psychological or spiritual. There are countless translations of Homer's original in many contemporary languages. Translations have been both in prose and in verse and styles have varied from the classic to the romantic and from the pompous and formal to the casual and colloquial. English translations of the *Odyssey* have included those of Thomas Hobbes, Alexander Pope, Samuel Butler, T. E. Lawrence and William Morris, as well as those used in my own text above by Robert Fagles, Stanley Lombardo, Walter Shewring and Emily Wilson. See https://en.wikipedia.org/wiki/English_translations_of_Homer.

There are now many retellings of the adventures of Odysseus and Penelope, especially by feminist authors, such as Margaret Atwood's

Penelopiad, Madeline Miller's *Circe*, Claire North's *Ithaca* and Luigi Malerba's *Ithaca Forever: Penelope Speaks*. There are loose adaptations in memoir like Daniel Mendelsohn's *Odyssey*, in film like Stanley Kubrick's *2001: A Space Odyssey* and the Coen Brothers' *Oh Brother, Where art thou?*, and in video games like *Super Mario Odyssey*. At my latest count, there were more than 10,000 items with '*Odyssey*' in their title in the Amazon catalogue. It would be easy to discard the *Odyssey* as a tedious cliché or an empty signifier if it weren't for the power of its imagery and the depth of its symbolism that continue to stir our emotions and shape the ways we make sense of our experiences and even our entire lives.

Doug Metzger offers a gripping narration of the *Odyssey*'s key episodes and a thoroughly scholarly and incisive commentary of some of the social, historical and literary issues it raises in his always fascinating podcast, *Literature and History*, available at https://literatureandhistory.com/index.php/episode-012-kleos-and-nostos. Another outstanding podcast with highly engaging commentaries of the *Odyssey* is Lantern Jack's *Ancient Greece Declassified*, available at https://www.greecepodcast.com/homers-meta-odyssey/. Episode 29 of this podcast is a stimulating conversation with classicist Olga Levaniouk on Penelope as a highly sophisticated and complex character, every bit of a match for Odysseus in versatility, sagacity and planning: https://www.greecepodcast.com/penelope-weaver-of-fate-w-olga-levaniouk/.

I can strongly recommend these two podcasts by outstanding scholars and, in the case of Lantern Jack, his guest interlocutors who comprise some of the world's most eminent classicists. Their podcasts, which come free and without advertisements, are models of classical scholarship for a wider public, combining wit, profundity and, at times, considerable beauty.

Among the many books that offer accounts of the sociology of the *Odyssey*, I would single out Finley's *The World of Odysseus* (1956/78).

The character of Odysseus in world literature is masterfully explored in *The Ulysses Theme* by Stanford (1963/92).

The way the 'refugee' is constructed in different discourses has been analysed with great insight by some distinguished theorists of organizations (Hardy and Phillips 1999; Hardy, Phillips and Clegg 2001; Phillips and Hardy 1997).

The story of the *Golden Venture* shipwreck has been exhaustively researched and told by Patrick Radden Keefe in his book *The Snakehead* (2009) and several articles in the *New Yorker*.

Chapter 7

There are several versions of the Narcissus myth from antiquity. In the classic version by Ovid in his *Metamorphoses*, his love for his self-image is his punishment for spurning Echo. In another version he is punished for spurning the love of another youth or for falling in love with his twin sister. In Ovid's account, Narcissus melts away under his own passion and turns into a gold and white flower, while in other versions he commits suicide before turning into a flower.

The concept of narcissism was first systematically expounded by Freud (1914/84) in an essay which has influenced many subsequent formulations, including those of psychoanalysts Kernberg (1970) and Kohut (1971), who made pioneering studies of narcissistic disorders and of the narcissistic character. The compilers of five editions of the US Diagnostic and Statistical Manual of Mental Disorders (DSM) have sought to refine and standardize the criteria for diagnosing what is now referred to as narcissistic personality disorder (NPD) (Association 2013).

The classic work on the culture of narcissism is Christopher Lasch's *Culture of Narcissism* (1980), which builds on the work of Freud,

Kernberg, Kohut, Fromm and others to develop a theory of narcissism as a generalized social phenomenon.

Several works including Schwartz 1990 and Maccoby 1981, 2000 have explored narcissism in organizational contexts and the propensity of narcissistic leaders to precipitate organizational decline and failure. Alvesson 2013 provides a sharp commentary on how an ethos of grandiosity has come to dominate many aspects of modern life, while Ritzer 1993/6, 1999 has developed the idea of cathedrals of consumption as the main institution through which contemporary capitalism seeks to re-enchant our lives. Sennett 1998 and Bauman 1996, 1998 have re-evaluated the character of contemporary work and the meaning of careers in a business culture that favours presentation and image over hard work and loyalty. The metaphor of the glass cage as a way of capturing the chief qualities of today's organizations has been central to my own work (Gabriel 2004, 2005).

Boorstin 1962 is a prophetic work on the power of image and its corroding consequences on the meaning of truth. Debord 1977 is the classic work of situationist theory that looks at our society as a society of spectacle, a theme that finds its apotheosis in the works of French postmodern philosopher Jean Baudrillard (1968/88, 1970/88, 1983). The power of the media to create alternative and infinitely seductive realities was explored by Neil Postman in his highly readable and disquieting *Amusing Ourselves to Death* (1986).

Chapter 8

My account of the Trojan War is naturally based principally on the *Iliad*. The fall of Troy is addressed twice in the *Odyssey* and is the main subject of the first part of the *Aeneid*. The events preceding the Trojan expedition are based on diverse sources by epic poets, tragedians and others. The story of Eris and the Golden Apple first featured in the *Cypria*, a now lost epic poem attributed to Stasinus, only small fragments of which have survived. These include a few lines on the Judgement of Paris. The *Cypria*, the *Iliad* and the *Odyssey* were parts of an epic cycle of eight poems, all in dactylic hexameters, of which only the *Iliad* and the *Odyssey* survive in full.

Homeric scholarship is a vast area with contributions from classicists, mythologists, archaeologists, philologists, linguists, historians and scholars from several other disciplines since antiquity. The so-called Homeric Question concerning the identity of the author(s) of the *Iliad* and the *Odyssey* has been a terrain of confrontations, sometimes acrimonious, among scholars for centuries. A good starting point for interested readers is offered by the eminent American classicist Gregory Nagy (1996); see also: https://chs.harvard.edu/curated-article/gregory-nagy-the-epic-hero/ and https://core.ac.uk/download/pdf/28932078.pdf.

A particularly fruitful cross-fertilization of the Homeric universe with the experiences of today's soldiers on the battlefield is provided by Jonathan Shay in his outstanding *Achilles in Vietnam* (1994). Shay, a psychiatrist with long experience of treating Vietnam veterans and a profound knowledge of Homer, achieves a remarkable double feat – he shows how the *Iliad*'s accounts of the battlefield provide unique insights into the experiences of today's warriors and also how these experiences offer a profound understanding of the metamorphosis of Achilles from noble and generous hero into a demented killing machine. He identifies the betrayal of 'What is Right' and the failure to grieve for the loss of a battlefield friend as crucial elements in a soldier's rage (what he calls 'berserkness') and its subsequent cause of insuperable psychopathologies.

The Argonauts' expedition is the topic of Apollonius of Rhodes's epic, *Argonautica*, a work often unfavourably compared to the

Homeric epics. Apollonius was a learned scholar and author. He lived the third century BCE and spent part of his life in Alexandria, where he held the post of librarian at the Library, the world's biggest treasure trove of knowledge at the time. A gripping narrative adaptation of *Argonautica* with an incisive and sympathetic commentary is provided by Doug Metzger in his invaluable podcast *Literature and History*, available at https://literatureandhistory.com/index.php/episode-038-the-epic-anti-hero.

Argonautica concludes with the Argonauts' return to Iolcus. The arrival of the youthful Iason in Iolcus is magnificently captured in Pindar's *Fourth Pythian Ode*. Other events in the lives of Iason and Medea are described in *The Library of Apollodorus* dating from the first or second century CE, in book 7 of Ovid's *Metamorphoses*, and in Euripides' terrifying tragedy, *Medea*. Euripides is the originator of the version in which Medea kills her own children, an account dismissed by Robert Graves in his *Greek Myths* (1955/2012). Among contemporary authors, Edith Hamilton's (2013) account of the Argonauts' expedition stands out. Doug Metzger provides a gripping account of Euripides' drama and a highly original and profound analysis at https://literatureandhistory.com/index.php/episode-033-woman-the-barbarian.

An extensive analysis of Agamemnon as a leader susceptible to hubris is provided by Porter 2019. The nature of Xerxes' hubris in *Persians* is discussed by Papadimitropoulos 2008 who offers references to several different ways of reading Aeschylus' play.

The hubris of today's leaders and managers is a topic widely discussed in contemporary literature. See, for example, Claxton, Owen and Sadler-Smith 2015; Kets de Vries 1990; Owen and Davidson 2009; Picone, Dagnino and Minà 2014.

The topic of leadership narcissism and resulting organizational failures are discussed by Maccoby 2000; Schwartz 1990; M. Stein 2003,

2013. The pretentious grandiosity that afflicts organizations and individuals in our times is explored by Alvesson 2013.

Chapter 9

For readings related to the *Odyssey*, see the section for Chapter 6 above.

There is a wide range of scholarly publications on the Sirens, their symbolism and evolution across the writings of Greek and Roman authors. A good starting point can be found in the 2006 selection of essays edited by Austern and Naroditskaya, *Music of the Sirens*, which offers a wide range of interpretations and perspectives on the Sirens. Extended extracts are available online at https://www.google.co.uk/ books/edition/Music_of_the_Sirens/5IBSGG9YegwC?hl=en&gbpv= 1&pg=PT25&printsec=frontcover.

Cicero's reading of the Sirens' episode can be found in Cicero 2001. Barker 1967 discusses Cicero's account, linking it to Dante's portrait of Ulysses.

Adorno and Horkheimer's reading of the episode can be found in *Dialectic of Enlightenment* (1947/97) and a discussion of their thesis can be found in Jameson 1990.

Blanchot 1982 and Salecl 1997 offer interesting interpretations of Kafka's short story.

The literature on the Covid-19 pandemic and its aftermath is already very substantial. An interesting account of the pandemic – its medical, social and psychological dimensions – is offered by Christakis 2020, who uses the plague described at the opening of the *Iliad* as a reference point for his own analysis.

Notes

Preface

1   The part of our mind that thinks mythologically works in different ways from
our reasoning mind and shapes our memories in distinctly personal ways. I
invited my fellow-walker on that memorable afternoon in Ithaca to comment
on my recollection. He responded thus: 'My recollection of the story is very
similar to yours, but it differs in one crucial respect: according to my memory,
the creature never barked. Moreover, this is one of the things that was so
unnerving about the episode – we saw it without hearing it. And it was almost
inconceivably large. It was covered in a fur that it had partially shed on many
occasions and was caked in mud after what I imagine were many solitary
winters up on the mountain side.'
2   Several of the myths discussed in this book have featured in my academic
writing over the span of several years, resurfacing and undergoing different
elaborations as my mythological thinking evolved and as circumstances
changed.

Introduction

1   For example, in a less well-known version by Hyginus, the story's central
character is Triopas, the name of Erysichthon's father in other accounts.
2   For a penetrating interpretation of the myth of Erysichthon as a critique of
consumer society, see Hopfl 2004.
3   It also generates numerous other words, including muscle, mouse and
myopia.
4   The Greek goddess of memory was Mnenosyne, mother of the Muses,
who numbered nine in most accounts, three or seven in others. The Muses

and the arts they represented (epic poetry, lyric poetry, music, tragedy and so forth) ensured that memories of great deeds and great sufferings were preserved across generations, celebrated and incorporated in different ritual practices.

5   Martin (1989: 95) traces the evolution of the word 'mythos' and examines closely its uses in Homer's *Iliad*, arguing that 'the best muthoi [myths] in this original sense would naturally involve the most powerful images, often resorting to genealogical recitation and claims about past status'.

6   If, like the author, you have ever been told a story in a foreign language which you only imperfectly command, then you will be aware how easy it is to lose the plot if you fail to understand even a single significant detail.

7   This is clear in the epigraph of this book.

8   Notice, too, that the priestess whose form Demeter assumes is named Nicippe, meaning 'victory of the horse'. It is an important feature of Greek myths that even minor characters have names.

9   'A tradition has been handed down by the ancient thinkers of very early times, and bequeathed to posterity in the form of a myth, to the effect that these heavenly bodies are gods, and that the Divine pervades the whole of nature ... They supposed the primary substances to be gods, we must regard it as an inspired saying and reflect that whereas every art and philosophy has probably been repeatedly developed to the utmost and has perished again, these beliefs of theirs have been preserved as a relic of former knowledge' (Aristotle, *Metaphysics* 12.1074b, trans. Hugh Tredennick).

10   Aristotle *Poetics* 1451b, trans. S. H. Butcher.

11   Aristotle's well-known and much debated theory of catharsis, the purging or cleansing of emotions experienced by audiences of tragic performances, alludes to the therapeutic power of myth. Aristotle astutely observed that by witnessing the sufferings of tragic characters on stage, audiences were able to experience powerful emotions that helped them manage their own fears and anxieties. For a discussion of the complexities and insights of Aristotle's concept of catharsis, see Nuttall 1996.

12   On the concept of narrative ecologies and a typology of such ecologies into narrative jungles, narrative monocultures, narrative temperate zones, narrative deserts and so forth, see Gabriel 2016, 2021.

13   The meaning of myth as popular untruth can be traced back to Plato, who refers to 'children's myths' (or what we would call 'fairytales') that are 'by and large untrue though they contain elements of truth' (*Republic* 377a, trans. Robin Waterfield).

14   See, for example, Davis 2017, D'Ancona 2017 and Ball 2017.

1 The Narrative Veil: Truths and Untruths, Facts and Fantasies

1 Birds are known to fly into large glass surfaces and walls. This is known as 'window strikes'. Many birds are unable to see glass and can mistake glass reflections of the sky or surrounding environment as an open space. Such collisions result in injuries and death. However, birds are not known to mistake images of fruit for real fruit.

2 Wilde 1889/1905: 9.

3 Wilde 1889/1905: 17.

4 Wilde 1889/1905: 3.

5 Benjamin 1968b.

6 For a useful classification of different types of hoaxes, see https://www.nspcc. org.uk/keeping-children-safe/online-safety/inappropriate-explicit-content/ fake-news/.

7 Raoul Hilberg and Yehuda Bauer, among several distinguished Holocaust scholars, both disputed the authenticity of the book from early on.

8 Maechler 2001.

9 Quote from Finkelstein 2000: 61, who discusses the case in some detail.

10 Maechler 2001: 281.

11 Jean Baudrillard, *The Gulf War Did Not Take Place* (Bloomington: Indiana University Press, 1995). In fairness to Baudrillard, he was paraphrasing the title of the famous play by Jean Giraudoux, *The Trojan War Will Not Take Place*, but the paraphrase as well as the use of a slogan as his book's title are typical examples of postmodern theorizing.

12 The argument that language is political and creates political realities lies at the heart of the work of Michel Foucault, another French philosopher who is identified with postmodernism but who rejected the title.

13 In 1966, Philip Rieff published *The Triumph of the Therapeutic*, a book that celebrated the rise of 'psychological man', the individual who seeks consolation for the sufferings that life dishes out, not in universal religious or political promises of salvation, but in personal therapy, analysis and self-inquiry. Rieff would have been surprised both at the vast escalation of the therapeutic discourses in the half-century that followed the publication of his book but also by the generally anti-scientific quality of these discourses.

14 Descartes, *Meditation II: Of the Nature of the Human Mind; and that it is more easily known than the Body* (trans. Elizabeth S. Haldane) https://yale. learningu.org/download/041e9642-df02-4eed-a895-70e472df2ca4/H2665_ Descartes'%20Meditations.pdf.

2 Iphigenia: Escaping from the Shadows

1 The Black Sea was known to the Greeks as *Áxeinos Póntos*. This is thought to derive from the Old Persian word *axšaina*, meaning 'dark-coloured'. Euripides himself refers to the sea at the place where Orestes' ship beached as black, '*pontos . . . melas*' (107).

2 This derived from the Tatar name of the peninsula, *Qırım*, its Russian and Ukrainian name being *Krym*, in all probability deriving from the Greek *Kimmerikos* (Cimmerian) *Bosporos* mentioned by Herodotus.

3 The peninsula was occupied at different times by different conquerors, including Romans, Mongols and Ottomans, from whom it was seized by Catherine the Great who annexed it to Russia in 1783. Its substantial Turkish-speaking population of Tatars was ethnically cleansed and deported by Stalin to Uzbekistan in 1944. The Crimea's history is marked by numerous wars, none bloodier and less conclusive than the 1853–6 Crimean War.

4 Writing several decades before Euripides composed *Iphigenia in Tauris*, the historian and geographer Herodotus, generally a sympathetic commentator on non-Greeks and arguably a not especially reliable narrator, describes the Taurians as a tribe living off 'war and plunder', sacrificing shipwrecked sailors and Greeks to their 'Maiden Goddess', whom they identify as Iphigenia, Agamemnon's daughter. He also mentions some other bloody customs of the Taurians like placing the severed heads of their victims on stakes next to their houses. This was thought to offer protection to the household (1954: 305).

5 Euripides, *Iphigenia in Tauris*, 221–4. I have used the translation by George Theodoridis, available online at https://www.poetryintranslation.com/PITBR/Greek/IphigeneiaTauris.php.

6 This chorus belongs to the same tradition as the chorus of Hebrew Slaves, 'Va Pensiero', in Verdi's *Nabucco* and the African-American Spirituals born of the unimaginable sufferings of enslaved people in North America and their longings for a return home.

7 Euripides, *Iphigenia in Tauris*, 1137–42.

8 Euripides, *Iphigenia in Tauris*, 80–2.

9 Euripides, *Iphigenia in Tauris*, 514.

10 Iphigenia derives from Greek *iphios* meaning 'strong' and *genes* relates to both birth and genealogy.

11 Euripides, *Iphigenia in Tauris*, 1061–81.

12 Hall 2013: 35.

13 Euripides, *Iphigenia in Tauris*, 1399–1403.

14 Euripides, *Iphigenia in Tauris*, 833–40.

15 Arguably neither Oedipus nor Orestes can match Medea's culpability of killing her two sons in Euripides' homonymous tragedy.

16 See Belfiore 1992: 359.

17 See Aristotle *Poetics* 16.1455a1 and Hall 2013: 69.

18 Aristotle *Poetics* 16.1454a33–1454b9.

19 Goethe achieves a reconciliation of Thoas and the Greeks without the intervention of Athena, by having Orestes realize that the object he was tasked to bring back to Greece by Apollo was his own (Orestes') sister and not the effigy of Apollo's sister. Some audiences may find this even less plausible than Euripides' solution. However, Thoas' words in his closing speech in Goethe's tragedy have a special poignancy in our times: 'The Greeks are wont to cast a longing eye upon the treasures of barbarians.'

20 What classicists refer to as 'aetiology'.

21 Homer uses the term *barbarophonos* to describe the Carians (*Iliad* II.867), sometimes translated as 'of uncouth speech'.

22 There are exceptions to the derogatory view of barbarians by Greeks, most especially those who had had extensive contact with non-Greeks and had taken the trouble to learn their language, customs and traditions, such as Xenophon.

23 Euripides, *Iphigenia in Aulis*, 1400–1.

24 This section is based on Hall's outstanding analysis of the Taurians 'tick(ing) almost all the boxes in the conceptual repertoire of postcolonial theory' in chapter XIII.

25 Hall 2013: 275.

26 One can easily imagine Thoas as the prototype on which subsequent gullible 'barbarian' rulers and their servants are portrayed in escape operas like Mozart's *Die Entführung aus dem Serail* and Rossini's *L'Italiana in Algeri*, where European captives flea from their Muslim captors.

27 Rorty 1993: 124.

28 Unlike Iphigenia, Orestes and Pylades who escape *from* the barbarian land, the barbarians themselves can *never escape from* the position in which they have been placed.

29 In recent times, various attempts have been made to decolonize the plot of *Iphigenia in Tauris* and reimagine the barbarian. Alfonso Reyes's poetic play, *Ifigenia Cruel*, reimagines the Taurians as a peaceful, pastoral people who practise human sacrifices to defend themselves against those seeking to conquer them. In Reyes's version, Iphigenia chooses to stay in her new country instead of returning to her murderous family in Greece.

30 Euripides, *Iphigenia in Tauris*, 1174.

31 Euripides, *Iphigenia in Tauris*, 1359.

32 The use of the plural may equally be Euripides' device to indicate the naiveté of the Taurians in their attempt to justify to their ruler the loss of the priestess

and the statue. But then Euripides is a dramatist whose work is full of ambiguities and ironies. This is the only instance in the play where the effigy is referred to as *xoanon*, indicating a statue made of wood.

33 https://gutenberg.ca/ebooks/andersen-shadow/andersen-shadow-00-h.html
34 For a fascinating interpretation, see Ursula Le Guin 1975.
35 Jung, to my knowledge, does not explicitly cite or refer to Andersen's *The Shadow*.
36 See, for example, Jung 1953, 1968; 2009.
37 Mudde 2014, Rosenthal 2020.
38 Hall 2013.
39 Author's translation. The entire poem and its translation by Edmund Keeley and Philip Sherrard can be found in the Cavafy Archive held at the Onassis Foundation, available online at https://www.onassis.org/initiatives/cavafy-archive/the-canon/waiting-for-the-barbarians.
40 https://cavafy.onassis.org/object/u-128/; author's translation.

3 Phaëthon: Flying High before Crashing

1   Ovid 1986: II 261–4, trans. A. D. Melville.
2   https://www.archbishopofcanterbury.org/news/latest-news/news-archive-2016/archbishop-justin-welbys-statement-his-father
3   This was recognized in the Roman law principle that stated: *Mater semper certa est, pater semper incertus est* ('The mother is always certain, the father is *always* uncertain').
4   Freud 1909/77.
5   The impostor theme is also rehearsed in myths and stories, in which the legitimacy of an individual is questioned, for a wide variety of reasons, such as that their claims are false or even that they have usurped their position by pretending to be someone other than who they are.
6   Winstanley 2004.
7   Diana Winstanley's own life (1960–2006) ended tragically. A dazzling mind, a passionate heart, a brilliant scholar, an infinitely compassionate teacher and colleague, a dedicated mother, she took her own life when the obligations and pressures of life overwhelmed her. She left behind psychological devastation for those who knew her, admired and loved her.
8   Ovid 1986: II 51–3.
9   The same can be said for its opposite, the pathological fear of flying that afflicts many individuals.
10 Few narratives capture the heroic qualities of space travel as well as Tom Wolfe's 1979 book *The Right Stuff*.

11 In the variant of the myth by Euripides accessible only through fragments (Diggle 2004), the dream of flying appears to be even more autonomous and primal than in Ovid's version, tied to the motive of escaping the constraints and limitations of life on earth. See https://www.hs-augsburg.de/~harsch/ graeca/Chronologia/S_ante05/Euripides/eur_phae.html.

12 Fraher and Gabriel 2014.

13 Ovid 1986: II 381–8.

14 This could be an example of what some regard as Ovid's sentimentality but it is also an example of his psychological astuteness.

15 Campbell 1949/88: 136.

16 Ovid 1986: II 90–4.

17 The transition from boyhood to adulthood is a central feature of Robert Bly's (1990) book, *Iron John*, in which he retells the Grimm brothers' story informed by Campbell's psychological insights. He argues that a father cannot ultimately initiate his son into adulthood by himself. This is a task in which another older man or a group of older men play the central role. This is something which Western culture systematically fails to provide. 'The boys in our culture have a continuing need for initiation into the male spirit, but old men in general don't offer it' (p. 14).

18 For example, he observed the adverse effects of deforestation in Attica during his own lifetime, partly due to the excessive need to build and equip the Athenian fleet of triremes. See *Critias* 111bc.

19 In addition to being one of Socrates' pupils, Critias was an important politician who emerged as the leading and cruellest figure in the Tyranny of the Thirty that would rule Athens after its defeat in the Peloponnesian War.

20 Plato *Timaeus* 22c, free translation by the author.

21 https://www.ipcc.ch/assessment-report/ar6/

22 Research carried out in 2020 by Oxfam and the Stockholm Environment Institute reported that the wealthiest 1 per cent of humanity are responsible for twice as many carbon emissions as the poorest 50 per cent, https://www. oxfam.org/en/research/confronting-carbon-inequality.

23 Diamond 2005.

24 For an inspiring account of the role of counter-narratives in combatting environmental devastation, see Rebecca Solnit '"If you win the popular imagination, you change the game": why we need new stories on climate' (2023). Available online at https://www.theguardian.com/news/2023/jan/12/ rebecca-solnit-climate-crisis-popular-imagination-why-we-need-new-stories?CMP=Share_AndroidApp_Other&fbclid=IwAR0E7yWojbBTbEr8X ntPwjXpjeJijfh_X-_3Wt6ZebducXs8u4Ewi7bChaw.

4 Oedipus and Thebes: Miasma, Contagion and Cleansing

1   Sophocles, *Oedipus Rex*, 1678–84, trans. Robert Fagles.
2   Sophocles, *Oedipus Rex*, 452–3, trans. Robert Fagles.
3   Notice, too, that, as Calasso 1983 argues, Oedipus is the only hero who does not touch the monster. 'Instead he looks at it and speaks to it. Oedipus kills with words; he tosses mortal words into the air as Medea hurled her magic spells at Talos. After Oedipus' answer, the Sphinx fell into a chasm. Oedipus didn't climb there to skin it, to get those colorful scales that allured travelers … Oedipus is the first to feel he can do without contact with the monster. Of all his crimes, the most serious is the one no one reproaches him with: his not having touched the monster' (p. 344).
4   The plot of *Oedipus Rex* was regarded by Aristotle as the greatest of any Greek play. He wrote that a 'plot ought to be so constructed that, even without the aid of the eye, whoever hears the tale told will thrill with horror and melt with pity at what takes place. This is the impression we receive from hearing the story of Oedipus' (*Poetics* 1453b, trans. S. H. Butcher).
5   Sophocles, *Oedipus at Colonus*, 465–6, my translation.
6   Jones 1955: 15.
7   Freud 1954: 227.
8   Many psychoanalysts draw a distinction between 'fantasy' and 'phantasy'. The first indicates a conscious or semi-conscious day-dreaming ('I dream of revisiting Venice') while the latter indicates an unconscious desire that surfaces from time to time in covert and disguised thoughts and wishes.
9   This is a core theme in Freud's 1913j own discussion in *Totem and Taboo*.
10 Edmunds and Dundes 1995. Folkloric versions of the Oedipus story can be found in different continents, including Africa, South America and Asia, and many cultures, including Serbian, Roma and even Burmese. See the contributions in the valuable 1995 collection edited by Edmunds and Dundes.
11 Sophocles was not only a member of a democratic state but one of her foremost citizens. A year after the first performance of *Antigone*, in 441 BCE, he was elected as one of the ten generals who ruled Athens. In this capacity, he participated in the Samos expedition and served under Pericles, with whom he almost certainly held conversations about government and the responsibilities of the ruler.
12 In the second of Sophocles' Theban plays, the blind Oedipus meets Theseus, the Athenian king, who offers him shelter in the city. This would also place Oedipus at least one if not two generations before the characters of the *Iliad* and the *Odyssey*.

13 Thebes is also the site of Euripides' dark play, *The Bacchae*, where the king of an earlier generation and the father of Jocasta, Pentheus, is punished by the new and young god Dionysus for banning his followers from worshipping him.

14 As a theorist of organizations, I first realized the theoretical power of the concept of miasma in connection with organizations that go through a long and profound period of dislocation following a bout of redundancies and lay-offs carried out by a leader intent on clearing out dead wood and restoring the organization to financial health. Mass downsizing is now a common occurrence in organizational life afflicting even highly profitable organizations like the Tech Giants. Such organizations can be gripped by miasma manifested in generalized depression, inability to fight or resist the changes, self-blaming, survivors' guilt and a feeling of pollution or uncleanliness. Such organizations are tainted by the presence of 'murderers', i.e. managers who have initiated a series of dismissals referred to as 'axemen' etc., and 'corpses', i.e. employees who have been dismissed or are about to be dismissed and 'disappear', once alive, now discarded. See Gabriel 2012.

15 See Halliday 2001.

16 Polianski 2021.

17 Sophocles, *Oedipus Rex*, 27–38, trans. Robert Fagles.

18 Sophocles, *Oedipus Rex*, 110–12, trans. Robert Fagles.

19 Vegetti 1995: 260.

20 Dodds 1968: 36.

21 Parker 1983 relied extensively on the classic works by van Gennep (1960) and Mary Douglas (1966/2002, 1975).

22 Parker 1983: 60.

23 Parker 1983: 4.

24 It is not accidental that one of the most painful consequences of the Covid-19 pandemic in its early days was that it denied the opportunity of survivors to bid farewell to their dying loved ones or to offer them appropriate funerals.

25 Freud 1917e/1984.

26 Freud 1917e/1984: 254.

27 See, for example, Yalom 1998.

28 Butler 2004.

29 Butler 2004: xviii.

30 Vernant 1978.

31 Lifton 1986: 481.

32 Kitromilides 2013.

33 If in the puritan eyes of the north, Greece was the southern parasite threatening to introduce miasma into its institutions, in Greece itself various

groups, at the height of the crisis, were cast in the role of the parasite. In an endless merry-go-round of recrimination and scapegoating various groups of corrupt politicians, indolent civil servants, lazy retirees, selfish plutocrats and, of course, refugees and migrants were routinely blamed for the desolation that afflicted the country.

34 Volkan 2003: 82.

5 Zeus and the Frogs: Craving for Strongman in Times of Uncertainty

1 'On Governmental Authority' (1523), available online at https://www. lolonline.org/hp_wordpress/wp-content/uploads/2020/06/Luther-Secular-Authority-To-What-Extent-It-Should-Be-Obeyed.pdf.

2 Aristophanes' *Frogs* was produced in 405 BCE, a year before Athens was defeated by Sparta, at a time of great anxiety, since defeat was imminent and could have led to the total destruction of the city and the massacre and enslavement of her population. In Aristophanes' play, written shortly after the death of Euripides, Dionysus descends to the underworld to bring back a tragedian in the hope that his wisdom will save the city. Following a contest between Euripides and Aeschylus, Dionysus opts to bring back Aeschylus who represents the old-fashioned virtues rather than the innovating Euripides.

3 http://www.perseus.tufts.edu/hopper/text?doc=Perseus%3Atext%3A1999.02 .0119%3Abook%3D1%3Apoem%3D2

4 Strongman leaders are almost all male, and use their raw and brutal masculinity as part of their appeal. In future, there will undoubtedly be female variants of the type. However, given the current monopoly of the strongman model by male leaders, I ask the reader's indulgence in referring to them with the male pronouns throughout this chapter.

5 The process of othering is discussed in detail in Chapters 2, 6 and 9.

6 See Ben-Ghiat 2020 and Rachman 2022.

7 Weber 1978: 241.

8 https://en.wikipedia.org/wiki/Cult_of_personality#:~:text=The%20term%20 %22cult%20of%20personality,Romanticist%20%22cult%20of%20genius%22

9 https://www.nytimes.com/2015/12/06/us/politics/95000-words-many-of-them-ominous-from-donald-trumps-tongue.html?smprod=nytcore-iphone&smid=nytcore-iphone-share&_r=0

10 I have analysed the ways infantile fantasies about our parents are later projected onto other figures of authority in Gabriel 1997.

11 http://mythfolklore.net/aesopica/phaedrus/12.htm
12 https://smartthinking.org.uk/the-kids-arent-alright-2/. For the full report, see https://www.ukonward.com/wp-content/uploads/2022/09/kids-arent-alright-democracy.pdf.
13 In times of what Durkheim would have called *anomie*. See Durkheim 1951.
14 https://www.gutenberg.org/files/25512/25512-h/25512-h.htm#riley_I_XXIV
15 https://www.perseus.tufts.edu/hopper/text?doc=Perseus%3Atext%3A1999.0 2.0119%3Abook%3D1%3Apoem%3D6
16 Jung 2009.
17 http://answers.google.com/answers/threadview?id=758865
18 For a critical account of the 'poem', its different variants and the pastor's role in its genesis and during the rise of the Nazis, see https://marcuse.faculty.history.ucsb.edu/projects/germanhistory/essays/1946-present.First_they_came_for_the_communists_....Harold_Marcuse.essay.Marcuse2014Niemoeller Quote147final.docx.

6 Odysseus and Nausicaa: Encounters with the Uprooted Other

1 In a view first put forward by Victorian novelist and critic Samuel Butler, Nausicaa could be the author of the entire *Odyssey*. The view that the *Odyssey* was written by a woman was further developed in *Homer's Daughter*, a 1955 novel by Robert Graves, celebrated author of *The Greek Myths* (1955/2012). It is now widely believed that large parts of the *Odyssey* were almost certainly composed by women.

2 The issue of the *Odyssey's* authorship as well as the authorship of the *Iliad* has preoccupied scholars for centuries. A good starting point for the layman is Doug Metzger's insightful summary on his enlightening and entertaining podcast transcript, available online at https://literatureandhistory.com/index.php/episode-011-who-was-homer.

3 Eric H. Cline in *1177 B.C.: The Year Civilization Collapsed* (2014/21) provocatively offers a precise date for this collapse which, he argues, was the result of a confluence of factors – environmental, geo-political, military and economic.

4 A remarkable finding in marine archaeology dating from the Late Bronze Age period (around 1300 BCE) is the Uluburun shipwreck discovered near Kas, Turkey. The ship was probably heading west when it sank, possibly from Cyprus or Canaan. Divers recovered much of its cargo which included tin and copper ingots, glass beads, elephant tusks, tortoise shells, cobalt, agate and

jewellery. What is particularly intriguing is that these goods originated from distant regions including the Baltic Sea, sub-Saharan Africa, Sicily and Mesopotamia. This diverse array of items suggests a vast network of trade spanning different continents and cultures. The discovery of the Uluburun shipwreck has significantly contributed to our understanding of the economy of the Late Bronze Age and has shed new light on the historical context of the Homeric epics. See Cline 2014/21.

5   The word 'nostalgia' was coined by the Swiss physician Johannes Hofer in 1688 to describe the morbid symptoms of Swiss mercenaries who spent long periods away from home.

6   When meeting strangers, Odysseus' default approach is to spin a yarn about his origin and identity. Even when he meets his old father Laertes in book XXIV, he invents an elaborate yarn, when there is no rational reason to lie about his identity. In light of the many tall stories that Odysseus dispenses throughout the *Odyssey*, some commentators since ancient times have suspected that even the bulk of his account of his seafaring adventures – the Cyclops, the Sirens, Circe, Calypso and all the rest – is nothing but a fanciful invention. This view found its chief exponent in the Roman satirist Juvenal in the second century CE.

7   For a thorough account of the character of Odysseus in world literature through the ages, see Stanford 1963/92.

8   *Iliad* IX.312–13, trans. Caroline Alexander.

9   An intriguing interpretation of the episode with the Cyclops is offered by Horkheimer 1947/97.

10 *Odyssey* XIII.299–311, trans. Emily Wilson.

11 This is something that resurfaced in our times when, in the course of the Troika's tutelage of the Greek economy during the depths of the country's financial troubles, Greeks were accused of being systematic liars, tax-dodgers and the like.

12 See, for example, the 2011 work of classicist Olga Levaniouk whose detailed analysis of book XIX of the *Odyssey* gives birth to a very different Penelope from that of more conventional readings, a Penelope who in effect is the chief orchestrator of Odysseus' return to the throne of Ithaca.

13 An incisive discussion of the Penelope question can be found in the Lantern Jack's podcast interview with Olga Levaniouk, available online at http://greecepodcast.com/episode29.html. There are several feminist readings of Penelope (e.g. Doherty 1995; Katz 1991) and several contributions in Cohen 1995.

14 *Odyssey* XXIII.300–2, trans. Walter Shewring.

15 *Odyssey* VI.126–37, trans. Stanley Lombardo.

16 *Odyssey* VI.140, trans. Walter Shewring.

17 *Odyssey* VI.175–83, trans. Emily Wilson.

18 *Odyssey* VIII.493–505, trans. Robert Fagles.

19 Nietzsche, *Beyond Good and Evil* (2020: 82; trans. modified).

20 See Phillips 1997 and Hardy and Phillips 1999.

21 In 2015, Sweden accepted more than 160,000 refugees from the Islamic State campaign of terror in Syria, Iraq and Afghanistan, while Germany accepted over a million.

22 Hosting ranges from detaining people in overcrowded refugee camps and prisons to helping reunite them with relatives or kindred communities and gradually start new lives.

23 https://www.unhcr.org/5ee200e37/

24 The quote is translated from the interview Angelopoulos gave to Jane Gabriel in her 1993 Channel Four documentary, *Balkan Landscapes: The Gaze of Theo Angelopoulos*, available online at http://www.tainiothiki.gr/en/59-movies/517-balkan-landscapes-the-gaze-of-theo-angelopoulos.

7 Narcissus and Echo: A Culture of Narcissism or a Culture of Echoes?

1 Christopher Lasch and Jessica Benjamin among others.

2 Freud 1914/84.

3 Freud 1914/84: 94, translation adjusted for gender inclusivity.

4 Freud referred to them as cerebral and somatic narcissism.

5 Identities, individual as well as group, have become one of the most widely discussed topics today, the subject of much agonizing and struggling. Some of the debates regarding identity were explored in Chapter 3.

6 Gabriel and Lang 2015: 1.

7 The interdependence of mass production and mass consumption is summed up in the Fordist Deal, the deal Henry Ford pioneered by offering his employees ever higher standards of living in exchange for tedious repetitive labour. See Gabriel and Lang 2015.

8 Korczynski and Ott 2006.

9 Lasch 1991: 521.

10 Many authors have made this argument, notably Sennett 1998, Bauman 1996, 1998, and Gabriel 2005.

11 Alvesson 2016.

12 Long before the rise of celebrity culture and social media influencers, Erich Fromm (1947/65) pointed out how a marketing orientation comes to dominate our social lives.

13 This has been a dominant theme in the work of sociologist George Ritzer (1993/6, 1999).

14 The strength and weaknesses of narcissistic managers has been explored by Maccoby 1981, 2000, Schwartz 1990 and others.

15 Weber 1958.

16 Lasch 1980.

8 The Trojan War and the Argonautic Expedition: Heroic Missions, Leadership and Hubris

1 Readers will forgive me using the Greek version of the hero's name in deference to the name's original meaning 'healer' but also to an indissoluble family connection. Iason's original name was Diomedes – he was named Iason by the wise centaur Cheiron. Iason, the healer, is highlighted in Pindar's account of his exploits in the famous *Fourth Pythian Ode*. In it, Pindar unmistakably invokes Iason's healing qualities to urge the dedicatee of the ode, King Arcesilas of Cyrene, winner of the chariot race in Delphi in 462 BCE, to heal the rift with his exiled political opponent Damophilus. It should be noted that 'Iason' was also a common epithet for Heracles.

2 Robert Graves dismisses Euripides' invention out of hand, mentioning that he was allegedly bribed by the Corinthians to write a tragedy that would absolve them of the guilt of killing Iason's children.

3 There are other types of Greek myths – for instance, those involving relations between a mortal and a god which tend to end badly for the mortal, those that involve outrageous acts by gods or humans, love affairs and much else besides. The heroic genre is easily recognizable by virtue of having a central character who, usually with the assistance of a divinity, performs various extraordinary deeds with courage and cunning. Heracles is the archetypal protagonist of heroic myths, but Theseus, Perseus and Bellerophon are exemplars of the genre.

4 Diomedes, Patroclus and Achilles are the other Greek heroes to be given an *aristeia* in the *Iliad*. Patroclus' *aristeia*, unlike the others, ends in his death. Hector is accorded a long *aristeia* when he storms the Greeks' fortifications and begins to burn some of their ships.

5 The account of Agamemnon at the start of the next book of the *Iliad* is even more pitiful. Looking at the joyful campsites of the Trojans, celebrating their earlier victories with pipes and flutes, and the deadly silence of the Greeks' own camp, he tears his hair 'by handfuls' and visits the tent of old Nestor in great distress to seek help.

6 Although Greek myths frequently feature greed, missions do not openly aim for material gain and profit. Loot and concubines were seen as the deserved bonus of successful campaigns. They were sometimes the subjects of acrimonious squabbles, but they were not the central point. The division of the spoils is a central theme in the *Iliad*, where the core dispute between Agamemnon and Achilles results from when the former seeks to deprive the latter of his 'earned' plunder, the girl Briseis. Throughout the *Iliad*, there are many references to the division of the war booty which included material treasures and female prisoners. This privileged the greater warlords and especially Agamemnon who kept for himself the lion's share. In a famous passage, Thersites, representing the 'common foot soldier' urges the Greek kings to return to their countries, their huts being 'full of bronze' and 'the choicest women' (book II.225, p. 46 in the Penguin translation by E. V. Rieu).

7 In this portrait of Agamemnon, I am indebted to the sharp, if rather hostile, account painted by Porter 2019.

8 Doug Metzger in his inimitable podcast *Literature and History*, available online at https://literatureandhistory.com/index.php/episode-038-the-epic-anti-hero.

9 It is telling that, burdened by the responsibilities of leadership, Iason spends sleepless nights, while Agamemnon, in book II of the *Iliad*, is reproached in his dream for sleeping too much (Hunter 1988: 445).

10 Idmon was killed by a wild boar and Tiphys, the steersman, died of an illness. A third Argonaut, Hylas, the friend of Heracles, disappeared in a land inhabited by nymphs – after a copious search for him, he was abandoned by the Argonauts and Heracles left the expedition.

11 The irony often goes unnoticed that Euripides has been castigated across the ages for his misogyny, not least by a man who knew him well, Aristophanes.

12 This maybe accounts for the play's failure with the public when it was first performed in 431 BCE. The play came last of the four performed at that year's Dionysia festival.

13 The Greek word for resource is *poros* and we learn from an allegory in Plato's *Symposium* 203b–e that Poros was a god, the son of Metis, who was tricked by Penia (Poverty) into having a child that turned out to be Eros (Love).

14 Iason and the Argonauts had delivered him from the ghastly Harpies that starved him by eating his food.

15 Some characters of these myths were short on courage and this was often pointed out to them. Paris' lack of courage is a frequent theme in the *Iliad* and his weapon of choice, the bow and arrow, is typical of the coward. While courage is extolled at every opportunity in the *Iliad*, the repulsive but enigmatic character Thersites points out that courage is nothing but a pretext for plunder and crumbles in the face of superior force. He insults his fellow

soldiers for being 'women' and only fighting out of fear of Agamemnon. Thersites is brutally beaten and ridiculed by Odysseus for insulting the supreme commander, but Homer allows ambiguity as to whether his words are those of a coward or of someone who speaks truth to power.

16 Deception or Apate is herself a goddess in the Greek Pantheon. She is daughter the Nyx (Night), and sister of Eris (Discord). She is a minor deity to be sure but one on good terms with Hera who used her help to avenge Zeus' infidelity with Semele. A related deity is Trickstery (Dolos), also a child of Nyx, whose name gives Dolios, one of Hermes' epithets.

17 This view which can be found in some of Euripides' dramas is discussed in detail in Plato's *Laws* vii 803e.

18 Hermes is also the nearest the Greeks had to a god of peaceful resolution of disputes. As the god of commerce, he represented both the mutually beneficial nature of commerce and its perennial enticement to chicanery and cheating.

19 Atē is pronounced *a-tee*, the accent on the first syllable to rhyme with 'chatty'. It features in several of Shakespeare's plays, including in *Julius Caesar*, when Mark Antony, says:
'And Caesar's spirit, raging for revenge,
With Ate by his side come hot from hell,
Shall in these confines with a monarch's voice
Cry "Havoc!" and let slip the dogs of war.'

20 *Iliad* XIX.85–94, trans. Caroline Alexander.

21 *Iliad* IX.496.

22 *Iliad* XVIII.110. A minor but indicative and well-known instance of *atē* seizes Glaucus, chief of the Lycians, one of the main allies of the Trojans. At one point, he challenges the Greek hero Diomedes to a duel, but after prolonged introductions, they discover that their grandfathers had been close friends. Instead of fighting, they pledge friendship and as a sign of this friendship they exchange armour. However, in a moment of exorbitant largesse prompted by *atē*, Glaucus exchanges his golden armour worth a hundred oxen for Diomedes' bronze armour worth nine oxen (*Iliad* VI.234–6).

23 There is an overlap between *atē* and hubris. The main difference is that *atē* refers to a specific 'moment of madness' that seizes a person, whereas hubris can be manifested in a variety of actions and words over a prolonged period of time. A related term that forms the cornerstone of Aristotle's theory of tragedy is 'hamartia', which indicates more specifically an error of judgement, a mistake. The word was eventually embraced by Christian theology to denote 'sin', something that is not part of Aristotle's original conception. Hamartia, like *atē* and hubris, brings about a character's downfall in tragedy.

24 Dodds 1968: 31.

25 The story is told to great effect by Ovid in book 6 of his *Metamorphoses*.

26 A full translation by Ian Johnston is available online at http://johnstoniatexts. x10host.com/aeschylus/persianshtml.html.

27 *Persians* 932–5, trans. Ian Johnston.

28 The historical Darius is unlikely to have felt this way. It was he who had conceived the great campaign against Greece, but died before he had had a chance to start it.

29 *Persians* 1004–6, trans. Ian Johnston.

30 *Persians* 745–6, trans. Ian Johnston.

31 *Persians* 80, trans. Ian Johnston.

32 For a fine discussion of Xerxes' hubris, see Papadimitropoulos 2008.

33 *Nicomachean Ethics* 1140b8.

34 It is also not uncommon for a person to make the same mistake, such as repeating different calamitous financial decisions or business ventures or repeatedly making disastrous choices of partner. This is a phenomenon of considerable interest to psychologists since Freud 1920/84 first discussed it in *Beyond the Pleasure Principle*.

35 See, for example, Owen 2009 and other references listed under 'Reading On'.

36 Quoted in Boyle 2000: 37.

37 See, for example, the detailed ethnography of the situations facing managers in their daily lives provided by Watson 1994.

38 See, for example, Stein 2013, Tourish 2013 and Stein 2007.

39 Boorstin 1962: 240.

40 Entertainer Jimmy Saville and Liberal politician Cyril Smith were just two examples of serial child abusers whose crimes only came to light after their deaths.

41 In the *Iliad* itself, Diomedes injured Aphrodite and the god of war, Ares, using his spear. Most other mortals would have been severely chastised for such acts, and yet he appears to evade punishment, maybe because a different goddess had been on his side at the time.

42 *Iliad* VI.494, trans. Stanley Lombardo.

43 In recent times there have been major novels by distinguished authors such as Pat Barker, Natalie Haynes, Madeline Miller, Margaret Atwood and, a little earlier, the doyenne of the genre, Mary Renault.

9 Odysseus and the Sirens: Songs, Noise and Silence

1 Homer, *Odyssey* XII.183–201, trans. Samuel Butler.

2 However, Ovid in book V of the *Metamorphoses* claimed that the Sirens had been human companions of Persephone. They had prayed for wings to search

for her after she had been abducted by Pluto, the god of the underworld, and the gods granted their wish. In other versions, they had been punished by Demeter, Persephone's mother, for having failed to protect her.

3   For instance, Odysseus does not inform his crew of the imminent danger that Scylla and Charybdis pose to them, as soon as they have moved on from the Sirens. Six of his sailors will lose their lives gobbled by the fiendish Scylla.

4   See Sawyer and Sawyer 2020.

5   See Cicero 2001.

6   See Horkheimer and Adorno 1947/97.

7   https://www.goodreads.com/quotes/876969-my-old-friend-what-are-you-looking-for-after-years

8   Kafka 1999b. Full text available online at https://www.yeyebook.com/en/franz-kafka-the-silence-of-the-sirens-short-story-text-eng/.

9   Notice how, in the earlier extract, even the minor characters Eurylochus and Perimedes are referred to by name.

10 Kafka 1999a: 383.

11 I shall refer to Homer's hero as Odysseus and to Kafka's as Ulysses.

12 Kafka 1999b: 431.

13 Benjamin 1968a.

14 Kafka 1999b: 431 (trans. modified).

15 See, for example, Salecl 1997 and Blanchot 1982.

16 Before the emergence of what Milan Kundera has semi-disparagingly described as 'Kafkology'.

17 Benjamin 1968a: 118.

18 See Levin 1990.

19 Cited by Self 2012, also available online at https://www.theguardian.com/books/2012/oct/05/kafka-was-author-unmusical-will-self. While Kafka's lack of musicality is an object of some debate, his extreme sensitivity to noise, a condition he shared with Darwin, Goethe and Chekhov, and one that prompted him to wear earplugs, is not.

20 Salecl 1997.

21 Freud 1920/84.

22 Freud 1913/85.

23 Sapienza 2015: 123, trans. Marianne Gabriel.

24 Smith 2020: 70–1.

25 Stanford 1963/92: 121.

26 Smith 2020.

27 https://www.athensvoice.gr/politics/632713_post-tis-imeras-alexandros-karagiannis. Translation by the author.

28 Seferis, 'The Last Post' in Greek, available online at http://ebooks.edu.gr/ebooks/v/html/8547/2702/Keimena-Neoellinikis-Logotechnias_B-Lykeiou_

html-empl/index_c_02_05.html; and in English, available online at https://pwchaltas.com/2015/05/31/translation-of-george-seferis-the-last-station/. Translation by the author.

Epilogue

1 Nothing sums the heroic character of Greek myths better than Sarpedon's famous speech to his cousin Glaucus in the *Iliad* (XII.312–28) in which he contrasts the immortality enjoyed by the gods to the honour and glory of the warrior. Excellence on the battlefield, even when it leads to death, is the supreme value of the hero, against which all else melts away. The theme of heroic excellence is masterfully explored by Nagy 1999, *The Best of the Achaeans: Concepts of the Hero in Archaic Greek poetry*.

2 The heroic character of most myths has persisted through the ages. When mythology chooses as its subjects real historical or quasi-historical figures, it cannot resist the temptation of mythologizing warriors and conquerors like Alexander the Great, Roland or King Arthur.

3 This is what theorists of organization refer to as 'institutional myth' (Amis, Mair and Munir 2020; Meyer and Rowan 1977).

4 *Republic* 607a, trans. Robin Waterfield.

5 Plato's criticism of Homer's portrayal of the gods is by no means the earliest. Criticizing the prevailing images of gods, the pre-Socratic philosopher, poet and Homer-performer Xenophanes (*c.* 570–*c.* 478 BCE) famously claimed that people make gods in their own image. He wrote: 'Homer and Hesiod have attributed to the gods all sorts of things that are matters of reproach and censure among men: theft, adultery, and mutual deception' (B11), available online at https://plato.stanford.edu/entries/xenophanes/.

6 Plato's critique of Homer, Hesiod and the tragedians is in books II, III and X of the *Republic*.

7 Many centuries after Plato, in 1830, following a performance of Auber's grand opera *La Muette de Portici* in the Theatre de la Monnaie in Brussels, a crowd stormed the local courthouse setting off the revolution that led to Belgian political independence.

8 The themes of last judgement, reincarnation and salvation that are central to Plato's myth of Er influenced different world religions including early Christianity, Judaism and Gnosticism. I discuss the myth of Er in the Appendix to give readers a flavour of Plato's use of a myth he invented with the intention of lending support of his philosophical arguments.

9 Discussing Plato's myths, Julia Annas (1982: 122) is of the view that 'for [Plato], as for Aristotle, "the lover of myth is a lover of wisdom, in a way" (*Metaphysics* 982b 18–19)'. The myth of Er and the other myths deployed by Plato can then be viewed as aiming for a kind of reconciliation of the 'ancient quarrel between poetry and philosophy' (*Republic* 604b, trans. Robin Waterfield).

Appendix

1 These are eloquently and sympathetically drawn out by Annas 1982.
2 This is also central to the other two eschatological myths written by Plato, those that conclude the *Gorgias* and the *Phaedo*.
3 Notice, too, that Socrates uses two words we encountered earlier, 'miasma' and 'phronesis', as he urges Glaucon, his interlocutor, to keep his soul untainted and use his good judgement to follow the course of justice.

References

Agamben, G. (1998). *Homo Sacer: Sovereign Power and Bare Life*. Stanford: Stanford University Press.

Alvesson, M. (2013). *The Triumph of Emptiness: Consumption, Higher Education, and Work Organization*. Oxford: Oxford University Press.

Alvesson, M., and Gabriel, Y. (2016). 'Grandiosity in contemporary management and education.' *Management Learning* 47(4): 464–73. doi:10.1177/1350507615618321

Amis, J. M., Mair, J., and Munir, K. A. (2020). 'The Organizational Reproduction of Inequality.' *Academy of Management Annals* 14(1): 195–230. doi:10.5465/annals.2017.0033

Annas, J. (1982). 'Plato's Myths of Judgement.' *Phronesis* 27(2): 119–43. http://www.jstor.org/stable/4182147

Armstrong, K. (2005). *A Short History of Myth*. Edinburgh: Canongate.

Association, A. P. (2013). *Diagnostic and statistical manual of mental disorders: DSM-5* (Vol. 5). Washington DC: American Psychiatric Association

Austern, L. P., and Naroditskaya, I. (2006). *Music of the Sirens*. Bloomington: Indiana University Press.

Bachvarova, M. R. (2015). *From Hittite to Homer: The Anatolian Background of Ancient Greek Epic*. Cambridge: Cambridge University Press.

Ball, J. (2017). *Post-truth: How Bullshit Conquered the World*. London: Biteback.

Barker, E. (1967). *Traditions of Civility: Eight Essays*. Hamden, CT: Archon Books.

Baudrillard, J. (1968/88). 'The system of objects.' In M. Poster (ed.), *Jean Baudrillard: Selected Writings* (pp. 13–31). Cambridge: Polity Press.

Baudrillard, J. (1970/88). 'Consumer society.' In M. Poster (ed.), *Jean Baudrillard: Selected Writings* (pp. 32–59). Cambridge: Polity Press.

Baudrillard, J. (1983). *Simulations*. New York: Semiotext(e).

Bauman, Z. (1996). 'From pilgrim to tourist – or a short history of identity.' In S. Hall and P. Du Gay (eds), *Questions of Cultural Identity* (pp. 18–36). London: Sage.

Bauman, Z. (1998). *Work, Consumerism and the New Poor*. Buckingham: Open University Press.

Beck, U. (1992). *Risk Society: Towards a New Modernity*. London: Sage.

Belfiore, E. (1992). 'Aristotle and Iphigenia.' In A. O. Rorty (ed.), *Essays on Aristotle's Poetics* (pp. 359–77). Princeton: Princeton University Press.

Ben-Ghiat, R. (2020). *Strongmen: Mussolini to the Present*. New York: W. W. Norton & Co.

Benjamin, W. (1968a). 'Frantz Kafka.' In H. Arendt (ed.), *Walter Benjamin: Illuminations* (pp. 111–41). London: Jonathan Cape.

Benjamin, W. (1968b). 'The storyteller: Reflections on the works of Nikolai Leskov.' In H. Arendt (ed.), *Walter Benjamin: Illuminations*. London: Jonathan Cape.

Beresford-Kroeger, D. (2010). *The Global Forest*. New York: Viking.

Blanchot, M. (1982). *The Sirens' Song: Selected Essays of Maurice Blanchot* (S. Rabinovitch, trans.). Bloomington: Indiana University Press.

Bly, R. (1990). *Iron John: A Book About Men*. New York: Addison Wesley.

Boorstin, D. J. (1962). *The Image: or, What Happened to the American Dream*. New York: Atheneum.

Boyle, D. (2000). *The Tyranny of Numbers: Why Counting Can't Make us Happy*. London: HarperCollins.

Butler, J. (2004). *Precarious Life: The Powers of Mourning and Violence*. London: Verso.

Buxton, R. (2022). *The Greek Myths that Shape the Way We Think*. London: Thames & Hudson.

Čadková, D. (2023). 'Mythological heroes on Czech stages and politics: the case of Phaethon and Antigone.' *Classical Receptions Journal*. doi:10.1093/crj/clad005

Calasso, R. (1983). *The Marriage of Cadmus and Harmony*. London: Jonathan Cape.

Campbell, J. (1949/88). *The Hero with a Thousand Faces*. London: Palladin Books.

Cartledge, P. (1993). *The Greeks: A Portrait of Self and Others*. Oxford: Oxford University Press.

Christakis, N. A. (2020). *Apollo's Arrow: The Profound and Enduring Impact of Coronavirus on the Way We Live*. New York: Little, Brown Spark.

Cicero, M. T., and Annas, J. (2001). *On moral ends [De finibus bonorum et malorum ('On the ends of good and evil')]*. Cambridge: Cambridge University Press.

Claxton, G., Owen, D., and Sadler-Smith, E. (2015). 'Hubris in leadership: A peril of unbridled intuition?' *Leadership* 11(1): 57–78. doi:10.1177/1742715013511482

Cline, E. H. (2021). *1177 B.C.: The Year Civilization Collapsed* (revised and updated edn). Princeton: Princeton University Press.

Cohen, B. (ed.) (1995). *The Distaff Side: Representing the Female in Homer's Odyssey*. Oxford: Oxford University Press.

D'Ancona, M. (2017). *Post-truth: The New War on Truth and How to Fight Back*. New York: Random House.

Davis, E. (2017). *Post-Truth: Why We Have Reached Peak Bullshit and What We Can Do About It*. London: Little, Brown.

de Beauvoir, S. (1953). *The Second Sex*. London: Jonathan Cape.

Debord, G. (1977). *Society of the Spectacle*. Detroit: Black and Red.

Diamond, J. M. (2005). *Collapse: How Societies Choose to Fail or Succeed*. London: Penguin Books.

Diggle, J. (2004). *Euripides: Phaethon* (Vol. 12). Cambridge: Cambridge University Press.

Dodds, E. R. (1968). *The Greeks and the Irrational*. Berkeley: University of California Press.

Doherty, L. E. (1995). *Siren Songs: Gender, Audiences, and Narrators in the Odyssey*. Ann Arbor: University of Michigan Press.

Douglas, M. (1966/2002). *Purity and Danger*, Routledge Classics Edition. London: Routledge.

Douglas, M. (1975). *Implicit Meanings: Essays in Anthropology*. London: Routledge.

Durkheim, E. (1951). *Suicide*. New York: Free Press.

Edmunds, L., and Dundes, A. (1995). *Oedipus: A Folklore Casebook*. Madison: University of Wisconsin Press.

Eliade, M. (1963). *Myth and Reality*. New York: Harper & Row.

Fanon, F. (1967). *The Wretched of the Earth*. London: Penguin Books.

Fineman, S. (2014). *The Blame Business: The Uses and Misuses of Accountability*. London: Reaktion Books.

Finkelstein, N. G. (2000). *The Holocaust Industry: Reflections on the Exploitation of Jewish Suffering*. London: Verso.

Finley, M. I. (1956/78). *The World of Odysseus* (2nd edn). London: Chatto & Windus.

Fraher, A. L., and Gabriel, Y. (2014). 'Dreaming of Flying When Grounded: Occupational Identity and Occupational Fantasies of Furloughed Airline Pilots.' *Journal of Management Studies* 51(6): 926–51. doi:10.1111/joms.12081

Freud, S. (1909/77). 'Family romances.' In *On Sexuality* (Vol. 7, pp. 217–27). London: Pelican Freud Library.

Freud, S. (1913/85). 'The Theme of the Three Caskets.' In J. Strachey (ed.), *Penguin Freud Library* Vol. 14 (pp. 233–49). London: Penguin Books.

Freud, S. (1913j). *Totem and Taboo* (Standard edn, Vol. 13). London: Hogarth Press.

Freud, S. (1914/84). 'On Narcissism: An introduction.' In *On Metapsychology: The Theory of Psychoanalysis* (Penguin Freud Library, Volume 11, pp. 59–97). London: Penguin Books.

Freud, S. (1916–17/73). *Introductory lectures on psychoanalysis* (Vol. 1). London: Pelican Freud Library.

Freud, S. (1917e/1984). 'Mourning and melancholia.' In *On Metapsychology: The Theory of Psychoanalysis* (Vol. 11, pp. 245–68). London: Pelican Freud Library.

Freud, S. (1920/84). 'Beyond the pleasure principle.' In *On Metapsychology: The Theory of Psychoanalysis* (Vol. 11, pp. 269–338). London: Pelican Freud Library.

Freud, S. (1921/85). 'Group psychology and the analysis of the ego.' In *Civilization, Society and Religion* (Vol. 12, pp. 91–178). London: Pelican Freud Library.

Freud, S. (1923/84). 'The ego and the id.' In *On Metapsychology: The Theory of Psychoanalysis* (Vol. 11, pp. 341–406). London: Pelican Freud Library.

Freud, S. (1954). *The origins of psycho-analysis: Letters to Wilhelm Fliess, drafts and notes, 1887–1902* (M. Bonaparte, A. Freud, and E. Kris, eds). New York: Basic Books.

Friedländer, S. (1997). *Nazi Germany and the Jews: The Years of Persecution 1933–1939*. New York: HarperCollins.

Fromm, E. (1947/65). *Man for Himself: An Inquiry Into the Psychology of Ethics*. New York: Fawcett Premier.

Fry, S. (2018). *Mythos: The Greek Myths Retold*. London: Penguin Books.

Füredi, F. (2006). *Culture of Fear Revisited: Risk-taking and the Morality of Low Expectation* (4th edn). London: Continuum.

Gabriel, Y. (1997). 'Meeting God: When organizational members come face to face with the supreme leader.' *Human Relations* 50(4): 315–42.

Gabriel, Y. (2004). 'The Glass Cage: Flexible work, fragmented consumption, fragile selves.' In J. C. Alexander, G. T. Marx, and C. L. Williams (eds), *Self, Social Structure and Beliefs* (pp. 57–76). Berkeley: University of California Press.

Gabriel, Y. (2005). 'Glass cages and glass palaces: Images of organizations in image-conscious times.' *Organization* 12(1): 9–27.

Gabriel, Y. (2012). 'Organizations in a State of Darkness: Towards a Theory of Organizational Miasma.' *Organization Studies* 33(9): 1137–52.

Gabriel, Y. (2015). 'The caring leader – What followers expect of their leaders and why?' *Leadership* 11(3): 316–34. doi:10.1177/1742715014532482

Gabriel, Y. (2016). 'Narrative ecologies and the role of counter-narratives: The case of nostalgic stories and conspiracy theories.' In S. Frandsen, T. Kuhn, and M. W. Lundholt (eds), *Counter-narratives and Organization* (pp. 208–26). London: Routledge.

Gabriel, Y. (2021). 'Narrative Ecologies in Post-truth Times: Nostalgia and Conspiracy Theories in Narrative Jungles?' In R. Rhodes and H. S. (eds),

What Political Science Can Learn from the Humanities (pp. 33–55). London: Palgrave Macmillan.

Gabriel, Y., and Lang, T. (2015). *The Unmanageable Consumer* (3rd edn). London: Sage.

Gennep, A. van (1960). *The Rites of Passage* (M. B. Vizedom and G. L. Caffee, trans.). London: Routledge & Kegan Paul.

Glassner, B. (2018). *The Culture of Fear: Why Americans are Afraid of the Wrong Things* (2nd paperback edn). New York: Basic Books.

Graves, R. (1955/2012). *The Greek Myths*. London: Penguin Books.

Gray, J. (2018). 'The rise of post-truth liberalism.' https://unherd.com/2018/09/the-rise-of-the-post-truth-liberals/

Grint, K. (2010). 'The Sacred in Leadership: Separation, Sacrifice and Silence.' *Organization Studies* 31(1): 89–107.

Hageneder, F., and Harper, L. (2020). *The Living Wisdom of Trees: A Guide to the Natural History, Symbolism and Healing Power of Trees*. London: Watkins.

Haidt, J. (2022). 'Why the Past 10 Years of American Life Have Been Uniquely Stupid.' *The Atlantic*, 11 May. https://www.theatlantic.com/magazine/archive/2022/05/social-media-democracy-trust-babel/629369/

Hall, E. (1989). *Inventing the Barbarian: Greek Self-Definition Through Tragedy*. Oxford: Oxford University Press.

Hall, E. (2013). *Adventures with Iphigenia in Tauris: A Cultural History of Euripides' Black Sea Tragedy*. Oxford: Oxford University Press.

Halliday, S. (2001). 'Death and miasma in Victorian London: an obstinate belief.' *British Medical Journal* 323(7327): 1469–71. <Go to ISI>://000172979900019

Hamilton, E. (2013). *Mythology*. New York: Little, Brown and Co.

Hardy, C., and Phillips, N. (1999). 'No joking matter: Discursive struggle in the Canadian refugee system.' *Organization Studies* 20(1): 1–24.

Hardy, C., Phillips, N., and Clegg, S. (2001). 'Reflexivity in organization and management theory: A study of the production of the research "subject".' *Human Relations* 54(5): 531–59.

Herodotus (1954). *Herodotus: The Histories* (A. De Sélincourt, trans.). London: Penguin Books.

Hopfl, H. (2004). 'Demeter and the curse of consumption.' In Y. Gabriel (ed.), *Myths, Stories and Organizations: Premodern Narratives for Our Times* (pp. 192–204). Oxford: Oxford University Press.

Horkheimer, M., and Adorno, T. (1947/97). *Dialectic of Enlightenment* (J. Cummings, trans.). New York: Herder and Herder.

Hunter, R. L. (1988). '"Short on Heroics": Jason in the Argonautica.' *The Classical Quarterly* 38(2): 436–53. http://www.jstor.org/stable/638989

James, P., and van der Sluijs, M. A. (2016). 'The Fall of Phaethon in Context: A New Synthesis of Mythological, Archaeological and Geological Evidence.' *Journal of Ancient Near Eastern Religions* 16(1): 67–94.

Jameson, F. (1990). *Late Marxism: Adorno, or, the Persistence of the Dialectic*. London: Verso.

Jones, E. (1955). *Sigmund Freud: Life and Works* (Vol. II).

Jung, C. G. (1953). *The Collected Works of C. G. Jung* (H. Read, M. Fordham, and G. Adler, eds). New York: Pantheon Books.

Jung, C. G. (1968). *The Archetypes and the Collective Unconscious* (Vol. 9). London: Routledge.

Jung, C. G., and Shamdasani, S. (2009). *The red book = Liber novus* (1st edn). New York: W. W. Norton & Co.

Kafka, F. (1999a). 'Excursion to the Mountains.' In N. N. Glatzer (ed), *The Complete Stories* (p. 383). London: Vintage.

Kafka, F. (1999b). 'The Silence of the Sirens.' In N. N. Glatzer (ed.), *The Complete Stories* (pp. 430–2). London: Vintage.

Katz, M. A. (1991). *Penelope's Renown: Meaning and Indeterminacy in the Odyssey*. Princeton: Princeton University Press.

Keefe, P. R. (2009). *The Snakehead: An Epic Tale of the Chinatown Underworld and the American Dream*. New York: Doubleday.

Kernberg, O. F. (1970). 'Factors in the psychoanalytic treatment of narcissistic personalities.' *Journal of the American Psychoanalytic Association* 18(1): 51–85.

Kets de Vries, M. F. R. (1990). 'The organizational fool: Balancing a leader's hubris.' *Human Relations* 43(8): 751–70.

Kitromilides, Y. (2013). 'Stories, Fables, Parables, and Myths: Greece and the Euro Crisis, Toward a New Narrative.' *Journal of Economic Issues* 47(3): 623–37. doi:10.2753/jei0021-3624470302

Kohut, H. (1971). *The Analysis of the Self*. New York: International Universities Press.

Korczynski, M., and Ott, U. (2006). 'The menu in society: Mediating structures of power and enchanting myths of individual sovereignty.' *Sociology* 40(5): 911–28. doi:10.1177/0038038506067514

Kyriakou, P. (2006). *A Commentary on Euripides' Iphigenia in Tauris*. Berlin: de Gruyter.

Lasch, C. (1980). *The Culture of Narcissism*. London: Abacus.

Lasch, C. (1991). *The True and Only Heaven: Progress and Its Critics*. New York: W. W. Norton & Co.

Le Guin, U. K. (1975). 'The child and the shadow.' *The Quarterly Journal of the Library of Congress* 32(2): 139–48.

Levaniouk, O. (2011). *Eve of the Festival: Making Myth in Odyssey 19*. Washington DC: Center for Hellenic Studies.

Lévi-Strauss, C. (1958/76). 'The story of Asdiwal.' In C. Lévi-Strauss (ed.), *Structural Anthropology* (Vol. 2, pp. 146–97). London: Penguin Books.

Lévi-Strauss, C. (1963). *Structural Anthropology* (Vol. 1). London: Penguin Books.

Lévi-Strauss, C. (1966). *The Savage Mind*. Oxford: Oxford University Press.

Lévi-Strauss, C. (1978). *Myth and Meaning: The 1977 Massey Lectures*. London: Routledge.

Levin, T. Y. (1990). 'For the record: Adorno on music in the age of its technological reproducibility.' *October* 55: 23–47.

Levita, D. J. de (1965). *The Concept of Identity*. New York: Basic Books.

Lévy-Bruhl, L. (1923/78). *Primitive Mentality*. New York: AMS Press.

Lifton, R. J. (1986). *The Nazi Doctors: Medical Killing and the Psychology of Genocide*. London: Macmillan.

Lindholm, C. (1988). 'Lovers and leaders: A comparison of social and psychological models of romance and charisma.' *Social Science Information* 27(1): 3–45.

Lovelock, J. (1979). *Gaia: A New Look at Life on Earth*. Oxford: Oxford University Press.

Lovelock, J. (2006). *The Revenge of Gaia: Why the Earth is Fighting Back – and How We Can Still Save Humanity*. London: Allen Lane.

Mabey, R. (2007). *Beechcombings: The Narratives of Trees*. London: Chatto & Windus.

Maccoby, M. (1981). *The Leader*. New York: Simon & Shuster.

Maccoby, M. (2000). 'Narcissistic leaders: The incredible pros, the inevitable cons.' *Harvard Business Review* 78(1): 69–77.

Maechler, S. (2001). *The Wilkomirski Affair*. Basingstoke: Picador.

Martin, R. P. (1989). *The Language of Heroes: Speech and Performance in the Iliad*. Ithaca: Cornell University Press.

Martin, R. P. (2016). *Classical Mythology: The Basics*. London: Routledge.

Mbembe, A. (2003). 'Necropolitics.' *Public Culture* 15(1): 11–40.

Memmi, A. (1991). *The Colonizer and the Colonized* (expanded edn). Boston: Beacon Press.

Menchú, R., and Burgos-Debray, E. (1984). *I, Rigoberta Menchú: An Indian Woman in Guatemala* (E. Burgos-Debray, trans.). London: Verso.

Meyer, J. W., and Rowan, B. (1977). 'Institutionalized organizations: Formal structure as myth and ceremony.' *American Journey of Sociology* 83(2): 340–63.

Mitchell, J. (1975). *Psychoanalysis and Feminism*. London: Penguin Books.

Mudde, C. (2014). 'Fighting the system? Populist radical right parties and party system change.' *Party Politics* 20(2): 217–26. doi:10.1177/1354068813519968

Nagy, G. (1996). *Homeric Questions*. Austin: University of Texas Press.

Nagy, G. (1999). *The Best of the Achaeans: Concepts of the Hero in Archaic Greek Poetry* (rev. edn). Baltimore: Johns Hopkins University Press.

Nietzsche, F. W. (2020). *Beyond Good and Evil: The Philosophy Classic* (H. Zimmern, trans., C. Janaway and T. Butler-Bowdon, eds). Hoboken, NJ: John Wiley & Sons.

Nuttall, A. D. (1996). *Why Does Tragedy Give Pleasure?* Oxford: Oxford University Press.

Ovid. (1986). *Metamorphoses* (A. D. Melville, trans.). Oxford: Oxford University Press.

Owen, D., and Davidson, J. (2009). 'Hubris syndrome: An acquired personality disorder? A study of US Presidents and UK Prime Ministers over the last 100 years.' *Brain: A Journal of Neurology* 132(5): 1396–406. doi:10.1093/brain/awp008

Pallua, J. V. (2019). 'What can the mythical frog tell us? The symbolism and role of the frog in history and modernity.' *Folklore: Electronic Journal of Folklore* 77: 63–90. https://www.ceeol.com/search/article-detail?id=822155

Papadimitropoulos, L. (2008). 'Xerxes' hubris and Darius in Aeschylus' *Persae.' Mnemosyne* 61(3): 451–8. doi:10.1163/156852507x194746

Parker, R. (1983). *Miasma: Pollution and Purification in Early Greek Religion.* Oxford: Clarendon Press.

Phillips, N., and Hardy, C. (1997). 'Managing multiple identities: Discourse, legitimacy and resources in the UK refugee system.' *Organization* 4(2): 159–85.

Picone, P. M., Dagnino, G. B., and Minà, A. (2014). 'The Origin of Failure: A Multidisciplinary Appraisal of the Hubris Hypothesis and Proposed Research Agenda.' *The Academy of Management Perspectives* 28(4): 447–68. doi:10.5465/amp.2012.0177

Polianski, I. J. (2021). 'Airborne infection with Covid-19? A historical look at a current controversy.' *Microbes Infect* 23(9–10): 104851. doi:10.1016/j.micinf.2021.104851

Porter, A. (2019). *Agamemnon, the Pathetic Despot: Reading Characterization in Homer.* Washington DC: Center for Hellenic Studies.

Postman, N. (1986). *Amusing Ourselves to Death.* London: Heinemann.

Powers, R. (2018). *The Overstory.* New York: W. W. Norton & Co.

Rachman, G. (2022). *The Age of the Strongman: How the Cult of the Leader Threatens Democracy Around the World.* New York: Other Press.

Rieff, P. (1966). *The Triumph of the Therapeutic.* New York: Harper & Row.

Ritzer, G. (1993/6). *The McDonaldization of Society* (2nd edn). London: Sage.

Ritzer, G. (1999). *Enchanting a Disenchanted World: Revolutionizing the Means of Consumption.* Thousand Oaks, CA: Pine Forge Press.

Rorty, R. (1993). 'Human rights, rationality and sentimentality.' In S. Shute and S. Hurley (eds), *On Human Rights* (pp. 112–34). New York: Basic Books.

Rosenthal, L. (2018). '"Othering" Nationalism: The Bookends of the Industrial Age.' *Populism* 1: 1–11. doi: https://doi.org/10.1163/25888072-01011004

Rosenthal, L. (2020). *Empire of Resentment: Populism's Toxic Embrace of Nationalism.* New York: The New Press.

Said, E. W. (1985). *Orientalism.* London: Penguin Books.

Said, E. W. (1994). *Culture and Imperialism.* London: Chatto & Windus.

Salecl, R. (1997). 'The Sirens and Feminine Jouissance.' *Differences* 9(1): 14–28.

Sapienza, G. (2015). *Appuntamento a Positano.* Turin: Einaudi.

Sawyer, L., and Sawyer, B. (2020). 'Leadership in ancient and modern military: Carelessness and moral injury.' In L. Tomkins (ed.), *Paradox and Power in Caring Leadership* (pp. 98–108). Cheltenham: Edward Elgar.

Schwartz, H. S. (1990). *Narcissistic Process and Corporate Decay.* New York: New York University Press.

Self, W. (2012). 'Franz Kafka: was the author completely unmusical?' *The Guardian,* 5 October. https://www.theguardian.com/books/2012/oct/05/kafka-was-author-unmusical-will-self

Sennett, R. (1998). *The Corrosion of Character: The Personal Consequences of Work in the New Capitalism.* New York: W. W. Norton & Co.

Shay, J. (1994). *Achilles in Vietnam: Combat Trauma and the Undoing of Character.* New York: Touchstone.

Sievers, B. (1994). *Work, Death and Life Itself.* Berlin: de Gruyter.

Smith, R. S. (2020). 'Myth, Poetry and Homer in Seneca Philosophus.' In M. Garani, A. Michalopoulos, and S. Papaioannou (eds), *Intertextuality in Seneca's Philosophical Writings* (pp. 50–80). London: Routledge.

Spivak, G. C. (1988). 'Can the subaltern speak?' In Nelson, Cary, and Grosberg (eds), *Marxism and the Interpretation of Culture* (pp. 271–313). Urbana: University of Illinois Press.

Stanford, W. B. (1963/92). *The Ulysses Theme.* Dallas: Spring Publications.

Stein, H. F. (1998). *Euphemism, Spin, and the Crisis in Organizational Life.* Westport, CT: Quorum Books.

Stein, H. F. (2001). *Nothing Personal, Just Business: A Guided Journey Into Organizational Darkness.* Westport, CT: Quorum Books.

Stein, M. (2003). 'Unbounded irrationality: Risk and Organizational Narcissism at Long Term Capital Management.' *Human Relations* 56(5): 523–40. <Go to ISI>://000183958000001

Stein, M. (2007). 'Oedipus Rex at Enron: Leadership, Oedipal struggles, and organizational collapse.' *Human Relations* 60(9): 1387–410. doi:10.1177/0018726707082852

Stein, M. (2013). 'When Does Narcissistic Leadership Become Problematic? Dick Fuld at Lehman Brothers.' *Journal of Management Inquiry* 22(3): 282–93. doi:10.1177/1056492613478664

Stoll, D. (1999). *Rigoberta Menchu and the Story of All Poor Guatemalans*. New York: Routledge.

Tourish, D. (2013). *The Dark Side of Transformational Leadership: A Critical Perspective*. London: Routledge.

Vegetti, M. (1995). 'The Greeks and their Gods' (C. Lambert and T. L. Fagan, trans.). In J.-P. Vernant (ed.), *The Greeks* (pp. 254–84). Chicago: University of Chicago Press.

Vernant, J.-P. (1978). 'Ambiguity and Reversal: On the Enigmatic Structure of Oedipus Rex.' *New Literary History* 9(3): 475–501. doi:10.2307/468451

Volkan, V. D. (2003). *Appendix 4. Post-Traumatic States: Beyond Individual PTSD in Societies Ravaged by Ethnic Conflict*. http://www.irss-usa.org/pages/documents/PSGuide.pdf

Watson, T. J. (1994). *In Search of Management: Culture, Chaos and Control in Managerial Work*. London: Routledge.

Weber, M. (1958). *The Protestant Ethic and the Spirit of Capitalism* (T. Parsons, trans.). New York: Charles Scribner's and Sons.

Weber, M. (1978). *Economy and Society* (G. Roth and C. Wittich, trans. and eds, vols 1 & 2). Berkeley: University of California Press.

Wilde, O. (1889/1905). 'The Decay of Lying, originally published in *Intentions*, New York: Brentano.' http://virgil.org/dswo/courses/novel/wilde-lying.pdf

Winstanley, D. (2004). 'Phaethon, the Struggle for Identity, and the Reins of Power.' In Y. Gabriel (ed.), *Myths, Stories and Organizations: Premodern Narratives for Our Times* (pp. 176–91). Oxford: Oxford University Press.

Yalom, I. D., and Yalom, B. (1998). *The Yalom Reader: Selections from the Work of a Master Therapist and Storyteller*. New York: BasicBooks.

Zipes, J. (2008). 'What makes a repulsive frog so appealing: Memetics and fairy tales.' *Journal of Folklore Research* 45(2): 109–43.

Index